A CENTURY OF ARAB POLITICS

A CENTURY OF ARAB POLITICS

From the Arab Revolt to the Arab Spring

Bruce Maddy-Weitzman

ROWMAN & LITTLEFIELD
Lanham • Boulder • New York • London

Senior Acquisitions Editor: Marie-Claire Antoine
Associate Editor: Monica Savaglia
Marketing Manager: Kim Lyons
Production Editor: Elaine McGarraugh
Cover Designer: Neil Cotterill

Credits and acknowledgments of sources for material or information used with permission appear on the appropriate page within the text.

Published by Rowman & Littlefield
A wholly owned subsidiary of The Rowman & Littlefield Publishing Group, Inc.
4501 Forbes Boulevard, Suite 200, Lanham, Maryland 20706
www.rowman.com

Unit A, Whitacre Mews, 26-34 Stannary Street, London SE11 4AB

British Library Cataloguing in Publication Information Available

Library of Congress Cataloging-in-Publication Data

Maddy-Weitzman, Bruce.
A century of Arab politics : From the Arab revolt to the Arab Spring / by Bruce Maddy-Weitzman.
pages cm.
Includes bibliographical references and index.
ISBN 978-1-4422-3691-2 (cloth : alk. paper) -- ISBN 978-1-4422-3692-9 (pbk. : alk. paper) -- ISBN 978-1-4422-3693-6 (electronic)
1. Arab countries--Politics and government--20th century. I. Title.
DS36.88.M324 2016
909'.0974927082--dc23
2015030520

♾ ™ The paper used in this publication meets the minimum requirements of American National Standard for Information Sciences Permanence of Paper for Printed Library Materials, ANSI/NISO Z39.48-1992.

Printed in the United States of America

CONTENTS

LIST OF MAPS

ACKNOWLEDGMENTS

In one way or another, we are all products of our environment. In my case, I have had the great and good fortune to spend my professional life within the friendly confines of Tel Aviv University's Moshe Dayan Center for Middle Eastern and African Studies. Since arriving there thirty-six years ago as an aspiring graduate student, I have benefited immeasurably and matured as a scholar thanks in large part to the wisdom and guidance of teachers, mentors, and colleagues. Their substantial presence in the bibliography of this study reflects only a small portion of their contribution. No one could have asked for a more stimulating and supportive environment, reinforced by the solidarity and assistance of administrators and staff throughout the years. In particular, I will forever be grateful for the training and guidance of Daniel Dishon, of blessed memory. His penetrating writings on regional Arab politics during the 1970s had aroused my interest in the subject even before arriving at the Center, and the opportunity to work with and learn from him was priceless. This particular project was greatly enhanced by the constructive criticism and encouragement of two longtime friends and Center colleagues, Ofra Bengio and Asher Susser. Naturally, I am solely responsible for any remaining shortcomings. Special thanks go to Marie-Claire Antoine, senior acquisitions editor at Rowman & Littlefield, for initiating the conversation that led to this book. Thanks also to production editor Elaine McGarraugh and the entire team for shepherding the manuscript to publication, and to Robert and Cynthia Swanson for preparing the index.

This book is dedicated to the memory of another dear friend and colleague, Joseph ("Yossi") Kostiner. Yossi's contributions to the field of modern Middle East history are universally recognized. All who knew him would agree that his talents as a scholar were matched by his generosity of spirit, particularly toward students and younger colleagues, not to mention his ubiquitous sense of humor and fundamental human decency. I was honored when he invited me to collaborate with him in researching the dynamics of Arab regional politics, a journey that took us to places, physical and intellectual, that I never would have reached otherwise. Along the way, we received funding to support our work from the United States Institute of Peace and the Israel Foundation Trustees. Unfortunately, life interfered in various ways, and our planned joint study of contemporary Arab politics did not come to fruition. I have no doubt, however, that this particular study is informed by our years of collaboration, and I extend my belated thanks to the supporting foundations. Sadly, it is now five years since Yossi prematurely left this world, but his contribution to the Center and Department of Middle Eastern History remains ever-present, and his persona an enduring model of emulation.

INTRODUCTION[1]

This book is a political history of the rise and decline of the Arab regional order over the course of a century of upheaval and conflict, from the 1916–1918 "Great Arab Revolt" that helped bring an end to the four-hundred-year reign of the Ottoman Empire in the predominantly Arabic-speaking lands in the Near East and North Africa, to the contemporary upheavals of the "Arab Spring." The first half of that century was very much the story of pan-Arabism as an idea and a movement, which decisively shaped regional politics and collective identities, notwithstanding its limitations and ultimate failure to achieve the cherished goal of Arab

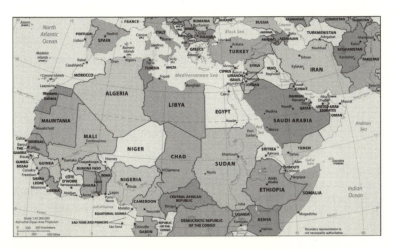

Figure I.1   Middle East and North African countries. Library of Congress.

unity. The second half was characterized by the strengthening and legitimation of Arab territorial states, only to witness the progressive decline of the political significance of Arab nationalism, the decline in Arab power, individually and collectively, and the unraveling of many of the Arab states that it had spawned. In the Fertile Crescent/Levant region, this even included the effective erasure of the post-World War I boundaries and sovereign order that had been established there.

At its peak, pan-Arabism offered a compelling and powerful vision of unity that promised to restore the Arabs' proverbial place in the sun, i.e., achieving power, dignity, and prosperity commensurate with their idealized image of the past. It was a vision that profoundly shaped, and in multiple and contradictory ways, the twin processes of state formation and nation formation in ex-Ottoman Arab lands. But the realization of that vision proved to be elusive, foundering on the shoals of deep-rooted socio-historical factors that made it impossible to triumph over the varied and competing interests of Arab states. The failing fortunes of pan-Arabism paved the way for the pragmatic acceptance of the colonially created state order, the entrenchment of the territorial state and accompanying formulations of territorial nationalism,[2] and the unapologetic pursuit of *raison d'état* by the various Arab states. These developments were accompanied by the fashioning and propagation of a modern standard Arabic language, the central marker of modern Arab identity, throughout a defined "Arab space," from the Atlantic Ocean to the Persian Gulf. Thus the stage seemed to be set for a more "normal" Arab state system, in which the cherished values of common Arab national identity would be fully commensurate with state sovereignty. However, the triumph of territorial Arab states over the vision of integral pan-Arabism proved to be limited in value, as recent years have witnessed a dramatic unraveling of the Arab order. Arab state-building projects proved to be severely deficient, characterized by what Hisham Sharabi called "neo-patriarchy,"[3] a distorted form of secular modernity that enabled ruling Arab elites to dominate Arab societies but without acquiring the requisite degree of institutional legitimacy necessary for addressing the fundamental needs of their increasingly embittered and alienated publics. Indeed, the absence of legitimate and effective governing institutions all but guaranteed that the Arab Spring upheavals that began in Tunisia in December 2010 and cascaded back and forth across the Arab Middle East and North Africa would not produce a stable and pluralist political order (Tunisia being a conspicuous, albeit still fragile exception). The Arab collective appeared to have reached a Shakespearean moment, "to be or not to be," as religious, sectarian, and ethnic affiliations fueled civil wars and even effectively erased state boundaries, particularly in the historic birthplace of Arabism, the Levant/Fertile Crescent region.

A subsidiary theme of this book is the changing salience of inter-Arab relations. The twenty-two members of the League of Arab States (*jam`iyyat al-duwal al-`arabiyya*) can be categorized according to a number of criteria, including regime type, ethnic and religious makeup, degree of "Arabness," historical trajectories, and varying degrees of social cohesion and "stateness." Nonetheless, scholars have long recognized the existence of an Arab state system: Paul Noble has likened the intensity and multiple effects of their interactions to a "vast sound chamber" in which ideas and actions reverberate widely,[4] and to a "set of interconnected organisms separated only by porous membranes."[5]

How did this system emerge and what were its central features? An overarching theme of the grand narrative of Arab nationalism accepted by generations of Arabs and Westerners alike was Britain's perceived betrayal of promises to support Arab independence and unity to its World War I Arab allies, resulting in the carving up of the allegedly "natural" Arab political space into unnatural territorial units that lacked the requisite bases for social and political cohesion. The more radical current of pan-Arabism, whose political heyday was the 1950s and 1960s, but whose worldview was formed earlier, championed this view, and used it as a weapon to delegitimize the newly independent, narrowly based, and weak regimes. But more and more scholars understand the limitations of this narrative, for it is as much an ideological construct as a reflection of what actually transpired. Elie Kedourie provided an unmatched account of the "Anglo-Arab Labyrinth" during and immediately after World War I, rejecting the Arab nationalist narrative of betrayal, while faulting British diplomacy for its ignorance, amateurism, and confusion.[6] Israel Gershoni, Philip Khoury, and others have shown that there is not one Arab nationalist experience, but rather many.[7] Moreover, Ilya Harik cogently questioned the alleged illegitimacy of separate Arab entities, arguing that a majority of the member states of the Arab League, from North Africa to the Gulf, albeit not in the Fertile Crescent, had acquired a considerable degree of legitimacy that predated the arrival of colonialism.[8]

In any case, the "fit" between the new Arab states and Arab nation-hood was problematic. Beginning in the 1920s, the ongoing tension be-tween *raison d'état* (*wataniyya*—territorial nationalism) and *raison de la nation Arabe* (*qawmiyya*—pan-Arab nationalism) was a permanent and defining feature of regional Arab politics. The combination of the lack of "stateness,"[9] and therefore legitimacy for ruling elites, and the construc-tion and dissemination of a hegemonic, albeit contested ideology of Arab nationalism, created a highly elastic system, in which ruling elites and opposition movements alike competed fiercely over both concrete and symbolic interests and resources. Relations between Arab states would be characterized by high degrees of conflict and bouts of cooperation, under-pinned by an increasingly shared adherence to a common Arab identity and bedeviled by competing efforts over who could best define and repre-sent that idea and advance the goals of the nation. Arab nationalism would both unite and divide, creating a heady but often toxic brew. One result was that the Arab League, the supreme collective Arab institution founded in 1945 by seven countries—Egypt, Syria, Iraq, Transjordan, Lebanon, Saudi Arabia, and Yemen—would remain weak and ineffec-tive, and thus unable to fulfill its declared role of promoting closer sus-tained cooperation among its members in accordance with supreme Arab national values. Another was the collective Arab failure vis-à-vis the cause of Palestine, which had become the litmus test of one's fidelity to those values.

A third was that for approximately a decade, beginning in 1955, the ascendant radical current of pan-Arabism embodied by Gamal ʿAbd al-Nasir and the pan-Arab Baʿth Party raised the inter-Arab temperature to the boiling point, challenging ruling elites and the very legitimacy of territorial Arab states. And even the dichotomy between integral pan-Arabism and the territorial state is only part of the story. Arab nationalism and the adherence to pan-Arab norms were also crucial in terms of state building and for the forging of a degree of social cohesion.[10] As Malik Mufti has shown, this was true for Iraq and Syria in the late 1950s and early 1960s, where unionism was an effective defensive mechanism to ensure their respective pan-Arab Baʿthi regimes' hold on power.[11]

The defeat of Arab armies by Israel in the June 1967 War constituted the Waterloo for the vision of pan-Arab unity and revolution, and a pro-found trauma for its legions of followers. The practical value of pan-Arabist ideology waned in the decades afterward, as Egypt recalibrated its regional policies, power within the Arab firmament increasingly shifted to the oil-rich, conservative states of the Arabian Peninsula and Persian Gulf, alliances were reshuffled, state institutions controlled by ruling elites became more entrenched, and their bureaucratic-authoritarian power penetrated more deeply into society. Concurrently, pan-Arab sentiment was increasingly folded into Islamist opposition movements that challenged the incumbent regimes and sought to Islamize their respective states and societies.[12] Nonetheless, inter-Arab affairs would remain highly charged for some time, and Arab summit conferences would constitute an important arena for rival leaders seeking to advance their particular agendas and block their rivals.

In essence, the unresolved conflict with Israel was all that was left to unite the Arab world and that did not last for very long, as Egypt departed from the Arab ranks in the late 1970s, and was officially cast out of the collective Arab fold for a decade. The Iran-Iraq war dealt a further severe blow to tattered Arab norms, as Syria supported Iran against a fellow Arab state. Iraq's subsequent invasion of Kuwait in 1990 and the alliance of most Arab states with the United States against Iraq were nothing less than an earthquake for the Arab region. The last semblance of meaningful collective Arab action came in 2002 with the issuing of the Arab Peace Initiative, an endorsement of the end of conflict with Israel, albeit subject to a number of problematic conditions. Although it was born out of disagreement and compromise, with no mechanism to promote its implementation, it nonetheless still serves as a reference point of sorts for Arab-Israeli peacemaking. By contrast, efforts by the Arab League to staunch the bloodshed in Syria in 2011–2012 failed miserably, highlighting the depths to which the Arab order had sunk.

Arab societies in the post-1967 era generally tended to share a multidimensional set of identities, some of which were more "core" in character, and others more peripheral. Egyptians, Jordanians, Palestinians, Iraqis, and Tunisians, for example, were the proud possessors of their respective territorial identities as they were also, at one and the same time, Arabs and Muslims, Christians, Sunnis, or Shi'is, and so on. In the new circumstances, it was the more secularist purveyors of existing territorial identities who competed with the Islamists. To be sure, the secularizing nationalist regimes of the mid-twentieth century in countries like Egypt, Iraq, and Syria had maintained the relevance of religion in public life by dabbling on occasion, for their own purposes, in Islamic politics. But overall, they effectively blocked the Islamists, who were crushed under-foot by military dictatorships.

Throughout the last quarter of the twentieth century and into the first decade of the twenty-first, the increased state capacity of authoritarian Arab regimes guaranteed the maintenance of the institutional order. As the vision of pan-Arab unity and social revolution waned from the 1960s onward, more concerted and deliberate efforts were made by many of the Arab regimes to actively promote a sense of genuine territorial identity and consciousness, ostensibly overriding religious identities and bridging longstanding sectarian, ethnic, or tribal fault lines. At long last, the en-trenchment of Arab territorial states seemed irreversible, enabling and legitimizing the unencumbered pursuit of their respective *raisons d'état*, which in turn promised to make inter-Arab relations more "normal," i.e., one concerned with concrete economic and security issues, and not those related to identity.[13]

However, the decline of pan-Arabism and the loss of hope that it represented left Arab regimes bereft of an important legitimizing tool, while leaving them with the arduous task of meeting their populations' practical and symbolic needs. As a series of reports produced by teams of Arab intellectuals during the first decade of the new century starkly showed, Arab regimes were not delivering. The reports highlighted many state shortcomings; the concept of "stalled" states and societies had al-ready entered into the lexicon.[14] And when the spark was lit by a young, despairing, unemployed Tunisian in December 2010, the resulting "Arab Spring" protests spread like wildfire.

According to some, the Arab nationalist idea was actually rejuvenated by the new media, and the uprisings created a newly meaningful regional bond, constituting a second "Arab awakening," similar in impact to the emergence of modern Arab identity a century earlier. Marc Lynch ob-served that "a radically new Arab political space" had been created by "a new generation of Arabs." They had "come of age watching al-Jazee-ra . . . connecting with each other through social media; and internalizing a new kind of pan-Arabist identity," as they shared complaints about their authoritarian leaders, their stalled economies, and their stagnant poli-tics.[15]

However, this excitement, dominated by ideological tendencies and no little wishful thinking, was off the mark. As Stephen Humphreys had already noted, Arab nationalism was "even in its heyday, a new plant . . .

with very shallow roots in the political tradition of [the] region."[16] Martin Kramer's erudite analysis of the rise and decline of Arab nationalism went even further, speaking of a case of "mistaken identity."[17] Taking the middle ground, one could argue that "being" Arab remains a meaningful category of collective cultural identity for a majority of Arabic speakers, albeit with minimal political effect, and most Arab states will continue to define themselves as such. They will also maintain their membership in the Arab League, notwithstanding its limited effectiveness, which is largely a function of the lack of political will, mutual distrust, and internal weaknesses among its members. As opposed to the experience of pan-European institution building, all-Arab cooperation remained largely negative, rather than positive in purpose. At the same time, the instrumental value of Arab identity for Arab states' foreign policies has lessened, and is at best an implicit and not an explicit focus of domestic debates; there it is folded into the debates about the role of Islam in political life and in the shaping of collective identity. Arab nationalism, therefore, has lost its role both as a platform for secular politics and as a cohesive force overriding more traditional forms of collective identity. In the Fertile Crescent, these were being expressed in dramatic fashion in 2014–15: the boundary between Syria, traditionally the "beating heart of Arabism" (*qalb al-nabid lil-`uruba*), and Iraq, which Saddam Husayn had proclaimed to be "the eastern flank of the Arab homeland," had been essentially erased, not by pan-Arabism but by a murderous, self-proclaimed Islamic caliphate; and the long-suppressed Kurds of the region had now succeeded in carving out a space for autonomous action, thus further calling into question the viability of the post-World War I territorial arrangements and raising new questions about the future of the venerable but increasingly fraying Arab collective.

Organizationally, the book is divided into two sections. The first, which discusses the rise of Arab nationalism as an idea and a movement, its impact on Arab state formation, and the resulting intense competition and rivalries between Arab states over both concrete and symbolic assets, is told in a chronological fashion, from the late nineteenth century up until the debacle of the June 1967 war with Israel. The second section covers the themes of the post-1967 period: the entrenchment of territorial states less beholden to pan-Arab values and norms but still engaged with one another in a highly conflictual regional environment, the declining salience of Arab identity as a meaningful political category, and the ultimate failure of many Arab states to establish stable, successful, and legitimate political systems. Separate chapters examine these themes as they applied to three key state actors—Egypt, Iraq, and Syria—and the Palestinian movement. As for the Gulf and Maghreb regions, local, state-centered identities and institutions had never been seriously challenged by radical pan-Arabism. Hence, the developments there and the regional policies of these countries during the post-1967 years, particularly Saudi Arabia's expanding regional role and initiatives at Arab summit conferences, are folded into the other chapters. The Kurdish ethno-national project is discussed in the chapter on Iraq, as well as in the book's final chapter. The latter focuses on the upheavals of the "Arab Spring" years that have resulted in an unraveling of the Arab regional order.

I

The Emergence of Arab Nationalism: One Nation, Many States

I

ARAB NATIONALISM

Modest Beginnings

Arabism, as an idea and as a movement, emerged at the end of the nineteenth and beginning of the twentieth centuries, within the general ferment that characterized the last decades of the Ottoman Empire. While having a number of strands, its overall message up until World War I was the strengthening of Arab collective identity as part of a larger effort to reform and maintain the Empire. Like other such movements, it was built on the foundations of a core ethnic group.[1] As a collective, the Arabs emerged onto the pages of history in the seventh century AD as the bearers of a new religion, Islam, with a universal message expressed in the Arabic language and canonized in a holy book, the Qur'an.[2] Unlike Christianity, Islam came in as a winner: The first Islamic empire was established by conquering Arab rulers in Damascus in AD 661, only forty years after the prophet Muhammad first began disseminating his message in the Arabian cities of Mecca and Medina. But while the Arabic language spread across the Near East and North Africa and Arabs retained an honored place in the expanding Islamic civilization, being Arab ceased to have political significance.

Ottoman military expansion in the sixteenth century rendered the predominantly Arabic-speaking lands of the Near East (Egypt, the Fertile Crescent, and Arabian Peninsula) and the North African Mediterranean littoral (excluding Morocco) integral parts of the Ottoman Empire. The Empire's fundamental legitimacy was based on its Sunni Islamic character, with the ruling sultan's primary task being to defend the faith and its far-flung territories. Like all empires, the Istanbul-based Ottoman Empire was multi-ethnic and multi-confessional. Its *millet* system provided considerable space for *dhimmi*s—protected Christian and Jewish religious minorities—to administer their own affairs.[3] The large majority of ethnic Arabs were Muslims, primarily Sunni, with pockets of mostly marginalized Shi`is; Arabic-speaking Christians were of sizeable numbers in Egypt and the Fertile Crescent, and the Jews of these lands also spoke varieties of Judaeo-Arabic. Overall, in Bruce Masters's words, the Arabs of the Empire were culturally distinct, but not politically, and the perception of their cultural alterity was mutual.[4] Consequently, prior to the last decades of the Empire, ethnic Arabs posed no challenges to the Ottoman political and social order. The opposite, in fact, was the case: Local Ottoman-Arab elites were an integral part of that order. And while ethnic Arabs may have been aware of their cultural distinctiveness vis-à-vis the Ottoman Turks, other components of their collective identities were far more relevant.

However, the Ottoman world would gradually be undermined and with it, the nature of the collective identities of its subjects, including Arabic speakers, would be called into question. The reason, of course, was the giant leap forward of Christian European states, technologically, economically, and militarily, beginning in the late seventeenth century. The balance of power thus shifted decisively, resulting in their relentless pressure on, and conquest of Ottoman lands in central and southeastern Europe, the Caucasus, and North Africa throughout the nineteenth century. Ottoman responses were hardly passive: The implementation of far-reaching reforms, collectively known as the *tanzimat*, were designed to both modernize and centralize the Empire, for the purpose of emulating Europe's success in order to rebuff the threat that it posed. Particularly noteworthy for understanding the evolution of collective identities in the Empire were the imperial edicts issued under European pressure in 1839 and 1856, which proclaimed the equality of all Ottoman subjects, i.e., its non-Muslim communities, thus introducing the concept of common Ottoman citizenship into the public discourse. In practice, though, this remained a distant and unrealizable notion, and as the century unfolded, ethnic nationalism became the dominant ideology among most of the Empire's Christian subjects, albeit not in the Arabic-speaking lands.

The suspension of the Ottoman constitution in 1876, just months after its propagation, and the reassertion of absolute powers by Sultan Abdulhamid II was a severe blow to Ottoman reformers. Concurrently, European penetration and domination came in all forms and directions, from the support for separatist nationalist movements in the Balkans and among Ottoman Armenians, to economic domination in North Africa and the Levant, and military invasion and occupation of Tunisia (1881) and Egypt (1882). European debates over the future of the Ottoman Empire (widely seen as the "sick man of Europe") were intimately bound up with concerns over the European balance of power. For Muslim intellectuals, the matter was existential, and more acute than ever.

ARABISM AND ARAB NATIONALISM—FIRST STIRRINGS

The origins of Arabism, namely the notion that speakers of Arabic constituted a distinct human collective whose cultural and ultimately political demands needed to be addressed, can be found within this larger context. Narratives propagated in the decades after World War I by Arab nationalist ideologues and practitioners engaged in state- and nation-building projects presented these developments in a teleological manner. As is usually the case with nationalist movements, Arab nationalism's emergence was described as a natural and inevitable reawakening of ancient bonds for the purpose of attaining Arab independence and unity, thus restoring the Arabs' proverbial place in the sun.[5] Eventually, however, scholars began addressing the matter in a more dispassionate fashion, producing a variety of explanations and insights, and generating a number of historiographical debates about what happened and why. More and more, scholars have come to understand that the notion of a master narrative of the origins of Arab nationalism needs to be supplemented, if not supplanted, by an approach that decenters it both in time and place.[6] For example, Arabism as a marker of national identity in North Africa would develop much later than in the Fertile Crescent.

While avoiding the older master narrative, one must nonetheless begin any discussion on the origins of Arabism (*'uruba*) by focusing on the Ottoman Syrian lands (*bilad al-Sham*) and Egypt, particularly after the British occupation. Time-wise, it is useful to distinguish between two periods: the decades between the suspension of the 1876 constitution by

Sultan Abdulhamid and its restoration in 1908 by the Young Turk Revolution, and the six years that followed, until the outbreak of World War I in August 1914. The initial gestation of the idea of Arabism occurred during the first period; the concretization and politicization of Arabism developed during the second. Throughout both periods, however, "Arabism" was distinct in meaning from "Arab nationalism." Arabism posited a strengthening of Arab identity within a reformed Ottoman Empire. As C. Ernest Dawn showed in his seminal studies on the subject, Arabism was a fluid term, and most of its adherents saw no contradiction between their ideas and being loyal to the Empire.[7] The doctrine of Arab nationalism (*qawmiyya `arabiyya)*, on the other hand, demanded independence: on the eve of World War I, it was an idea with very few advocates.[8]

For decades after the publication in 1938 of George Antonius's *The Arab Awakening*, its explanation for the rise of modern Arab nationalism was seen as definitive by both Western and Arab scholars. Arab nationhood, he postulated, had ancient roots, had manifested itself in numerous and diverse fashions over the centuries, and was chafing under the Ottoman yoke, waiting for the spark that would launch its revival. This spark, he said, was provided during the second half of the nineteenth century by the literary activity of Christian Arab intellectuals in the Levant (modern-day Syria and Lebanon), many of whom had received a modern education in Western missionary schools.[9] Together, he said, they spurred a cultural *nahda* ("awakening"), involving the modernization of the Arabic language and articulation of a common Arab identity, which ultimately laid the foundations for the subsequent Arab Revolt and drive for independence during World War I.

To be sure, these intellectuals did contribute to the fashioning of a modern, proto-national, and even secular Arab self-view. Nonetheless, it is now generally accepted that the central explanatory thread explaining the rise of Arabism was its connection to the promotion of Islamic reform (*islah*).[10] Muslim intellectuals were acutely aware of the Ottoman Empire's weak and vulnerable standing vis-à-vis ever-encroaching Christian European powers, whose influence had wrought profound changes on their societies—socially, economically, and demographically.[11] Consequently, they sought ways to both explain the secret of Western power and to find ways to overcome it, even as they themselves were the products, at least in part, of those changes. Moreover, most Christian Arab writers shared the injured self-view common to Muslim intellectuals.

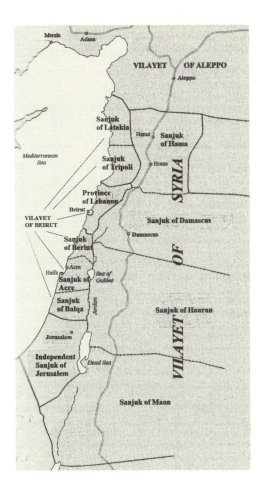

Figure 1.1.   The Levant in the Ottoman Empire before World War I.

Indeed, according to Hasan Kayali, in the period prior to 1908, "Christian Arabs contributed more to the resuscitation of the liberal movement that eventually became known as the Young Turk movement than they did to the fostering of Arabism." [12]

Three luminaries particularly stand out: Jamal al-Din al-Afghani, Mohammed `Abduh, and Rashid Rida. All three championed *salafism*, namely the need to emulate the pious ancestors (*al-salaf al-salih*) of early Islam. [13] The *salafi* current believed that by shedding the layers of allegedly un-Islamic practice that had accumulated over the centuries (e.g., Sufism, medieval scholasticism, saint worship, and veneration of tombs), the Islamic faith could be restored to first principles. Islam of the Qur'an, according to salafis, was a religion based on reason, enabling it to adapt to changing circumstances. It was only through this kind of reform that Islamic society would be able to mobilize its energies and rescue itself, politically, militarily, and spiritually.

For Jamal al-Din al-Afghani (1838/9–1897),[14] the focus was on politics and power. The solution to the Muslim world's plight, in his view, was to renew Muslim solidarity through the promotion of pan-Islam, in order to resist the West.[15] His charisma and peripatetic activities won him a considerable following among Muslim circles but also many enemies. Together with `Abduh (1849–1905), they disseminated their ideas through the influential journal al-`Urwa al-Wuthqa ("the indissoluble bond"). However, `Abduh was cut from an entirely different cloth. As a respected religious jurist in Cairo, particularly in the first two decades after Britain's occupation of Egypt, and eventually the Mufti of al-Azhar, the venerable institute of higher learning in Sunni Islam, `Abduh's focus was on internal reform, and particularly education. More than anyone else, it was `Abduh who actively sought to reconcile Islam with modernity's emphasis on both technological innovation and representative government. Rashid Rida (1865–1935), for his part, was initially a member of `Abduh's circle, and together they published the journal al-Manar. Rida was a native of Tripoli, a city in today's northern Lebanon. Like others from bilad al-Sham opposed to Abdulhamid, Rida made his way to the more relaxed confines of British Egypt. There, he actively promoted his ideas for decades, beginning with a call for the maintenance of Ottoman territorial integrity, resistance to imperialism, and opposition to Abdulhamid's authoritarian ways.[16] They would eventually evolve in the direction of stricter adherence to Islamic precepts, along the lines of the more puritan Wahhabi Islam championed by the Al Sa`ud chieftaincy in Arabia.

Inevitably, the salafi current's emphasis on the "straight path" (al-sirat al-mustaqim) of early Islam as a model to be emulated drew attention to those who had been there at the creation, namely the Arabs. Indeed, notwithstanding its universal message, Islam was originally a religious creed propagated by an Arab prophet and for the Arabic-speaking tribes of the Arabian Peninsula. One member of `Abduh's circle, the Aleppo-born, Cairo-based `Abd al-Rahman al-Kawakibi (1855–1902), drew a number of conclusions that emphasized the role of the Arabs in reforming the Empire. His solution to the Ottoman Empire's plight was to separate the political functions of the state from its religious ones. Political power, he said, could only be maintained by a just government, namely one that governed according to the will of the people, and not Hamidian despotism.[17] The spiritual leadership of the Empire, on the other hand, should be conferred upon a descendant of the Quraysh, the Prophet Muhammad's tribe, for it was the Arabs, and particularly the peninsular Arabs, who were best equipped to lead the spiritual regeneration of Islam necessary for the Empire's survival. Among their favorable attributes, he said, were their "purity of descent, richness of language, courage, pride, loyalty and fidelity, magnanimity, generosity, love of freedom, and ability to bear hardship."[18] Kawakibi also pulled no punches regarding what he believed to be the superiority of the Arabs over the Turks, insisting that it was the Turks who had corrupted Islam and thus were responsible for the current perilous state of affairs.

Abdulhamid, who was claiming the caliphate for himself in order to bolster his legitimacy, would obviously not countenance such thinking; nor would the Young Turk authorities who deposed him. In any case, Kawakibi's treatises had no immediate discernible impact. Later scholarship highlighted the derivative nature of his ideas and the connection between his writings and his apparent efforts to promote the Egyptian Khedive Abbas Hilmi Pasha as the temporal head of Islam. But in foregrounding the Arabs and belittling the Turks, in highlighting the just rule of the *rashidun*, the "rightly guided caliphs" of early Islam, and in promoting an institutional expression of Arab leadership, Kawakibi can be considered the first true intellectual precursor of modern Arab nationalism.[19]

A few years later, Naguib Azoury (c. 1870–1916) published eighteen issues of a periodical, *Le Reveil De La Nation Arabe*. Claiming to represent a secret society, he lambasted Turkish rule and called for full Arab independence. Azoury has often been mentioned in the same breath as Kawakibi, but as a disgruntled Maronite Christian ex-Ottoman official, he was a marginal figure who represented no one but himself. As the book's title and place of publication (Paris) indicates, it was written for a European audience; it advocated the establishment of an Arab empire, ideally ruled by a prince of the Khedival family (the ruling dynasty in Egypt), albeit under the tutelage of an "enlightened" European power, preferably France.[20] This hardly qualifies him as an authentic "founder" of Arab nationalism.

Nonetheless, the increasingly constricted Ottoman Empire was hardly immune from the phenomenon of mass politics that was coming to dominate Europe, aided by the spread of new media—newspapers and periodicals. Ironically, it was the Ottoman authorities themselves who played a key role in expanding the pool of politically conscious citizens through the expansion of state schools in its Arabic-speaking territories, both civilian and military. These schools played a key role in shaping a nationalist self-view of young Arab Muslim men, where they imbibed the ideas of Islamic reform, modernity, and political activism in the service of the Ottoman nation (*umma*).[21] Eventually, with the fall of the Empire, they would replace "Ottoman" with "Arab."

Arabism as a more explicitly political ideology emerged following the 1908 Young Turk revolution. Ironically, the enhancement of ethnic communal consciousness was one of the consequences of the Committee of Union and Progress (CUP) policies of liberalization of public life and expansion of educational opportunities that were designed to promote greater social cohesion and national integration. Arab deputies in the newly restored Ottoman parliament actively participated in the discussions over the Empire's future, including the budding challenge of Zionism.[22] While being especially concerned with issues pertaining to Arab regions of the Empire, their overall orientation was distinctively unionist.[23] Nonetheless, small secret societies of politically conscious Arabs were also founded; *al-jam`iyya al-`arabiyya al-Fatat*, founded in Paris in 1909 and made up primarily of Syrian civilians, and *al-`Ahd*, founded in Istanbul in 1913, which would also have branches in Baghdad and Mosul.[24] In addition, Beirut newspapers gave voice to their concerns and demands.[25] The most noteworthy event regarding the growth of Arabism prior to World War I was the convening of an Arab Congress in Paris on June 18–24, 1913. Most of the participants were Syrians, many of whom lived outside of the Empire. Their demands centered on calls for decentralized administration that would ensure the primacy of Arabic in provincial administration and schools and a more equal place for Arabs alongside their Turkish Muslim brethren through, among other things, specified quotas for Arabs as governors, district administrators, and senators.[26] However, Muslim Congress members from Beirut made sure to stop in Istanbul on the way home and proclaim their fealty to the Sultan, indicating their opposition to the pro-European, Christian separatist component of the Beirut reform group. In any case, the CUP soon eliminated the liberal opposition in Istanbul, with which Arab decentralizers had found common cause, leaving them with no political avenue to pursue their agenda.[27]

What had prompted these developments? The long-held explanation posited the emergence of political Arabism as a response to Turkification policies pursued by the ruling CUP clique in Istanbul. Arab sensibilities were said to have been wounded by the authorities' insistence on the exclusivity of the Turkish language in all official business, and by the replacement of local Arab officials with Turkish ones. The CUP's supposedly overt secularization policies were also said to have contributed to Arab alienation.[28] However, more recent scholarship challenges this simple dichotomy, while still leaving room for interpretation. Dawn's detailed research emphasizes that what was occurring was primarily an intra-elite conflict, in which the new CUP rulers replaced Arab administrators in *bilad al-sham* who had been loyal to Sultan Abdulhamid with other members of that same elite.[29] In addition, the small but unmistakable rising middle class generally favored CUP centralization policies, opposing only the insistence on the exclusivity of Turkish in the imperial administration.[30] At bottom, the question of Turkish versus Arabic was more of degree than anything else; Turkish had always been the primary language of administration. Those who favored decentralization were mainly those who had lost out in the quite ordinary administrative reshuffle, although the CUP did alienate some of its former Arab allies when it started compromising with conservative notables. What was new was that opposition demands were being couched in ethno-linguistic terms. Hence, it appears that the rise of the Beirut Arabic press does not fit neatly into the Andersonian model of nationalism's growth through the spread of print capitalism in vernacular languages,[31] or reflect the needs and Arab nationalist sensibilities of a rising middle class. Nonetheless, increased emphasis was now made on "being Arab" and "being Turk" among the politicized public in both Istanbul and the Levant, and even within the CUP leadership. The fact that both Greeks and Armenians were demanding that their languages be recognized as state languages was not lost on Arabs either.[32] Turkification policies, to the extent that they were advanced, were more of a by-product of the CUP's efforts to centralize their rule than the reason for those efforts. But they were nonetheless advanced in state and administrative agencies and secondary education.

The story of Arabism was quite different in other parts of the Ottoman world, thanks to the interplay of local, regional, and international forces. Italy's occupation of Ottoman Libya in 1911–1912 generated armed resistance, which Egyptians, Tunisians, and others rushed to join in the name of defending Islam and the realm of Empire against Western imperialism. For Egyptian nationalists, led by Mustafa Kamil, the defense of Ottoman Libya and their proclaimed loyalty to the Ottoman sultan was more a function of their anti-British position than a desire to be reincorporated into the Empire: by this time, the idea of an independent territorial state in Egypt had struck deep roots among the political classes. In Iraq, by contrast, plans by the Ottoman government in 1909 to grant a monopoly on river transportation to a British company aroused broad opposition throughout Iraqi society, which led to the resignation of the grand *vezir* and the cancellation of the plans. However, politically conscious Arab Iraqis would soon be divided into centralization and decentralization camps.[33] In any case, the overall level of Arab national consciousness was very low, as testified to by a future Iraqi statesman, Tawfiq al-Suwaydi.[34]

The Hijaz, the region of Islam's holiest sites, and the Arabian peninsula as a whole, had been remote, tribal, and still nomadic, to an extent, in social organization, and largely immune from the great forces that had fundamentally challenged the Ottoman order during the nineteenth century, apart from the sacking of Mecca by the forces of the Egyptian khedive, Mohamed Ali, in 1813. Notwithstanding the presence of an Ottoman governor, the real authority in the Hijaz belonged to one or another of the grand Hashimite *sharifian* families charged with maintaining the holy places and managing the pilgrimage. By the end of the century, however, the centralization impulses that had guided the thinking of Ottoman rulers for decades were starting to be felt in the Hijaz. As elsewhere, the 1908 Young Turk revolution accelerated matters. Moreover, the Hijaz railway's Damascus-Medina line was completed that same year, enabling the Ottoman authorities to have a heavier footprint in the region. Economically, too, the railway posed a threat to the caravan trade and pilgrimage traffic controlled by the tribes, who rose in revolt. Two years later, Medina would be administratively separated from the rest of the Hijaz, in order to further centralization policies there.[35]

The central actor of the forthcoming drama, Sharif Husayn bin `Ali, was appointed emir of Mecca in 1908. His top priority was to preserve and enhance his position in the face of Ottoman centralizing pressures, local rivals and dissident tribes, the growing strength of `Abd al-`Aziz bin Sa`ud in the northeast of the peninsula, and the dominance of European powers. He was about as far away from the notion of Arabism and the political efforts to advance it as one could be. Ironically, it was over his shoulders that the mantle of Arab leadership would eventually be draped.

In sum, Arabism in August 1914 was certainly a minority movement, and the advocates of Arab nationalist separatism were few and far between. But the war that broke out in Europe would change everything.

2

WORLD WAR I AND ITS AFTERMATH

The Arab Revolt and Unrealized Expectations

World War I was a watershed in the history of the Middle East, resulting in the collapse of the Ottoman Empire and subsequent redrawing of the regional map. The Empire had entered the conflict in November 1914 on the side of the Central Powers (Germany and Austria-Hungary). By the time the war concluded four years later, Ottoman forces had been pushed out of its Arabic-speaking provinces in the Near East by British forces, assisted by Arab tribal units operating under the banner of Mecca's Hashimite guardian, Sharif Husayn; its capital Istanbul was occupied by the victorious Allied powers, and what remained of the country was on the verge of dismemberment, as envisaged in the August 1920 Treaty of Sèvres. The Sèvres treaty also confirmed what had been decided three months earlier at the San Remo conference: the division of the lands of *bilad al-sham* and Mesopotamia into Mandated entities: Iraq and Palestine (including Transjordan) under British tutelage, and Syria and Lebanon, the latter being effectively separated from the rest of Syria, overseen by France. By mid-1923, the map of the Near East had been almost definitively redrawn and enshrined in the Treaty of Lausanne, sanctified by the League of Nations, and the process would be completed in 1925, with the assignment of most of the ex-Ottoman *vilayet* of Mosul to British Mandated Iraq. In contrast to the newly consecrated Mandated territories, a viable Turkish national state, led by Kemal Attatürk, had emerged in a trial by fire, following the rolling back of Greece's invading army from western and central Anatolia by Turkish forces, thus compelling the Western powers to accept the existence of an independent Turkey.

For subsequent generations of Arab nationalists, the single overriding theme of these monumental developments was that of loss and betrayal. In return for initiating a revolt against the Ottomans in July 1916, Sharif Husayn and his sons were understood to have received a firm commitment from Great Britain to support Arab independence and unity following the Ottoman defeat, only to have Britain renege on its pledge in favor of a secret pact that had concurrently been signed with France, the Sykes-Picot Agreement, that carved up the region according to British and French interests, and against its inhabitants' desires for independence and unity. "Sykes-Picot" would henceforth enter into the political lexicon of the Middle East as a synonym for imperialism running roughshod over indigenous peoples' interests and aspirations. And to make matters even worse, as far as Arab nationalists were concerned, the British issued the Balfour Declaration on November 2, 1917, in which Great Britain committed itself to the establishment of a Jewish national home in Palestine, inaugurating what is now a century-old conflict.

The job of the historian is to explain what happened and why. Indeed, innumerable works have been written about these transformative events. Nonetheless, the debates over what transpired remain lively, offering various interpretations of the motivations and actions of the key players.

George Antonius's *The Arab Awakening* faithfully articulates the consensus Arab nationalist version of the events. By the eve of the war, he wrote, Arab nationalism had congealed as an idea and a movement: The desire to be free of the yoke of Turkish domination was widespread, and Arab officers in the Ottoman army who belonged to the *al-`Ahd* secret society were waiting in Damascus for the signal from Sharif Husayn's son, Faysal, to rise up in rebellion. The fact that this never occurred was ascribed to the harsh repression of the Ottoman governor of Syria, Jamal Pasha: Twenty-one suspected Arab nationalists were publicly executed in Damascus and Beirut on May, 6, 1916, and numerous Arab officers were transferred out of the region. Nonetheless, he insisted, the Hashimite-led Arab Revolt, undertaken at great risk, represented the general will of the Arab nation, and made a significant contribution to the war effort. The climax came with Faysal leading his troops in a victorious entry into Damascus on October 1, 1918, followed by the momentary realization of the dream of Arab unity on March 8, 1920, when the General Syrian

Congress proclaimed him king of a united and independent Syria, in all the lands of *bilad al-sham*. Concurrently, a similar declaration was issued by the Iraqi Congress in Damascus, proclaiming Iraqi independence and `Abdallah, Faysal's older brother, as king of Iraq. Sati` al-Husri, a key figure in the propagation of Arab nationalist ideology during the interwar period, echoed Antonius's versions of events. Faysal's government, he wrote, "was the offspring of the Arab Revolt and the beacon of its hopes…a modern Arab Government in every sense of the term, fully conscious of its Arabism, working unceasingly for Arab nationalism, and appreciating to the utmost the requirements of contemporary life."[1]

The bitter fall was not long in coming: On July 24, 1920, French forces occupied Damascus and put paid to Faysal's kingdom, asserting their prerogatives initially agreed to by Britain in the Sykes-Picot Agreement and firmed up at San Remo. For Arab nationalists, Britain's assent to France's deposal of Faysal, however reluctant, offered the ultimate proof of its bad faith. So did the Balfour Declaration. Their reading of Britain's original commitment to Sharif Husayn was that Palestine was clearly included in the territory designated for the future independent Arab state. The Declaration stood in obvious contradiction to that alleged commitment, as did the subsequent (1922) League of Nations-issued Mandate for Palestine, which explicitly included the establishment of a Jewish National Home as part of its *raison d'étre*.[2] More generally, the Mandate system in general seemed to be a thinly disguised implementation of Sykes-Picot. Instead of establishing a unified independent Arab state in Greater Syria and a companion state in Iraq, which Arab nationalists insisted was the natural order of things, the region was broken up into multiple entities, which were to be patronizingly guided by France and Britain toward independence.

This essentially black-and-white, linear, and moralistic account of what happened contains serious flaws. Sharif Husayn, we now know, was hardly a passive or innocent player in the game. Rather he harbored ambitions of his own, both temporally—to be king of a sovereign Arab nation, and not just over his immediate Hijaz environs—and spiritually— to be recognized as caliph of the Muslim world. Indeed, the initial overture to him by Britain's Lord Kitchener in November 1914 dangled the idea of shifting the seat of the caliphate from Istanbul to Mecca (a partial echo of the idea tendered a decade earlier by Kawakibi). To be sure, British officials didn't deem it to have much practical significance. For

Sharif Husayn, though, it held great potential. At the same time, he was keenly aware of his vulnerability. The Ottoman garrison in Medina could easily depose him from power if the order was given, and the Ottoman authorities were watching his behavior closely for any sign of insubordination or encouragement of insurrection. Conversely, British naval power was literally on his doorstep, in the Red Sea, backed by British forces in Egypt. Hence, it would be only natural for Sharif Husayn to explore his options and not rush to make any irreversible decisions. Indeed, it appears that it was only after he believed that the Ottomans were planning to depose him that he crossed the Rubicon and threw in his lot with Britain.[3] Moreover, even after he did so, he engaged in continuous diplomatic maneuvering to try to ensure the optimal outcome.

Sharif Husayn's alliance with Britain was forged through his correspondence with Britain's High Commissioner in Cairo, Sir Henry McMahon. Sharif Husayn needed to be convinced that rebelling against the Ottoman sovereign would be worth his while: that he would be provided with sufficient gold and supplies to ensure the loyalty of the tribal forces whom he would mobilize, that Britain would ultimately ensure his safety and survival, and that the reward—namely, the establishment of Arab rule in the Fertile Crescent under his family's leadership, and hopefully the caliphate—would be commensurate with the risk involved. For Britain, the possibility of peeling away Istanbul's Arab subjects and opening a second front was attractive. The question was whether the Sharif could deliver on his promise of leading a large-scale revolt, and how far Britain could go in committing itself to his postwar vision.

A close examination of the correspondence reveals the wide initial gaps between the two sides' positions, the efforts made to narrow them, and the remaining opacity of Britain's commitment to meeting Husayn's postwar aspirations, which stemmed in no small measure from a lack of coherent policy formulation in London. The language of McMahon's crucial letter of October 24, 1915, the source of much of the subsequent debate over what exactly Britain promised to Husayn, was "vague, involved, roundabout, and obscure."[4] Britain excluded a number of areas from Husayn's proposed domain: those that it termed "not purely Arab," namely "the portions of Syria lying to the west of the districts (*wilayat*)[5] of Damascus, Hama, Homs, and Aleppo," i.e., the coastal regions of Syria, Mt. Lebanon, and the Lebanese coast, and into southern Anatolia ("the districts of Mersina and Alexandretta"); and the provinces of Basra and Baghdad, areas of vital British economic and strategic interests and thus requiring special administrative arrangements. In addition, the letter said, Britain's existing treaties with the Arab chieftains of the Persian Gulf principalities were to be preserved, and independence would be supported for those (unspecified) areas in which Britain was "free to act without detriment to her Ally, France." As McMahon subsequently explained to his superiors, this qualification provided for "possible French pretensions" to the four Syrian towns that Britain had made the core of the region designated for Arab independence.[6] The qualification would also apply to Palestine. Subject to these modifications, the letter declared, Great Britain was "prepared to recognize and support the independence of the Arabs within the territories included in the limits and boundaries proposed by the Sharif . . . and [would] assist them to establish . . . the most suitable forms of government in those territories." It would also have exclusive right among European governments to provide advisors and officials to ensure sound administration.[7]

Sharif Husayn, for his part, while happy to receive the pledge of British support for Arab independence in Syria and more than willing to accept its future patronage, was hardly ready to accept the territorial limitations enumerated by McMahon. In his reply of November 5, 1915, he quickly assented to the exclusion of the Mersina and Adana regions, but utterly rejected McMahon's exclusion of the coastal regions of Syria, Lebanon, and northern and central Palestine: "The two *wilayat* [Ottoman provinces] of Aleppo and Beirut and their sea coasts are purely Arab," he declared, "with no difference between a Muslim and a Christian Arab." Similarly, he insisted, the Mesopotamian *wilayat* (Baghdad and Basra) must be included within the future Arab kingdom, having been the seat of the caliphate since the time of the fourth caliph `Ali (the city of Kufa, 170 kilometers south of Baghdad), although the Sharif was willing to allow Britain to maintain its troop presence and administration there for a short period of time, in return for suitable financial compensation. Its existing treaties with the Gulf sheikhs would be respected. Husayn made no mention of the *sanjaq* of Jerusalem, an Ottoman district that was accorded a special administrative status within the province of Syria (*al-Sham*) and encompassed part of central and southern Palestine, presumably to avoid raising British hackles, but it had been included in the initial map of his demands that had been presented to the British, and he no doubt hoped to include it within his domain, sooner or later.

Two more rounds of letters would be exchanged in December 1915 and January 1916, with neither side altering their conflicting positions regarding the areas west of the Syrian towns or the future role of France. McMahon emphasized that the interests of Britain's ally were involved and thus required careful consideration, and that the British-French alliance would be even stronger after the war. Husayn responded that he would claim Beirut and its coastal regions at the earliest opportunity after the war, and that conceding even a single foot of territory to France or any other power was "out of the question." Throughout, it was Britain that urged speedy action by the sharif to unite Arab parties behind him and initiate the revolt, while the latter remained cautious, fearing the possible negative repercussions.

What emerged, in essence, was an alliance based on sufficient mutual interests and partial understandings, alongside an agreement to disagree about the desired nature of the postwar arrangements. Both sides were keenly aware that the devil would be in the details of the postwar settlement, which had not yet been worked out, and would presumably be shaped by developments on the ground. At the same time, McMahon's admittedly imprecise language offered the sharif some assurance that Britain would be sympathetic to a postwar order that would take his aspirations into account. Ultimately, with the Ottoman threat to his position increasingly salient, the sharif took the plunge, proclaiming the revolt on June 10, 1916.

The politicking was only just beginning, as Great Power interests and rivalries interacted continuously with local factors and concerns. In May 1916, the Sykes-Picot Agreement was signed, albeit not publicized. It divided the Levant/Fertile Crescent Region into five regions. Two were to be ruled directly: the Syrian coastal region (corresponding to the *wilaya* of Beirut and part of the *wilaya* of Aleppo) by France (known as the "Blue" zone), and the Baghdad-Basra region by Britain (the "Red" zone). Two were to be the bases for Arab rule, albeit under European supervision: inland Syria, centering on the four cities of Damascus, Homs, Hama, and Aleppo, by France (Area A), and the mostly desert interior to the east and south by Britain (Area B); and one, which included part of the Ottoman *sanjak* of Jerusalem and the southernmost part of the *wilaya* of Beirut (i.e., central and part of northern Palestine) would be ruled by an international condominium (the "Brown" zone). As Kedourie pointed out, and contrary to popular belief, the agreement did not stand in complete and blatant contradiction to McMahon's statements to Husayn. Indeed, it gave concrete expression to McMahon's reservations regarding France's interests in the coastal regions and in general.[8] Nonetheless, as we have seen, Husayn wasn't buying the package and was determined to advance his own agenda. When push came to shove, Great Britain would find it impossible to reconcile the demands of its number-one ally, France, and its new client-ally, the Hashimite family, through which it hoped to advance its interests in the post-Ottoman Near East.

The Balfour Declaration stirred Arab opposition and would contribute immeasurably to the Arab nationalist self-view of having been fundamentally wronged. But the immediate and overriding issue, from the time that Faysal led his units into Damascus and established a nascent government

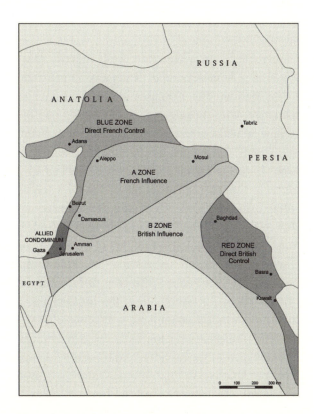

Figure 2.1.   Sykes-Picot Agreement 1916. Reproduced from www.passia.org with permission (Mahmoud Abu Rumieleh, webmaster).

in Syria under British patronage until his forcible eviction two years later by French forces, was the future of Syria.

British policy on the fate of Syria, and the validity of the Sykes-Picot Agreement in general, was certainly a question mark in the eyes of all the parties. Britain's ambitions in Mosul and Palestine stood in blatant contradiction to its commitments to France in Sykes-Picot.[9] However, the favorable balance of power produced by the war enabled Britain to discard the agreement's stipulation that the oil-rich Mosul region would be included in the French zone of influence (Area A), and that Jerusalem and a surrounding portion of Palestine would be internationalized. Faysal was clearly hoping that Britain would behave similarly in Syria, and at least some British officials were in fact working to that end. However, French interests and influence, particularly in the coastal regions (the "Blue" zone), were manifest, based on moral/religious, political, and economic pillars,[10] and Paris was determined to assert its predominance in both the Blue zone and the Syrian interior.

Meanwhile, the task of quickly fashioning a viable and coherent Syrian national entity based on a common Arab identity that could resist French inroads was a herculean and ultimately impossible task within such a short time period. The Damascene Ottoman elite families were concerned primarily with preserving their status, and hence looked askance at the new arrivals, who to them were uncouth Bedouin from the desert. Matters weren't helped by the fact that activists from across the region, including Iraq, the Hijaz, and Palestine, flocked to join Faysal's new government, or that the officer corps of Faysal's forces were made up of ex-Ottoman officers, mostly from Iraq, who consequently assumed senior positions in the nascent administration. Syrian complaints against the Iraqi "aliens" and about being "strangers in their own country" were matched by Faysal's associates' expressions of frustration over Syrian "parochialism."[11] There were also significant differences between older and younger members of the Syrian elite: the former, who had been an integral part of the pre-war Ottoman Arab world, were more amenable to a localized "Syrian" nationalist vision that would better enable them to preserve their status than to the broader "Arab" one, which was attracting younger members of the Syrian upper classes, and expressed in the pan-Arab *Hizb al-Istiqlal al-`Arabi*.[12] And as James Gelvin has cogently noted, the pan-Arab, essentially secular nationalist discourse being promoted by Faysal's government did not resonate with the broader, poorer, recently urbanized, and increasingly politicized sectors of society, whose material situation was deteriorating rapidly. Their clear, simple, and populist messages ("Complete independence for Syria within its natural boundaries, no protection, no tutelage, no mandate")—chanted in planned demonstrations and spontaneous riots, and scrawled on walls throughout Syria as graffiti—were far more in tune with the actual beliefs and desires of the populace at large than the country's leadership. [13]

The short-lived Faysal government lurched from crisis to crisis, being unable to cope with a host of postwar economic hardships, increased lawlessness, and urban overcrowding, owing to the influx of refugees, particularly destitute Armenians uprooted by the 1915 massacres in Anatolia. A second wave of refugees, mostly from the Syrian countryside, began with the breakdown of rural security in the wake of the "Evacuation Crisis," following the September 15, 1919 Anglo-French agreement in which Britain relinquished its temporary military control of the coastal regions and Lebanon's Biqa` valley to France, and the interior to Faysal's administration, pending a permanent understanding between the two contesting parties. As is so often the case in multi-ethnic, multi-confessional societies, the breakdown in order and governmental services resulted in rising intercommunal tensions. Worst of all, for most Syrians, was the Faysal government's imposition of compulsory military service and efforts to impose new taxes. [14]

As the situation deteriorated in the first half of 1920, the Faysal government's "moral and political authority collapsed," with popular committees and local organizers moving to fill the gap. [15] They grew in strength as the French threat loomed and Faysal desperately sought some kind of compromise. With his hands tied by French determination, British resignation, economic insolvency, and militancy at home, the die was essentially cast. Just four days before French troops entered Damascus, Faysal's forces brutally put down an insurrection prompted by his concessions to the French, one that cost nearly two hundred lives in Damascus alone, and hundreds elsewhere. [16] For Gelvin, the insurrection provides irrefutable evidence of the strength of populist nationalism at the time, and its distance from the elites, and heralded the advent of popular nationalist politics in the Arab Middle East that endures to this day. [17]

Following the climactic one-sided battle of Maysalun on July 24, 1920, Faysal and his entourage fled Damascus, making their way to Palestine with British assistance, and France consolidated its control over

Syria and Lebanon. On September 1, 1920, the latter was consecrated as "*Le Grand Liban*": France and its local Maronite allies had expanded the autonomously administered Ottoman *mutassarifate* of Mt. Lebanon to include the coastal cities of Beirut, Tripoli, Sidon and Tyre, and the Biqa` valley. The rest of Syria would be administratively divided into four entities, two centering on Damascus and Aleppo, one in the area known as the Druze Mountain in the southeast, and one in the Alawi northwest. Overall, France's actions in Syria and Lebanon reflected an overarching sectarian-based view of Near Eastern societies. Britain's vision, on the other hand, emphasized their common Arabness.

For the Hashimite Sharifians and their allies, and Arab nationalists in general, the dream of a large independent Arab state in *bilad al-sham* under Hashimite rule had been crushed by the Western powers, who had divided it into seven sections, including Palestine and Transjordan, leaving great bitterness and new political realities. At the same time, for Arab nationalism, as both an idea and a movement, it was only the beginning.

3

STATE-BUILDING AND NATION-BUILDING IN ADVERSE CIRCUMSTANCES

The foundations for what would be a highly charged, competitive, and largely conflictual inter-Arab system were laid during the ensuing quarter century, between Faysal's expulsion from Damascus and the end of World War II. It would be marked by halting and uneven state-building and nation-building processes throughout the region, which partly complemented and partly conflicted with one another. Moreover, these processes would occur under the influence of the Mandate powers' deep involvement in local affairs, the burgeoning Jewish-Arab conflict over Palestine, the rise of fascism and Nazism in Europe, and the ensuing world war.

For Arab nationalism, both as an idea and a political movement, the results would be transformational. Prewar political Arabism within a reformed Ottoman Empire was now superseded by an overarching doctrine of Arab nationalism, elaborated upon by intellectuals, publicists, and activists. It was widely disseminated in the education systems of newly emerging entities of the Near East and gradually extended into Egypt and French-ruled North Africa as well. This doctrine would be fundamental to local elites' efforts to build viable entities and achieve independence from European domination, but also render them vulnerable to criticism by political opponents both within and beyond their borders. Arab nationalism, which conditioned the legitimacy of these new entities on their fealty to the principle of broader Arab unity, would eventually achieve hegemonic status. Eventually, in Michael Barnett's words, there emerged

Arab states with a set of interests that flowed from the Arab identity. States became mutually vulnerable to the symbols of Arab nationalism, and Arab leaders tried to accumulate these symbols to deploy them against their rivals in the pursuit of their domestic and foreign policy objectives.[1]

This mutual vulnerability to the symbols of Arab nationalism would be particularly salient among the newly established, socially and economically fragmented Fertile Crescent entities.

One may conveniently divide the unfolding of these processes into two periods: 1920–1936, from the moment of Faysal's expulsion to the outbreak of the Arab Revolt in Palestine, and the concurrent signing of the Anglo-Egyptian and (aborted) French-Syrian treaties; and 1936–1945, covering the descent into the abyss of World War II to the war's end, the establishment of the seven-member League of Arab States, and the ignominious end of French-mandated Syria and Lebanon.

CENTERING AND DECENTERING ARAB NATIONALISM

As mentioned in chapter 1, recent scholarship on Arab nationalism points to its decentering, i.e., the variety of Arab nationalist experiences, and the multiple meanings appropriated by various actors across different social classes and ethno-religious communities in the newly emerging entities as they struggled for power and influence.[2] For Sunni Arabs in the multi-confessional societies of the Fertile Crescent, Arab nationalism seemed an appropriate way to ensure the preeminence that they had enjoyed during the hundreds of years of Ottoman rule. For at least some minorities, and particularly intellectuals and members of the younger generations, secular Arab nationalism seemingly provided a path to equality. And in North Africa, and particularly French colonial Algeria, an Arab-Islamic identity would become central to nationalists seeking to distinguish their societies from France's embrace. All of this is crucial to the story. Nonetheless, one must begin by emphasizing the central thread of the idea, its elaboration, and widespread dissemination.

During the 1920s and 1930s, as C. Ernest Dawn's important study shows, a coterie of Arab writers/activists fashioned a coherent "Arab national history" and disseminated it in school textbooks that were adopted throughout the region. The prewar Islamist modernism that emphasized the central role of the place of the Arabs in the rise of Islam and its necessary rejuvenation was joined to a larger Semito-Arab version of history in which pre-Islamic waves of Semitic people were said to have carried forth the message of civilization throughout the ancient Near East. According to this grand narrative, while it was Islam that had brought the Arabs to greatness, it was the Arabic language and this common history that had forged the Arab nation. However, the Arab nation had declined in the face of Aryan/Persian and Turco-Mongol imperialism, and excessive tribalism (`asabiyya, literally "tribal solidarity") and individualism. Moreover, according to this narrative, the Arabs had become corrupted by excess borrowing, a process that was nearly fatal. History was now said to be repeating itself, as Western imperialism threatened Arab existence, and only a national revival could rescue the nation. A kind of semi-Marxism was added to the mix as well, emphasizing the inherent equality of ancient Arab society and the need for social justice for the increasingly politicized masses.[3]

Israel Gershoni's analysis of the rise of nationalism in the Middle East provides some of the background for understanding the strength that this grand narrative of Arab identity and history possessed. As in many other societies, he wrote, nationalism was a "principal agent" for the introduction of Western modernity and progress, "forging a new and authentic collective identity, a 'new nation,' able to inculcate 'in its own way' a modern value system."[4] Focusing on language and territory (rather than on religion) as the dominant cohesive elements of society, nationalism became the main secularizing vehicle of politics in the Middle East of the twentieth century. Everywhere in the Muslim world, a process of consolidation of nation-states was in motion: In Egypt and the successor states to the Ottoman Empire, the process of marginalizing religion from high politics had been underway for more than a century. At the same time, for Arab nationalists, "becoming modern" clashed with the inherent tendency to look backward, toward the Golden Age of early Islam. To be sure, all modern nationalisms promote nostalgia for lost glories as essential components of their collective identities. But the strident condemnations of "excess borrowing" from other civilizations that allegedly corrupted the Arabs' essential identity both ignored the rich history of classical Islamic civilization that engaged in extensive cultural borrowing (as all civilizations do), and pointed to what would be a serious limitation in the Arab nationalist project—the inability to decisively separate religious truths and tenets from political life.

The person most closely associated with the doctrine of secular Arab nationalism, with its primary emphasis on a common language and history, was Sati` al-Husri. In developing these themes, he drew heavily on Johann Gottlieb Fichte, Johann Gottfried Herder, and other nineteenth-century German espousers of cultural nationalism, which posited the objective existence of national communities from time immemorial, regardless of transient political circumstances and boundaries.[5] Belonging to the nation, according to them, was not voluntary: The mission of nationalists was, first and foremost, to awaken the members of the nation to their "objective" belonging to the nation, and then develop the appropriate political and cultural strategies to achieve its goals. Although a later generation of Arab nationalist theoreticians would view Husri's views as overly conservative and lacking in militant revolutionary fervor,[6] his stress on the Arabic language and history as the essential elements of Arab nationalism would remain central to the Arab nationalist worldview.

Husri's pan-Arab outlook was epitomized by his career trajectory: director-general of the Education Ministry in Syria under Faysal's nascent government, and then in Iraq, where he played a central role in fashioning the nationalist self-view of Iraqi Sunni elites; a return to Syria in 1943, where he was charged with introducing a new history curriculum into secondary schools; and then a move to Cairo in 1947, to head the Cultural Directorate of the League of Arab States. Ironically, but not untypical of the times, Husri himself had not been an Arab nationalist before World War I, reflecting his background as the son of an Ottoman provincial official (the family was from Aleppo, a historic, ethnically and religiously mixed city in northern Syria; he himself was born in San`a`, Yemen, where his father was stationed). The idea of Arab nationalism clearly provided a concrete solution for Husri and other members of his class left adrift by the collapse of the Ottoman Empire. At the same time, he brought with him what Elie Kedourie termed "the cold centralizing passion of the Ottoman bureaucracy,"[7] one that was manifestly unsuited to Iraq's heterogeneous realities. Indeed, Husri prevented the opening of teacher training colleges in predominantly Shi`i and Christian areas, fearing that they would help consolidate sectarian feelings, and opposed proposed state subsidies to Jewish and Christian schools because they wouldn't be accompanied by his control over their curricula. He was biased against the Kurds as well. Husri was also a fervent advocate of compulsory military conscription, viewing it as a perfect complement to compulsory education.[8]

Of course, Husri was well aware of the linguistic realities on the ground: the huge gap between literary Arabic, based on the Qur'an, and the innumerable dialects of unwritten spoken Arabic, some of which vary so widely as to be mutually unintelligible. Some linguists even argue that Lebanese Arabic is a language in its own right, owning to the influences of Syriac.[9] The same also may be true for Moroccan (and Algerian) Arabic, which have been heavily influenced by Berber (Tamazight).[10] Hence, Husri and his successors in the emerging Arab states would make the standardization of Arabic and the Arabization of their societies a top policy priority. Similarly, there was a huge gap between an insistence on a common "Arab" history and the actual historical record, in which the hallowed ideal of Arab unity existed for only a century or so, during the so-called Golden Age of the "Rightly Guided" Caliphs (632–661) followed by the Damascus-based Umayyad Empire (661–750). But as has already been shown, and has been the case with nearly all nationalist movements, this did not prevent Arab activists and pedagogues from promoting a mobilized, national version of history.

THE PARTICULARS OF STATE-BUILDING AND NATION-BUILDING DURING THE INTER-WAR YEARS

Most of the modern Arab states that would emerge in the self-defined "Arab homeland" (*al-watan al-`arabi*) stretching from North Africa's Atlantic coast to the Persian Gulf possessed a considerable degree of legitimacy that predated the arrival of colonialism. This was true regardless of the specific premodern regime types: the Ottoman Regencies of Tripoli, Tunis, and Algiers, all run by military-bureaucratic oligarchies with only tenuous ties to Istanbul; the imam-chief system that prevailed in Morocco and Oman, in which religious and political legitimacy were invested in a single person; the Arabian chieftaincies of Najd, Hijaz, and the Persian Gulf littoral; and nineteenth-century dynastic Egypt and Maronite-dominated Mount Lebanon. In all of these cases, important foundations had been laid for what would become modern states. It was only the Fertile Crescent/Levant that lacked this long history of durable ruling elites that were largely independent of Istanbul.[11] Given the region's social, religious, and ethnic fragmentation, it was only natural that Arabism, Arab nationalism, and pan-Arabism would develop there, providing a possible tool to overcome "primordial" divisions and the absence of independent political traditions. At the same time, the fact that the doctrine would spread hither and yon, to Egypt and North Africa, and to the Arabian Peninsula, and become integral parts of the state-building and nation-building formulas there, testifies to its power and value at this particular moment in history.

Iraq

In the summer of 1920, a large-scale rebellion in the middle and lower Euphrates regions, some of it generated by Faysal's pan-Arab agents and some by Shi`i leaders, particularly Sayyid Abu Talib, posed a major threat to continued British control. In casting about for a solution that would enable Britain to establish its designated Mandate, British officials found what to them seemed to be an elegant answer: a monarchy, headed by their Hashimite ally, the recently deposed Faysal, accompanied by the ex-Ottoman Iraqi officers who had joined him in Damascus, which would hopefully be supported by the country's Sunni elite based in Baghdad and surrounding areas.[12] Such a solution essentially ignored the other ethnic and confessional components of Iraqi society—its Shi`is, Kurds, Assyrians, Turkomens, Christians, and Jews. Moreover, being Sunni would turn out to be insufficient: the Hashimite monarchy would never strike deep roots in Iraqi society, even among its Sunni Arab component and would fail to acquire a sufficient measure of legitimacy. Indeed, just before his death in 1932, Faysal himself would bemoan the lack of national cohesion and solidarity among his countrymen, and despair of ever achieving it.[13] The aftermath of the 2003 US war in Iraq seemed to confirm Faysal's pessimism, and even Kedourie's view that the idea of establishing a single united Iraq had been a bad one from the outset.[14]

Having quickly become aware of the difficulties in ruling Iraq, Britain sought a formula that would enable it to preserve its interests while avoiding excessive entanglement. Hence, only a decade after Sam Remo, Iraq was granted formal independence and joined the League of Nations, while Britain retained its military bases and close ties with a section of the political elite. Assyrian, Kurdish, and Shi`i communities were brutally repressed with impunity. The parliamentary political system established by Britain served merely as a cover for the Iraqi Sunni elite to enhance its wealth and power, at the expense of the public at large. Over time, there emerged a younger and increasingly politicized generation of Iraq army officers and political activists, one that would make militant pan-Arabism and anti-British imperialism central tenets in their worldview, leading to chronic political instability and the progressive, and ultimately poisonous, involvement of the military in politics.

For Iraq's Sunnis, both those aligned to Britain and the monarchy and those opposed to it, an Arab nationalist identity had instrumental value, as it was crucial to ensuring their own preeminent status in a society in which they constituted a numerical minority. There was also a regional aspect to their embrace of Arabism. In their view, Iraq could play a role in the Arab East analogous to that played by Prussia a half-century earlier, which united the various German-speaking principalities under its leadership. Geopolitical and demographic calculations were part of the picture as well. Instead of being almost entirely landlocked, and squeezed from the north by a rapidly rising Kemalist Turkey and from the east by Iran, extending Iraq's influence westward over Greater Syria carried the promise of a powerful state with a Sunni Arab majority. [15]

Syria

According to the emerging grand Arab nationalist narrative, Syria was "the beating heart of Arabism." Indeed, Arab nationalism would come to heavily shape the evolution of the Syrian polity during the years of the French Mandate, albeit in a more complex way than the received narrative would have.

Having severed Lebanon from the rest of Mandated Syria, France would further divide Syria into distinct regions—the Druze and 'Alawi mountains, Aleppo and Damascus. Unlike the British in Iraq, who put all of their eggs in the Sunni-Hashimite basket, France preferred a "divide and rule" approach to its new Mandated territory, in line with its understanding of the societies of the region as essentially sectarian-based, a view not bereft of logic. As it happened of course, the outcome in Syria was no better than in Iraq. The process of state-building and nation-building during the Mandate years was halting at best, and Syria would emerge in 1945 as a weak state and divided society, with an uncertain future and the object of rival regional ambitions.

As we have seen, the traditional Sunni Damascene elite had been extremely uncomfortable with Faysal's minions. Hence, once the dust had settled, and particularly after the 1925 revolt that began in Jebel Druze (Druze Mountain) and spread into portions of Damascus and other urban areas throughout the country,[16] it resumed its preeminent role, albeit this time under the supervision of French administrators. Although there would be considerable friction, their approach to the Mandate would be one of "honorable cooperation," in which they would seek to negotiate independence for Syria. By contrast, a younger group of mostly Damascus-trained lawyers rejected this strategy: Organized under the banner of the League of National Action, they lobbied during the mid-1930s for a more militant strategy to attain independence. However, they failed to build bridges to other social groups in the urban areas, let alone the rural ones.[17] Hence, Syria could hardly be called a coherent, economically, and socially integrated entity. Seeking some sort of glue to bind it together, and with the Iraqi example in mind, both the Mandate powers and neighboring regional actors floated numerous ideas regarding the possibility of establishing a monarchy in Syria. However, nothing came of it.[18] As for Lebanon's Sunni Muslims, the severance from Damascus was a bitter pill to swallow and would take years to grudgingly accept.

Transjordan

The sparsely populated (c. 300,000; mostly Bedouin), mainly desert territory east of the Jordan River wedged between Syria, Arabia, Iraq, and Palestine was nearly *terra nullis* as far as postwar plans had been concerned. Under the Ottomans, it had belonged to the *vilayet* of Damascus. According to Sykes-Picot, it would be part of Area B, namely, under Arab rule and British patronage. The Hijaz railway, running from Damascus to Medina, traversed the territory and was thus subject to the attacks of Faysal's forces. At the end of the war, it came under British military administration, which actually consisted of just a few junior officers, who eventually deferred to Faysal's representatives. Naturally, it was included in the territorial definition of Faysal's short-lived Syrian kingdom. But France made no effort to include it within Mandated Syria, and it was generally assumed that it would be included in the British Mandated areas, mainly Palestine but perhaps also Iraq. Zionist representatives at the Paris Peace Conference had included the area just west of the Hijaz Railway to the Jordan River in its proposed territorial delineation of the Jewish National Home.

It was `Abdallah, Faysal's older brother, who forced the issue. Smarting over his brother's preeminence in the firmament of postwar Arab politics and his own marginalization, he mobilized a few thousand tribesmen in late 1920 for the declared purpose of marching on Damascus and restoring Arab rule there. Arriving in the village of Amman (pop. 3,000), he compelled British officials to act, so as to avoid a confrontation with its ally France. The result, determined at the March 1921 Cairo Conference of British Middle East officials, headed by Colonial Secretary Winston Churchill, was an extension of Britain's alliance with the Hashimite family to `Abdallah.[19] Transjordan would be part of British Mandated Palestine but excluded from the area of Jewish settlement that was integral for establishing a Jewish National Home. One might even argue that by shepherding the establishment of the Hashimite kingdoms of Iraq and Jordan, Britain was remaining true to its original commitments to Sharif Husayn, although increasingly politicized Arab publics and the guardians of an evolving Arab nationalist grand narrative would certainly not agree. For them, the Hashimites would go from being the standard-bearers of Arab aspirations to collaborators with British imperialism.

In any case, over the ensuing decades, Transjordan would evolve into a separate entity, one that was weak and almost totally dependent on Great Britain, but headed by a monarch whose ambitions were regional in scope, and who would thus become an important player in inter-Arab politics. And in contrast to the difficulties faced by his brother and subsequent heirs in Iraq, Transjordan's small and heavily tribal population lent itself to accepting `Abdallah's rule as legitimate, as long as their interests were secured. Moreover, a cohesive civilian elite would gradually emerge to govern in partnership with `Abdallah, something that would be indispensable for maintaining stability in the nascent kingdom.

From the Kingdom of the Hijaz to the Kingdom of Saudi Arabia

Sharif Husayn's wartime proclamation of himself as "King of the Arab Lands" (*malik al-bilad al-`arabiyya*) had been brushed aside by Britain, but London did recognize him as King of the Hijaz. In the immediate postwar years, Husayn would attempt to ensure his dynastic rule there. However, establishing even a rudimentary state apparatus would be an extremely daunting task. Moreover, he faced a "local" challenge, the house of Al Sa`ud, headed by the talented and ambitious `Abd al-`Aziz bin Sa`ud, based in the Najd, in northeastern Arabia around Riyadh, and aligned with the puritan reformist Wahhabi Islamic current. Complicating things further for Husayn was the fact that `Abd al-`Aziz was also a British client/ally. Matters came to a head in 1924: Following Turkey's abolition of the caliphate, Husayn proclaimed himself caliph, which brought an end to any possibility of a Hashimite-Saudi understanding, and pushed `Abd al-`Aziz to take the offensive. Heavy British pressure on Husayn to step down in favor of his oldest son, `Ali, bore fruit. Ultimately, though, Britain could only watch as the Saudis advanced on the Hijaz, with the prize, of course, being Mecca. `Ali's forces abandoned it in mid-October 1924, Jeddah was occupied by Ibn Sa`ud's forces in December 1925, and the Hashimites lost their patrimony. [20] The dual kingdom of the Hijaz and Najd was established in 1927, and would be unified and renamed the Kingdom of Saudi Arabia in 1932. [21]

As was true with the Hashimites, state-building in Arabia would be an arduous task. It would be compounded by the opposition of the *Ikhwan* ("Brotherhood"), [22] the Wahhabi shock troops that had been central to `Abd al-`Aziz's conquests, to his pragmatic, albeit tentative measures at state-building and modernization. Until oil would be discovered in the 1940s, the annual pilgrimage to Mecca was the sole source of income, which `Abd al-`Aziz needed to pacify the tribes. The kingdom's southwestern border would be challenged by the Imamate of Yemen in a border war in 1934. As for Arab nationalism, it was a notion that was entirely foreign to the tribal world of the Arabian Peninsula—Saudi Arabia, the Yemeni imamate, and the British-protected emirates and chieftaincies adjacent to the Persian Gulf—and would penetrate there only slowly and by degrees.

Egypt

Egypt during the 1920s and 1930s presented a paradox, as far as Arab nationalism is concerned. On the one hand, Egypt possessed a degree of "stateness," including a well-defined territorial and cultural sense of self and a particular history that dwarfed all other entities in the Arabic-speaking lands. While having been a part of the Ottoman Empire since the early sixteenth century, it became a full-fledged actor on its own beginning in the early nineteenth century, under Muhammad `Ali, an Albanian-born officer who established a dynasty that would sit at the apex of Egyptian politics for 150 years, until being toppled in 1952. Occupied by Britain in 1882, Egypt became, ironically, a refuge and center for Arab intellectual and political opposition to Abdulhamid's heavy hand in the Levant. But the modern Egyptian nationalist movement, which emerged at the beginning of the twentieth century under British occupation and would attain a limited degree of independence in 1922, was very much Egypt-centered. Sa`d Zaghlul Pasha, the unchallenged leader of the Wafd, the political organization that was the repository and representative of Egyptian national sentiment during the 1920s, expressed a similar view in no uncertain terms; when asked by a visiting delegation from Iraq in 1925 his view about the ideal relationship between Egypt and the Arab East, he replied, famously, that "zero plus zero equals zero."[23] This aptly suited the secular-liberal current of Egyptian intellectual and cultural life, which was keen to promote a modern West-centered identity rooted in Egypt's Pharonic past and Mediterranean milieu, based on kinship, modes of speech and behavior, and a common history that embraced Egypt's substantial Coptic Christian community whose existence predated the Islamic conquests of Egypt.[24]

However, Egypt was also a central pillar of the Arab-Islamic milieu, the home of al-Azhar University, the supreme Sunni Islamic institution of higher learning. As such, it was a center for the Islamic reform current at the end of the nineteenth century, whose influence on early Arab nationalist thought and praxis was outsized (see chapter 1). And as Egypt in the 1920s and 1930s sought to fashion a modern political community,[25] the rise of mass politics in the context of economic and social upheavals and incessant political maneuverings led Egypt in a different direction than the one envisaged by the liberals, namely, neo-traditional forms of identity, emphasizing religious, spiritual, and other components of identity, in opposition to the Godless secular materialism of the West.[26] Egyptian political and cultural life would be filled with competing movements and visions during these years, none more important than the Society of Muslim Brothers (*Jama`at al-Ikhwan al-Muslimin*). Founded in 1928, the Muslim Brotherhood's emphasis on Egypt's Islamic essence inevitably contributed to the increasing "Arabness" of Egyptian self-definition among the traditional sectors. And by the mid-1930s, the notion that Arabism was fully compatible with being Egyptian had started to penetrate into more modern intellectual and cultural circles as well, spurred by frustration with the course of political life at home, and by increasing cultural and political contacts with the Arab East, this against the background of rising anti-British and anti-French sentiment throughout the region.[27]

North Africa

The Berber-speaking regions of North Africa west of Egypt had been initially conquered by Arab-Islamic warriors at the end of the seventh century and swiftly incorporated in the Islamic milieu. Successive Berber Islamic dynasties would rule the region and parts of Andalusia (Islamic Spain) between the eleventh and fourteenth centuries. Over time, the region would be partially Arabized as well, as additional waves of Arab tribes moved into the area from the east, as well as Andalusian Arabs fleeing the Christian Reconquista, and orthodox Maliki Islam became the accepted basis of religious praxis in the urban areas. By the mid-sixteenth century, a rough balance of power was established in the central and western Mediterranean between Christian European states and the Islamic empires—Sharifian Morocco and the Ottoman Empire, which nominally ruled the regencies of Tunis, Algiers, and Tripolitania. These recognizable territorial entities would form the basis of states in the modern area. Morocco—*al-Maghrib al-Aqsa*, the "Far West" in Islamic parlance—would remain the most Berber of all of the North African regions, with a majority of the population being Berber speakers right into the twentieth century and most of the rest being Arabized Berbers. Tunisia stood in extreme contrast to Morocco. It was the first region to be conquered and settled by Muslim Arabs, eventually becoming a crossroads for people and goods from all parts of the Mediterranean world—north, south, east, and west—as well as the most Ottoman-like of all of the North African entities, culturally, linguistically, and bureaucratically. There, the percentage of Berber communities dwindled into the single digits.[28]

The nineteenth and early twentieth centuries were transformational for North Africa, as the Ottomans were evicted by France from Algeria (1830) and Tunisia (1881), and from Tripolitania by Italy (1911–1912); Morocco would also fall under European domination, first economically and then politically, with the *coup de grace* coming in 1912, delivered by France. Overall, the French conquest and domination of North Africa, politically, militarily, and culturally, was often brutal and far-reaching. Independence movements would slowly emerge after World War I and begin to gather speed in the 1930s. In this regard, developments in North Africa partially paralleled those in the Arab East. The Islamic modernist current arrived from the east: one of its chief proponents was Shakib Arslan, the self-appointed heir to Jamal ad-Din Afghani's Islamic activism, who influenced the salafi-oriented young urban nationalists in the early 1930s in both Morocco and Algeria.[29] The dramatic anti-Spanish colonialist uprising of the Riffian Berber chieftain Muhammad bin `Abd al-Krim al-Khattabi in northern Morocco (1921–1926) resonated widely across the region and even beyond, including the young Paris-based student Ho Chi Minh. The unsuccessful rebellion against Italian rule in Libya and execution of its leader, `Umar al-Mukhtar, in 1931 also reverberated widely.[30] Despite the similarities and points of contact between North Africa and the Arab East, however, their very different historical experiences, both more remote and with regard to the colonial era, the existence in North Africa of relatively well-defined territorial entities, the "Berberness" of much of the region, the centrality of Islam as a unifying and mobilizing force against French rule, and the distance from the Fertile Crescent—the center of the budding Arab nationalist current—all meant that North Africa would be outside of the loop of regional Arab politics for some time to come.

1936—A Turning Point

Nineteen thirty-six was a pivotal year in the history of Arab regional politics, as developments drove the various Arab actors, both official and nonofficial, toward more intense involvement with one another, thus putting meat on the bones of budding Arab nationalist sentiment. In Egypt, Great Britain and the Egyptian authorities signed a twenty-year treaty that provided the country with a real measure of independence for the first time, enabling it to join the League of Nations, and engage in foreign policy, particularly toward its neighbors, for the first time. At the same time, the country's political parties and institutions were seen as primarily self-serving, resulting in the proliferation of extra-parliamentary movements and increasing polarization. In Iraq, military officers seized power from the politicians.[31] It was a stark indication that the state-building and institution-building processes of the new Iraqi state were not proceeding smoothly, as well as an onerous omen for the future of Arab political systems throughout the region. In Syria, a draft treaty to bring an end to the French Mandate was drawn up but failed to be implemented, raising bitterness among the increasingly politicized urban classes.[32] Finally, in Palestine, a sustained revolt broke out, as Palestinian Arabs sought to bring a halt to the Zionist enterprise and achieve independence from Britain.

If the practical meaning of Arabism had been somewhat vague up to this point, it now began to have more specific content, revolving around the quest for independence, the cause of Palestine, and the search for unity.[33] In particular, support for Arab Palestine became the litmus test for determining one's fidelity to the newly sharpened ideals of Arabism. The cause was genuinely popular among the increasingly politicized urban classes, who expressed themselves through protests, charitable donations, and political work. Indeed, their mobilization on behalf of Palestine was led by opposition political groups who sought to advance their positions and show the ruling elites as being deficient. The latter, whether in Egypt, Syria, or Iraq, would often be less than eager to overly confront their British and French patrons, but needed to take public opinion into account, as they sought to bolster their own legitimacy under the banner of Arabism.[34] Hence, the fateful intertwining of the Palestine question, the meaning of Arabism, and the domestic politics of Arab states had begun.

This intertwining would also have an important inter-Arab dimension, as various Arab actors would compete with one another to display their concern with Palestine, to bolster both their domestic and regional positions, vis-à-vis rivals at home and in the region. Doing so was essential, given the lack of "stateness" in these entities, and the problem of ensuring their legitimacy in the eyes of their increasingly restless and politicized publics enamored with the ideology of a common Arabism, which foregrounded *raison de la nation Arabe* over *raison d'état* (nationalism within defined territorial entities).

The regionalization of the Palestine question was now expressed in diplomatic terms as well. In October 1936, needing to bring an end to their six-month general strike, which was wreaking havoc on the Palestinian Arab economy, the Palestinian leadership accepted a mediation proposal tendered by four neighboring Arab monarchs—`Abdallah of Trans-jordan, King Ghazi of Iraq (son of Faysal, who had died in 1933), `Abd al-`Aziz of Saudi Arabia, and the Imam of Yemen, Yahya Muhammad. The mediation initiative was actually generated by Great Britain, which hoped that wider Arab involvement would have a calming and stabilizing effect as Britain sought a solution to the budding Jewish-Arab conflict in its mandated territory. Kedourie provocatively argues that by giving neighboring Arab states *locus standi* regarding the issue, Britain abdicated its sovereign responsibilities for the territory,[35] but given the value that involvement in the Palestine question had for Arab political elites and opposition movements alike, it is hard to imagine that Britain could have prevented outside Arab involvement in the Palestine question. In any case, from here on, it would be an integral part of the domestic politics of Arab states, and hence of inter-Arab politics as well. Just over two years later, at the London St. James Conference in February 1939, Egypt would also be present among the Arab delegations brought together by Britain, along with the Zionist leadership, in a last failed attempt to achieve an agreement before World War II. The conference had been preceded by a coordination meeting of Arab representatives in Cairo, a clear indication of Egypt's growing interest in Arab affairs, driven, as it were, by a self-view that required Egypt to be in the center of regional affairs, the dominant Wafd party's pragmatic, politically inspired drift toward an Arab orientation, and the personal ambitions of young King Farouk.

WORLD WAR II AND THE FORMATION OF THE LEAGUE OF ARAB STATES

Responses in the Arab world to the outbreak of World War II on September 1, 1939, and the course of the fighting during the next three years consisted mainly of watchful waiting in order to see which side would gain the upper hand. The eastward advances of Rommel's Afrika Korps in Libya, the political upheaval in Iraq, which led to temporary seizure of power on April 1, 1941, by pro-German anti-British Arab nationalists led by Rashid `Ali al-Kaylani, growing anti-British activity in Egypt, and Vichy France's assumption of authority in Syria and Lebanon all placed Britain on the defensive. However, its pushback was not long in coming, beginning in late May with the restoration of the status quo ante in Iraq

after a monthlong campaign, followed by a military operation that toppled the Vichy French authorities in Syria in June. Seeking to ensure
Arab support for the war effort, British Foreign Secretary Anthony Eden
declared on May 29, 1941 that his government was willing to support any
scheme to strengthen political, cultural, and economic ties that the Arabs
might agree upon.[36] However, there was little response. It was only after
the decisive defeat of Rommel's forces at El Alamein in Egypt's western
desert in early November 1942 that Britain's continued preeminence in
the region was assured. It was with that knowledge that Arab political
elites began preparing for the future. In Barnett's words, the mix of antic-
ipated independence (referring to French Mandated Syria and Lebanon
and British Mandated Palestine and Transjordan, as well as more genuine
independence for Egypt and Iraq) and Arab nationalist doctrine steered
the conversation among states and societies toward the future regional
order. A consensus quickly emerged that some kind of association was
necessary for an Arab revival on strategic, political cultural, and economic grounds.[37] The eventual outcome would be the creation on March 22,
1945, of the League of Arab States.

How did this come about? For years, the League's establishment was
viewed as having been inspired and directed by Great Britain. To be sure,
as Kedourie pointed out, there was indeed a widespread belief in British
circles about the "inevitable" triumph of pan-Arabism, compelling Britain to align with the movement. As a result, he said, Britain's simultane-
ous, if contradictory, encouragement of local Arab actors in Egypt and
the Arab East gave the decisive impetus to its formation.[38] Subsequent
research, however, shows that the primary impetus came from local actors, who ultimately compelled Britain to follow their lead, particularly
Egypt's.[39]

The Hashimites versus Egypt

Not surprisingly, the initial stirrings came from the Hashimite camp,
Britain's loyal allies and clients, and the original standard-bearers of Arab
independence and unity. By the end of 1942, Transjordan's `Abdallah
was renewing his long-standing call to reunify *bilad al-Sham/suriyya al-
tabi`iyya* ("natural Syria") under his leadership.[40] More importantly, in
January 1943, the resolutely pro-British Iraqi prime minister and regime
stalwart Nuri al-Sa`id propagated his Fertile Crescent project (also known

as Nuri's "Blue Book"), with the encouragement of a British official.[41] The plan's essence was the unification of "historical Syria" (Syria, Lebanon, Palestine, and Transjordan) and its joining together with Iraq in an "Arab League," whose permanent council would be responsible for defense and foreign affairs, currency, communications, customs, protection of minority rights, and education. Syrians would have the right to choose their form of government, a stipulation designed to mollify anti-monarchists in Syria; Nuri himself hoped that ultimately a throne could be established for the Iraqi Regent, `Abd al-Ilah (uncle to the boy king Faysal II). The Jews in Palestine would receive a semiautonomous administration under the plan, and the Maronite Christians in Lebanon would maintain their special status established during Ottoman times.

Overall, Nuri's plan was designed to place Iraq squarely in the center of Arab regional politics, in line with the Iraqi Hashimite vision, but also conforming to the overall aspirations of a generation of militant, anti-British Iraqi Sunni pan-Arabists. An additional favorable statement on February 29, 1943, by Eden regarding the postwar Arab regional order sent Nuri into diplomatic high gear to promote his program. At this point, however, he ran into an insurmountable obstacle—Egypt.

Nuri had included Egyptian prime minister Nahhas Pasha in his initial consultations with Arab leaders. In offering Egypt a ceremonial role in the all-Arab conference that he was preparing, Nuri was operating under the mistaken assumption that Egypt had no intention of being seriously involved in the Arab East, and would limit its regional ambitions to promoting the unity of the Nile Valley, joining Sudan to Egypt.[42] Instead, Nahhas took the initiative for a regional Arab framework out of Nuri's hands. Nahhas himself would be deposed by Farouk before finishing the job, but the overall Egyptian vision remained the same: a larger and looser regional framework that preserved the existence of separate Arab entities, thus blocking Hashimite ambitions to subsume Syria and Palestine under their wings.[43]

A preparatory conference in Alexandria on September 25, 1944, involving representatives of Egypt, Iraq, Syria, Transjordan, and Lebanon, laid the groundwork for the budding Arab League. At a crucial moment, Britain had actually warned Nahhas not to proceed, fearing an anti-British cast to the conference, but to no effect. Saudi Arabia and Yemen were both extremely suspicious about any regional grouping, but eventually concluded that the Egyptian-led regional framework was suitable to their needs, particularly the Saudis, whose primary concern at that point was Hashimite revanchism. The territorial status quo was also ideal for the republican nationalist leadership in Syria, which was poised to lead the country into independence, and for the Lebanese elites who a year earlier had concluded amongst themselves a "National Pact" that established the rules of power-sharing in an independent Lebanon. Indeed, the Alexandria Protocol that was issued at the end of the conference recognized Lebanon's independent existence based on the 1943 agreement. Hence, inter-Arab affairs were now primarily characterized by the rivalry between two blocs—a majority, Egyptian-led non-Hashimite camp that was committed to maintaining the territorial status quo, and a minority Hashimite camp (Iraq and Transjordan), which favored some kind of larger and tighter framework under the Hashimite banner, while disagreeing who should be its primary carrier. This division would remain a fundamental feature of Arab regional politics for the next decade, until Gamal `Abd al-Nasir's rise to prominence and adoption of a radically different vision for the Arab future.

The Arab League Charter (*mithaq jami`at al-duwal al-`arabiyya*), signed in Cairo with much fanfare on March 22, 1945, constituted a compromise between the competing blocs, albeit with a decisive tilt in favor toward the Egyptian-led group. League headquarters would be located in Cairo, and the organization's first secretary-general was to be an Egyptian diplomat, the longtime Arab nationalist advocate `Abd al Rahman `Azzam Pasha.[44] Primary emphasis was laid on the members' acceptance of each other's "independence and sovereignty" and "respect [for] the existing regime[s] in the other League States." The League's power to settle inter-Arab disputes was quite limited. Moreover, its decision-making powers in general were extremely constrained: Unanimous decisions would be binding on all members, while majority decisions were to be "binding only upon those states which have accepted them." In practice, this meant that recalcitrant parties could effectively block the implementation of controversial decisions. Hence, there would be a pronounced tendency to search for the lowest common denominator regarding most issues, so as to achieve consensual resolutions.

The new Egyptian-dominated League framework was a far cry from the Hashimite-centered unity efforts. However, Article 9 of the Charter offered Iraq and Transjordan some small comfort: member states "desirous of closer collaboration with each other and [of] stronger ties than those specified by this Charter have a right to conclude such agreements between themselves towards the realization of these efforts as they desire."[45] The challenge over the next decade for Iraq and Jordan, respectively, would be to persuade the government of Syria to move in that direction.

The Charter contained two annexes, one dealing with Palestine and one regarding Arab countries (*bilad*) that were not members of the League (i.e., the French-ruled North African entities, Allied-controlled Libya, and the British-protected Gulf principalities). Ties with the latter countries were to be developed in all possible ways to help them attain independence. Regarding Palestine, the Charter emphasized that legally, its existence and independence could not be questioned *de jure*, any more than could the independence of the other Arab countries. Until such time that Arab Palestine could exercise that independence, the League would appoint a Palestinian representative to take part in its work. The inability of the Palestinian Arab factions to agree on a common representative, and the assumption of that role by the League, marked a further symbolic stage in the transfer of responsibility for the issue to external Arab parties.

The creation of the Arab League was hardly a fulfillment of the pan-Arab dream. In the words of one veteran Iraqi statesman, it was "as much a truce between [its] leaders as it is the result of the movement for Arab unity for which we older Arab patriots have worked."[46] Moreover, its creation was very much a product of its times: Arab politics within and between the various entities was being conducted by extremely narrow elite groupings, concerned first and foremost with safeguarding and maximizing their own particular interests, both personal and political. It was some distance from the Ottoman Empire's "politics of notables" but was far from being a politics of mass movements.[47] But an eye had to be kept on the public, hence the centrality of Arabism. The ruling elites of the emerging Arab states lacked both external and internal legitimacy, thanks in large part to the colonial legacy, as well as to the internal societal fissures (intercommunal, social, class, etc.) and the growing attractiveness of the pan-Arab idea, particularly among the lower urbanizing classes. Hence, they were dependent on emphasizing an Arab identity to legitimize their policies and actions. The paradox, of course, is that the logical conclusion of Arab nationalism threatened to undermine the elites' bases of power. State-formation projects by the elites would thus

seek to combine material incentives, external threats, and the manipula-
tion of symbols.[48]

The inherent tension between the structure of the state and the idea of
the nation, both heavily influenced by, if not inherited from, the European
experience,[49] would bedevil Arab domestic and regional politics for
decades. Still, the intensity of this struggle could not have been fully
apparent in 1945. The Arab state system at its moment of birth was not
only low in the level of "stateness" (apart from Egypt) but also relatively
low in the level of "nationhood." Clifford Geertz's "integrative revolution," namely the efforts to aggregate and eventually transform primor-
dial (i.e., deep-rooted sub-national and supra-national—familial tribal,
communal, and religious) sentiments into the basis for a civil society, was
only in its infancy.[50] The new ideas of state and pan-Arab nationalism
had not found ways to effectively subordinate them; at times they even
reinforced them.

At the same time, the establishment of the Arab League marked a
historical watershed in Arab affairs. The contrast between the post-World
War I Mandate arrangements and the emergence in 1945 of a regional
grouping of seven independent Arab states formally committed to a set of
principles designed to advance collective Arab interests is striking.
France's "moment" in the Middle East had ended, Britain's was heading
in that direction, and Arab entities and societies were on the way to
acquiring an unprecedented degree of agency.

However, the obstacles to both successful state consolidation and genuine regional cooperation were formidable. On the economic plain alone,
there was no basis for the kind of functional cooperation that is vital for
forging more intimate links between sovereign states. A semblance of a
regional market, inherited from Ottoman times, had still been present in
the 1930s, although it was not serving as a "highway of learning," as in
Japan.[51] The worldwide depression and more assertive nationalist economic policies in the realms of tariffs, trade, and finance weakened even
this market. The Middle East Supply Center, established by the allies
during World War II, temporarily reversed these disintegrative trends,
boosting both industrial output and inter-Arab trade, but they weren't
maintained after the war.[52] Hence, at the dawn of the postwar era, the
path of greater inter-Arab cooperation was strewn with economic obstacles. And in the political realm, the continued absence of state cohesion
and weak governing institutions amidst the quickening pace of social

change, the mutual suspicions and rivalries of Arab leaders, the unfinished business with Great Britain, which was still very much present throughout the region, and finally, the budding crisis in Palestine, all ensured that Arab politics in the coming years would be highly charged, as rival elites sought to maximize their interests and rebuff their rivals. Working for unity was just a pious wish, useful mainly for strengthening regime legitimacy at home.

4

THE DYNASTIC ERA

Upheaval, Revolution, and Transition (1945–1954)

Two issues dominated the collective Arab agenda during the Arab League's first decade: the conflict over Palestine and the instability in Syria. The Arab states' political and military failure in attempting to prevent the establishment of an independent Jewish state was due in no small part to their lack of military and political coordination, highlighting the yawning gap between the expressed values of Arab solidarity and common purpose, and the reality of inter-Arab rivalries and pursuit of separate and often conflicting interests. The progressive weakening of the newly independent Syrian state, as manifested in repeated military coups, rendered it the object of intense competition between rival Arab countries, and provided a foretaste of what was to come during the latter part of the 1950s. The inexorable militarization of Syrian politics was also a portent of what was to come elsewhere. Indeed, Egypt quickly followed. The removal of King Farouk by a bloodless military coup in 1952 opened up a new chapter in Egyptian history and would have profound consequences for the Arab system as a whole.

Having survived the challenges and uncertainties of the World War II years, ruling Arab elites had momentary grounds for optimism at the beginning of the postwar era, albeit for different reasons. The establishment of the Arab League was most satisfying to the anti-Hashimite bloc: for Egypt, the League was a useful tool to promote regional leadership and check rival ambitions; for the Saudis, it provided an important layer of defense against any possible Hashimite threats; for the Lebanese, it promised to help stabilize the internal balance of power and ward off external meddling; and for the Syrians, the League was an immediately useful instrument for mustering diplomatic and public pressure against France's last-ditch use of force at the end of May 1945 to try to restore its preeminence in Syria and Lebanon. Unlike in the aftermath of World War I, this time Britain sided with the Arabs, forcing French forces to desist in their attacks and return to barracks.[1] They would finally leave Syria a year later, without any arrangements to ensure the continuation of French influence.

British policymakers had hoped that their actions in Syria would provide a new and more harmonious basis for British-Arab relations, in which Britain's strategic interests and influence could be preserved. However, they were quickly disabused of the notion. Efforts to negotiate new bilateral treaties, first with Egypt and then with Iraq, collapsed in the face of massive public opposition in both countries to anything that smacked of continued British domination. In Iraq, the deep anti-British feeling seriously damaged the legitimacy of Nuri al-Sa`id, Saleh Jabr (the prime minister at the time), the Iraqi Regent `Abd al-Ilah, and the rest of their political allies, and would ultimately lead to their downfall a decade later.

It was only with Transjordan, the entity most dependent upon it for its very existence, that Britain was able to amicably conclude a bilateral treaty, in 1946, that brought an official end to Mandatory rule and consecrated the country's formal independence.[2] The ramifications for Jordan's domestic stability would be felt in the mid-1950s. But for now, the British-Hashimite Jordanian relationship was not hindered by Jordanian domestic politics.

Having achieved formal independence, `Abdallah was eager to assert himself in both neighboring Syria and in Palestine, where the Jewish-Arab conflict was coming to a head. One of his contemporaries described him as "a falcon trapped in a canary's cage," someone whose ambitions as a scion of the Hashimite family could hardly be satisfied in the landlocked (except for `Aqaba at its far southern tip), sparsely populated, resource-bereft Transjordanian entity, where he was penned up by the British.[3]

Syria, of course, had been the ultimate prize that `Abdallah had set out to regain for the Hashimite family in 1920. Now that both Transjordan and Syria had had the formal shackles of the Mandates removed, he quickly renewed his designs, employing various means to try to undermine the consolidation of the new Syrian state under a republican regime. To be sure, his desires far outpaced his means, and the ground inside of Syria was distinctly not fertile for the kind of old-fashioned Hashimite patronage over Greater Syria that his brother Faysal had struggled to establish in 1918–1920. But `Abdallah's efforts were sufficient to generate harsh reaction in the anti-Hashimite camp of Arab states, especially from Syria's own leaders. Syrian President Shukri al-Quwatli not only characterized `Abdallah's actions as being in gross violation of the Arab League Charter, but also rhetorically turned the tables on him: it was `Abdallah's "princely throne" that was illegitimate, Quwatli said, because it had been "detached from the motherland," installed by a foreign mandate, and "based on neither constitution nor law."[4] Echoes of this debate would be heard decades later, in the context of a Syrian-Jordanian crisis in 1980–81 (see chapter 9).[5]

Similarly, `Abdallah's ambitions were not viewed with favor in Hashimite Iraq. Since the 1930s, the Iraqi Sunni political classes, both pro- and anti-British, had advocated Iraq's regional leadership with an eye on Syria, and viewed `Abdallah with disdain. So did the Regent `Abd al-Ilah, `Abdallah's nephew.[6] In 1947 the two countries concluded a treaty of Brotherhood and Alliance between them, "pursuant to the terms of Article 9" of the Arab League Charter, which legitimized the forging of closer ties between League members. But the actual content was quite tepid.

The future of Palestine, however, was a different matter. Here `Abdallah's ambitions were more realizable, and Britain's interests partially overlapped with them. So did Iraq's. All of this would be part of the story of the 1948 Palestine War—which would pose the first serious challenge in the post-1945 era to the collective Arab principles to which all Arab countries officially adhered.

WAR IN PALESTINE

Countdown

World War II had occasioned a hiatus in the Arab-Jewish conflict over Palestine. But as the horrors of the Nazi Holocaust became known and hundreds of thousands of destitute Jewish refugees languished in displaced persons camps, the Jewish leadership in Palestine decided to force the issue, both on the ground and internationally. As the pace quickened in 1946, following the publication of an Anglo-American Commission report recommending the immediate admittance of one hundred thousand Jewish refugees to Palestine, Arab leaders struggled to formulate an effective response. Egypt's King Farouk convened the first official meeting of Arab heads of state at his Inshas estate near Cairo, and a follow-up Arab League Council meeting was held a week later in Bludan, Syria, which sharpened the Arab collective position on Palestine. To be sure, no operative consensus was reached, but the conference proved to be, in Barry Rubin's words, "a first step towards the 1948 war."[7]

In the face of increasing attacks by the Zionist militias against British forces and the utter inability to broker an agreed-on solution, Britain played for time by asking the United Nations, in February 1947, to examine the issue, hoping that the absence of a viable solution would enable Britain to secure its strategic interests within a unitary framework in Palestine. Much to its surprise, a majority of the UN Special Committee on Palestine (UNSCOP) that had been appointed to study the subject eventually recommended that Palestine be partitioned into two states, one Jewish and one Arab, with Jerusalem and its surroundings to be internationalized for a ten-year period, and the two states joined in an economic union. After intensive diplomatic maneuvering, the UN General Assembly confirmed the partition recommendation in a dramatic vote on November 29, 1947, by 33–13 and 10 abstentions, just barely more than the two thirds necessary for passage.

The partition resolution's adoption came as a shock to Arab political elites and the public alike. The first Arab-Israeli war essentially began on the morrow of the vote. It consisted of two distinct phases: 1) the intercommunal phase, between the Jewish and Palestinian Arab communities, with the latter supported by Arab volunteer units mostly organized as the "Salvation Army" (*jaysh al-inqadh*), which lasted until the end of the Mandate and withdrawal of British troops on May 14, 1948; and 2) the interstate phase, beginning the very next day, between the armies of five Arab states and those of the newly declared State of Israel. This second phase would continue intermittently until early January 1949. The outcome was a clear victory for Israel and a severe defeat for the Arab side, individually and collectively, with the conspicuous exception of Transjordan.[8] In the following months, armistice agreements between Israel and each of the four Arab states bordering on its territory would be concluded and a new, albeit fragile status quo established.

Nothing was inevitable about this outcome. As with all historical events, and especially armed conflicts, it depended on a variety of factors, both structural and human. In this regard, the inherent advantages that the Arab states and the Palestinian Arab community possessed in numbers and territory would not be translated into success on the battlefield for a variety of reasons, including the weakness of Arab political institutions, enduring inter-Arab suspicions and rivalries that inhibited the conduct of the war, and a relatively cohesive and highly mobilized Jewish-Zionist adversary that viewed the conflict in simple existential terms. But the outcome was not foreordained or written in stone.

The Intercommunal Phase of the War

Arab prime ministers convened in Cairo on December 8–17, 1947, amidst the heightened sense of urgency. A certain degree of bloodshed was deemed inevitable, but coherent collective policies were beyond reach. The anti-Hashimite bloc, particularly the Syrians and the Saudis, were deeply concerned about Hashimite intentions, and thus insisted on maintaining the Arab League's existing policy of supporting Palestinian irregular forces and volunteer units. For their part, Jordan and Iraq stressed that regular forces would be needed after the British left, a view bolstered by an analysis made by the head of the League's newly established Military Committee, Iraqi General Isma`il Safwat.[9] Throughout, the Iraqis, representing the one important Arab country not bordering Palestine, and thus having the least to lose, were the most militant in their rhetoric, regarding both the military and economic steps that needed to be taken. `Abdallah, for his part, was in the best position, having a small but well-trained force at his disposal, and being in immediate geographic proximity to Palestine (the distance between the Jordan River Allenby Bridge crossing and Jerusalem, for example, is approximately 50 kilometers).

For the other Arab states, and especially Syria, Transjordan's Arab Legion would become a double-edged sword. As it become increasingly clear in March–April 1948 that the Jewish forces were gaining the upper hand on the ground and that Britain was determined to withdraw on schedule, the Legion came to be seen as a vital part of the collective Arab

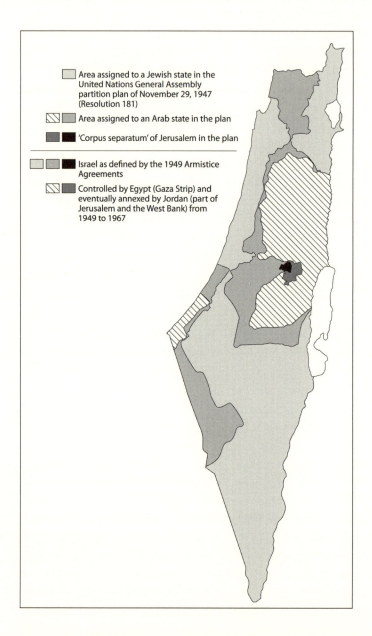

Figure 4.1.   UN 1947 partition plan for Palestine and 1949 Armistice Agreements.

war effort. But its entry into Palestine would give `Abdallah a chance to achieve his territorial ambitions, a prospect that was anathema to the anti-Hashimite camp. And the Syrians, especially, feared that a strengthened `Abdallah would then turn his eye on them. [10]

In order to try to limit `Abdallah's freedom of maneuver, Farouk engineered an Arab League resolution on April 12, 1948, that stipulated that any Arab military action in Palestine would be of a temporary nature, and that after liberation, Palestinians would elect their own government and control their own destiny. `Abdallah, for his part, raised no opposition, but clearly had no intention to adhere to it either. [11]

The collective decision to intervene with regular forces upon the termination of the Mandate was apparently made on April 24 at a League Political Committee meeting in Amman, but the operational details were not yet agreed upon. At the top of the list of questions was whether Egypt would participate in the war: an Egyptian representative wasn't even present at the meeting. As a result, Lebanon's prime minister Riyad al-Sulh and the Iraqi Regent `Abd al-Ilah traveled to Cairo to lobby for Egyptian involvement. The Iraqis, despite their regional rivalry with Egypt, did not want to leave their own forces exposed on the battlefield, while al-Sulh viewed Egypt's involvement as a crucial component of the collective Arab effort. Ironically, `Abdallah was supportive of the effort, as Egyptian involvement would provide his own upcoming actions with another layer of legitimacy.

Contrary to widely held perceptions of Arab overconfidence in the coming battle, the mood among Arab leaders was at times sober, and even pessimistic, with hope still being held out for a ceasefire and trusteeship formula that would forestall British evacuation and obviate the need for military intervention. Adding to their dilemma was concern for their own future, political and physical, in the event of either inaction or defeat.

The final plans for the invasion were only firmed up in the last days before the British withdrawal. Ironically, at this stage, the Jordanians and Egyptians were in agreement with regard to the battle plans. `Abdallah was named titular head of the combined Arab force. At his insistence, the original plan was altered to enable Jordanian forces to deploy in the Arab-populated central highlands north and south of Jerusalem (which was to be avoided for the time being, owing to `Abdallah's concern not to violate the UN Partition Resolution, which stipulated that Jerusalem and its surrounding environs were to be internationalized, and thus arouse the wrath of the international community), with Iraqi flanking support farther north and Egyptian forces tying down the bulk of Jewish forces to the south. Syrian and Lebanese forces were originally supposed to isolate the Jewish forces in the upper Galilee region, but the revised plan had Syrian forces moving to the southern end of the Sea of Galilee to attack Jewish settlements there, so as to provide flanking support to the Iraqis and Jordanians. Concurrently, Farouk decided to overrule the opposition of Egypt's top political and military echelons and committed the Egyptian army to the fight. Given his regional leadership pretensions, he could scarcely avoid this first test to collective Arab principles and leave the field clear to 'Abdallah.

To be sure, Cairo and Amman continued to have different strategic objectives. 'Abdallah was ready to acquiesce to the creation of a Jewish state (hopefully in a reduced area of territory), while the Egyptians hoped that a combination of war and diplomacy would leave the new Jewish state stillborn, and also limit 'Abdallah's gains. For the moment, though, each needed the other.

Thus, on May 15, the interstate phase of the first Arab-Israeli war began. An all-Arab coalition had been formed to fight the establishment of a Jewish state in Palestine, in the heart of the Arab world, notwithstanding the competing ambitions and interests, and mutually held suspicions of one another. The Arab League Secretary-General's cable to the UN Secretary-General explained the official, consensual position justifying Arab military intervention: the security of Palestine, it declared, was "a sacred trust" for the Arab states. Once peace and security were achieved, law and order restored, and a Palestinian sovereign state established, the intervention would end. [12] Obviously, 'Abdallah had other ideas, and they were no secret to the other members of the coalition. The mutual suspicions and rivalries among all of them would quickly resurface and seriously inhibit the conduct of the war.

The Interstate Phase

The first week of fighting seemed to be going according to the revised Arab war plan, at least as far as the Egyptians and Jordanians were concerned. The Egyptian army advanced into southern Palestine, while 'Abdallah's forces consolidated their positions in the central highlands and around Jerusalem. On May 18, following the breakdown of a shaky local cease-fire there, the Arab Legion moved into parts of the city itself, including the old walled city and its sacred sites, preventing it from falling into Israeli hands. Arab Legion forces would successfully block Israeli attacks on the besieged Jewish quarter, which surrendered on May 28. However, farther north, Syrian, Lebanese, and Iraqi forces were meeting stiff resistance while depleting their ammunition and supplies. More ominous still was the absence of coordination between the Arab armies. As for `Abdallah, having achieved his central goal, he was not interested in any further fighting. Initially, the Egyptians agreed, and a UN Security Council-sponsored four-week truce went into effect on June 11. However, at this point, the fundamental interests of Egypt, as defined by Farouk, and Transjordan began to diverge, and the Egyptians led the Arab League Council in rejecting a further extension of the cease-fire, resulting in a resumption of hostilities on July 9. While not unaware of the risks involved, an indefinite extension of the truce was tantamount to an admission of defeat in the eyes of their publics, something which Arab leaders couldn't countenance. Concerned with remaining within the Arab consensus, `Abdallah's ministers compelled him to go along.

The consequences were severe. In the ten days of fighting (July 9–18), Israeli forces widened their control of Tel Aviv's hinterland, capturing the neighboring towns of Lydda and Ramleh, and much of central Galilee. The Arab Legion's failure to dispatch significant forces from Latrun to Lydda (a distance of 20 kilometers) to support the Palestinian irregulars there[13] would take its place on the list of Jordanian "sins of betrayal" that would be compiled by its rivals at the end of the war. And from this point onward, the divergent interests of Egypt and Jordan would dominate their relationship, particularly against the background of the peace plan of UN mediator Count Folke Bernadotte that scrapped the UN partition plan's boundaries in favor of attaching all of the Negev to Transjordan and all of the Galilee to Israel. Politically, the Egyptians were keen to show their public that they had Palestinian interests at heart, which dovetailed with their opposition to Jordanian territorial aggrandizement. At Egyptian prodding, the Arab League Political Committee declared on September 20 its support for the creation of a "Palestinian government," prompting the Mufti's Arab Higher Committee to immediately proclaim the creation of the "Government of All Palestine," with its seat in Gaza. Although the Egyptians disliked the Mufti, it quickly extended it diplomatic recognition, as did all of the other Arab states, apart from Transjordan. Militarily, two Israeli offensives against Egyptian forces, in October and late December 1948–early January 1949, would reduce the Egyptian presence in Palestine to besieged units in the "Falljua pocket" in the northern Negev, and to a 300 square-kilometer strip of land around Gaza, adjacent to the Mediterranean Sea bordering the Sinai peninsula. The Gaza area's prewar population of 80,000 had now increased threefold, thanks to the influx of destitute refugees from Jaffa and southern Palestinian towns and villages. The Egyptian military setbacks were blamed in large part on Transjordan's failure to dispatch its troops to support the Egyptian forces. Farouk and the Egyptian media harped incessantly on `Abdallah's "betrayal" of the Arab cause, and some even suggested that the Jordanian inactivity was part of an Israeli-Jordanian conspiracy.[14]

Viewing the newly proclaimed Government of All Palestine as a strategic threat to his ambitions, `Abdallah began mobilizing Palestinian support for the formal extension of his authority westward. After much prodding, a gathering of Palestinian notables in Jericho on December 1, 1948, proclaimed `Abdallah to be king of a united Transjordan and Palestine. Farouk and the Syrians were angry, but Iraq's Nuri al-Sa`id and Lebanese leaders cautioned against pushing `Abdallah too far away, and perhaps into the arms of the Israelis. Egypt's restrictions on the Government of All Palestine's activities, its antipathy to the Mufti, and the decision not to press for the seating of the Gaza government in the Arab League all indicated that Egypt, too, was unwilling to push `Abdallah to the brink, notwithstanding its proclaimed fidelity to the Palestinian cause.

Israel's end-of-the-year offensive against Egyptian forces marked the first Arab-Israeli war's last round of fighting. Overall, the war constituted an unbridled failure for the Arab side, and came to be known in the Arab political lexicon as the *nakba* ("disaster"). A non-Arab state had been established in an area considered to be an integral part of the Arab patrimony, and 50 to 60 percent of the prewar Arab population of Palestine of 1.25 million persons had been rendered refugees.[15] Military and political coordination between the Arab states had been desultory, pointing to the huge gap between the expressed values of Arab solidarity and common purpose, and the reality of inter-Arab rivalries and pursuit of separate interests. The defeat also reflected badly on the Arab League as an institution.

ARAB-ISRAELI DIPLOMACY AND INTER-ARAB POLITICS: 1949–1950

The magnitude of the 1948 defeat had profound ramifications for the Arab world. While some intellectuals engaged in considerable soul searching and self-criticism of the shortcomings of Arab societies,[16] the collective failure served as a catalyst for political upheaval beginning almost immediately in Syria, to be followed by Egypt in 1952. In Iraq, the defeat would be added to the ruling oligarchy's long list of sins being compiled by opposition nationalists.

Regionally, the next year and a half were ones of almost continuous crisis, which threatened to change the inter-Arab balance of power. Three military coups in Syria within the space of nine months demonstrated that the institutions of the newly independent Syrian state were grossly inadequate to the task of nation-building and state-building. The intense involvement of neighboring Arab states in Syrian politics during this period was a centerpiece of Patrick Seale's history of the period.[17] However, Syria was not the only arena of intense Arab political maneuvering. The diplomatic aftermath of the first Arab-Israeli war, and particularly Jordan's efforts to consolidate its wartime games, would sorely test Egyptian leadership, and ultimately lead to a full-blown crisis. The larger question was whether Arab states had the right to pursue direct bilateral negotiations with Israel, or whether they were bound to a collective approach. This would be a recurring theme for the next half-century.

The question of bilateral versus collective negotiations with Israel was first raised at the beginning of 1949. Neither Egypt nor Jordan were keen on the latter, as they wanted the freedom of action to pursue their own policies, and not be bound by any of the other Arab parties' requirements. The island of Rhodes became the site of bilateral armistice negotiations between Israel and each of the Arab states, mediated by Ralph Bunche, a US State Department official representing the United Nations. Egypt would be the first to conclude an armistice agreement with Israel, in late February 1949, followed by Lebanon in late March, Jordan in early April, and Syria in mid-July. Broadly speaking, the armistice lines corresponded to the existing military lines at the moment of the war's end (with an important exception in the central sector, see below). In the aftermath of the 1956 Suez War, they gradually came to be considered Israel's legitimate international boundaries by the international community.[18]

The Israeli-Jordanian armistice agreement requires some comment. As the Rhodes armistice talks proceeded, Iraq made it clear that it intended to pull its forces out of Palestine unilaterally, and thus avoid the "stain" of having negotiated with the Jews. This position conformed to Iraq's traditional position during the long history of the Arab-Israeli conflict: its rhetoric would be the most militant, as Iraqi leaders' primary concern was their domestic political audience. (Subsequent post-monarchical regimes, especially that of Saddam Husayn, would also be very much concerned with Iraq's image in the region.) Nonetheless, in the 1948 war, Hashimite Iraq's actions on the ground were broadly in sync with their Hashimite Jordanian cousins. And now, Jordan stood to be the primary beneficiary from Iraq's withdrawal from the front, as it intended to take over its positions in the northern Samarian hills and just east of the central coastal plain. However, Israel had its own needs. The initial cease-fire agreement forbade any subsequent unilateral movement of troops, and Israel was keen on widening the narrow stretch of territory under its control north of Tel Aviv and to gain control of the road connecting the town of Hadera to Jewish agricultural settlements in the Jezreel Valley. It thus threatened the Jordanians with military action if they redeployed their troops without a prior agreement. Reluctantly, `Abdallah conceded. As a result, some 400 square kilometers that had been in Iraqi hands, encompassing fifteen or sixteen villages populated by twenty thousand persons, were handed over to Israel, as were agricultural lands belonging to villages that remained on the Jordanian side of the line.[19] In return, `Abdallah's forces now gained control of the rest of the Iraqi-held areas and a symbolic sliver of land from Israel. The Jordanian concession would forever be held up by militant Arab nationalists, and especially Palestinians, as a betrayal.

In early 1950, secret negotiations between Jordan and Israel resulted in a draft agreement of principles for a five-year nonaggression pact and provisions for the renewal of economic and commercial ties that had been severed with the end of the British Mandate.[20] Concurrently, Jordan moved to make official its two-year rule of the central hills of Palestine (the West Bank, i.e., that part of the area west of the Jordan River controlled by Jordan). The result was a prolonged rift that threatened to split the Arab League wide open.

For Egypt, it was an issue of principle: No Arab party could conclude a separate peace with Israel; peace could not even be considered in lieu of major territorial and other concessions by Israel (the Negev; refugee return); the boycott of Israeli products should be maintained and Israeli passports could not be recognized, and no oil tankers could traverse the Suez Canal to unload oil at the Haifa refinery. Hence, as news of progress in Jordanian-Israeli negotiations began filtering out, the Egyptian and Syrian media launched harsh attacks against Jordan. The pressure reinforced the reluctance of the Jordanian political elite to follow `Abdallah's lead in moving toward peace with Israel, and Jordan thus put the talks on hold so that it could concentrate on completing the incorporation of the West Bank into the kingdom. Nonetheless, the Egyptians kept up the pressure, publishing new evidence of Jordanian-Israeli wartime contacts in the press and employing the Arab League as a mechanism to embarrass Jordan and establish collective norms that were in line with its policies. To that end, it even began threatening to expel Jordan from the Arab League, a threat that was deemed serious enough to trigger a mediation effort by Iraqi and Lebanese leaders. The outcome was an Arab League Council resolution, passed unanimously on April 1, 1950, forbidding any member from negotiating for or concluding "a separate peace or any political, military, or economic agreement with Israel." A supplementary resolution laid out harsh penalties for any violator, including the severance of all political and economic relations and the closing of frontiers.[21] In doing so, the Council established a fundamental norm of behavior for Arab states. It would be nearly thirty years before it would be broken, ironically, by Egypt.

In any case, Jordan's immediate priority at this stage was to complete the West Bank's incorporation, beginning with parliamentary elections in both the West and East Banks. This, too, was against the wishes of the Egyptian-led anti-Hashimite bloc, and the Arab League Council quickly reaffirmed the validity of its April 1948 resolution that had declared any upcoming Arab occupation of Palestinian territory to be temporary and that political arrangements would be subject to the will of the inhabitants. However, the Jordanians were undeterred. On April 24, the newly convened parliament proclaimed the "complete unity of the eastern and western banks of the Jordan and their merging into one state" under the Hashimite crown, this in accordance with the "right of self-determination" and in view of the two Banks' "national, natural and geographic unity, as well as the necessities of their common interests and vital capacities." The proclamation also made sure to frame the action as being commensurate with the sacred ideal of overall Arab unity. Although the proclamation insisted that Palestinian Arab rights were being preserved and that the "final settlement of the just cause" [of Palestine] was not being prejudiced, Jordanian determination to hold onto the area for good was clear, no matter what the other Arab states said or did.[22]

The collective Arab response to Jordan's actions did not go beyond harsh declarations. While willing to acquiesce to Jordan's de facto control of the area, Egypt consistently opposed giving it a formal legal basis, for fear of undermining the central emotional motif of Arab nationalism, the cause of Palestine, and imply the formal acceptance of Palestine's partition. To that end, Egypt again activated the Arab League mechanism, proposing a trusteeship formula for the West Bank and threatening Jordan with expulsion from the League if it failed to accept it. A preliminary expulsion resolution was even passed by the Arab League's Political Committee. However, unlike with the peace negotiations with Israel, `Abdallah and his ministers were united in opposing the trusteeship formula. Moreover, none of the other Arab states were genuinely interested in pushing Jordan out of the League (and into Israel's arms), or had the capacity to pressure Jordan in any other way. As long as Jordan refrained from going too far toward Israel, Cairo would refrain from breaking up the League over the West Bank's annexation. Hence, the whole issue quickly faded from the collective Arab agenda. The single remnant of the controversy was that no Arab state ever officially recognized the annexation (the only two countries that did were Great Britain and Pakistan). It would take the June 1967 War to reopen the Arab debate on the status of the West Bank, and to give Palestinian nationalism a new lease on life, after a lengthy eclipse.

Concurrent with the new status quo on the West Bank, the possibility of a Jordanian-Israeli peace agreement faded away. The aging `Abdallah had, in a sense, become a prisoner of the situation that he had created. Demographically, Jordan now had a very large population of Palestinian origin, a considerable portion of which were embittered refugees, along with representation in the Jordanian parliament. He thus could no longer impose his will on a cabinet that paid close attention to public reaction at home and that of neighboring Arab states. Moreover, the need for a peace treaty had declined, following the US-British-French Tripartite Declaration of May 31, 1950, which provided guarantees maintaining the existing armistice lines. Sporadic contacts with Israel would continue during the next year, but without results, and `Abdallah's assassination on July 20, 1951, at the entrance to Jerusalem's al-Aqsa Mosque by a disgruntled Palestinian member of the Mufti Husayni's clan, put paid to any lingering possibilities for an Israeli-Jordanian agreement.

THE UPHEAVALS IN SYRIA

Round One

Syria's political, military, and economic weaknesses had confined it to a peripheral role in the 1948 Arab-Israeli war. These same weaknesses now resulted in the Syrian regime becoming the first victim of the collective Arab failure in Palestine. On March 30, 1949, it was overthrown in a bloodless coup led by the Army Chief of Staff, Col. Husni al-Za`im.[23] The coup inaugurated more than two decades of chronic instability, thrust into the center of an inter-Arab maelstrom.

The coup caught Arab leaders by surprise. As Patrick Seale recounts: "The question on everyone's lips was, 'Who is backing Za`im? Which way will he turn?'"[24] To one of the Hashimite monarchies, enabling them to advance their rival longstanding ambitions to "return" Syria to their control, or to the Egyptian-Saudi camp, thus keeping Syria out of the Hashimite clutches?

Some of Iraq's leaders, and especially Prime Minister Nuri al-Sa`id, were uneasy about the ripple effect that the military's intervention in Syrian politics might have on their own armed forces (a decade later these apprehensions would prove to have been justified). Nonetheless, they also perceived potential new opportunities and quickly sent a delegation to meet with Za`im and other Syrian politicians. It didn't take long for them to conclude that Za`im would be an unreliable partner. Some Syrian politicians were even eager that Iraq intervene by force to depose Za`im, an idea that appealed to the Iraqi Regent as a first step toward extending the Hashimite monarchy over the Syrian state. Nuri al-Sa`id, was less inclined to take risks. Supporting Za`im's opponents seemed like a good idea, but Iraqi military action was likely to draw international opprobrium, and might even trigger an Israeli military move in the West Bank to counterbalance the extension of Iraqi power toward Israel.

On April 9, Za`im surprised the Iraqis with an offer of a bilateral defense pact. Cautious but intrigued, Nuri sent a military delegation to Damascus to discuss the matter, and the Syrians responded by drafting an agreement to cover military cooperation and economic development. One week later, Nuri led a high-level delegation to Damascus to personally take Za`im's measure. But his meeting with him didn't go well, and Za`im informed him that Syria no longer feared "Jewish aggression," as it had received sufficient arms shipments from France. Za`im's moves turned out to be purely tactical, designed to strengthen his hand in the armistice negotiations with Israel and to achieve diplomatic recognition for his *coup d'état*. Nuri clearly sensed this, hence his focus was on Za`im's civilian opponents. In parallel meetings with Syrian politicians, he emphasized that if they really wanted closer ties with Iraq, the ball was in their court, requiring them to mobilize public opinion on behalf of forging closer ties.

Although it was he who had authored the Fertile Crescent scheme in 1943, Nuri's prevarication at this juncture was understandable. Still, he miscalculated Za`im's speed in embracing the primary regional opponent to an Iraqi-Syrian union—Egypt. Arab League Secretary-General `Azzam Pasha flew to Damascus on April 18 to urge Za`im to keep the Iraqis at bay, and also to restore constitutional procedures; like his old rival Nuri, `Azzam was of an earlier generation of Arab politicians who opposed the military's involvement in politics. Three days later, Za`im flew to Egypt to meet with Faouk and seal a Syrian-Egyptian alliance. It was apparently sweetened by a personal loan from Farouk to Za`im of between two and four million Egyptian pounds. Za`im symbolically proclaimed Farouk to be king of Syria, and himself as Farouk's viceroy in Damascus. Their joint statement also spoke of steps toward a Syrian-Egyptian merger (*indimaj*).[25] All of this was just for show. For Egypt and Saudi Arabia, the main thing was that the inter-Arab balance of power and territorial status quo had been preserved. Both countries would line up with Za`im in the coming months, providing political and financial support. The Lebanese leadership was of the same mind as Cairo and Riyadh, and was assuaged by something more concrete: on July 7, 1949, Za`im handed over to the Lebanese authorities the charismatic Antun Sa`adeh, the head of the opposition *Parti Populaire Syrién* (PPS), who had just attempted to spark a revolution in Lebanon. Sa`adeh was summarily tried and executed, dealing a mortal blow to a movement that had posed a Syrian-centered alternative to the larger project of Arab nationalism, one which portions of the Syrian elite and the opposition, particularly among the younger generation, had found attractive.[26]

Not surprisingly, Syrian-Iraqi relations were at a nadir in the following months, and Za`im suspected the Iraqis of plotting his downfall.

Rounds Two and Three

On August 14, 1949, the inter-Arab "struggle for Syria" was reopened by the overthrow of Za`im by a group of officers led by Col. Sami al-Hinnawi. Za`im's suspicions of Iraqi intrigue had been legitimate: Iraq had encouraged the plotters, although its actual role was secondary, thanks to Nuri's cautious response to requests for concrete assistance.[27] In any case, Hinnawi was now in charge, and he quickly had Za`im executed, along with his prime minister, Muhsin al-Barazi.

This coup suggested greater possibilities for Iraq than the previous one. To Baghdad's satisfaction, a civilian caretaker government was swiftly established, and it included a number of members of the Aleppo-based People's Party, which had previously advocated closer ties with Iraq in line with the city's historic economic links with the neighboring Mosul *vilayet* during Ottoman times. Nuri al-Sa`id's approach remained the same: the initiative for closer ties had to come from legitimate Syrian authorities, and the process had to move forward gradually, so as to successfully neutralize domestic (both civilian and military) and regional opposition.[28]

Iraqi and Syrian leaders held substantial discussions on the particulars of a Syrian-Iraqi framework in the following months. One major stumbling block was the extent to which the two countries' institutions should be unified. Another obstacle was the applicability of the existing Anglo-Iraqi Treaty to Syria. After months of talks, it became clear that further progress would have to await the upcoming November Syrian parliamentary elections, which ideally would result in a newly legitimized leadership capable of making the necessary decisions regarding the proposed union. But in the meantime, other Arab states, led by Egypt, began weighing in against the idea and advocated an inclusive Arab League collective security pact as an alternative to Syria's relying on Iraq to counterbalance Israel. In doing so, it strengthened the confidence of the anti-Iraqi elements in the Syrian army.

The prospects for a speedy adoption of an Iraqi-Syrian federation had thus receded, and the Syrian elections offered no definitive outcome either. Although the People's Party won the largest number of seats, it had not received a mandate for action, and in any case, the leadership was unsure of what course to pursue. The election boycott by Quwwatli's National Party had partially delegitimized the elections, and important elements of the army remained opposed to the union idea. All the Iraqis could do at this point was to continue cultivating pro-Iraqi elements in Syria, including the disbursement of funds.

The straw that broke the proverbial camel's back came on December 17, 1949: Syria's new Constituent Assembly approved the text of the oath of office to be taken by the country's president and assembly members. Proponents of closer ties with Iraq succeeded in omitting a pledge to preserve the republican regime, and including one to "work for the realization of the unity of the Arab states." The effect on the anti-union elements in the military was immediate. The next night, Hinnawi and a number of supporters were arrested by Col. Adib al-Shishakli, who had participated in the previous coup against Za`im. Col. Asad Tlas, Iraq's point man among the military, took refuge in the Iraqi embassy. As usual, the motives were a mixture of factors, but Shishakli's involvement with the PPS, whose vision of Greater Syria left room for union with Iraq, but only if Syria were a dominant partner and under a republican regime, pointed to the importance of the ideological dimension to the coup.

Although civilians were not touched at this stage, it was now abundantly clear that the center of gravity in Syrian political life was located in the barracks. Ironically, the veteran politician Hashim al-Atasi would be sworn in as president three weeks later using the unchanged oath of allegiance that had sparked the third military coup in nine months. Shishakli would confirm his decisive role a year later and remain the strongman of the country until 1954, when he was ousted, opening up another chapter in the tumultuous history of the Syrian state.

Meanwhile, for all of the upheaval during 1949, Syria's place within the inter-Arab framework ended up being the same as it had been, ensconced in the anti-Hashimite, Egyptian- and Saudi-led camp. The existing "cooperation" model of inter-Arab relations remained dominant, and the Hashimite-sponsored, geographically based "unity" model again failed to be consummated. Overall, the existing uneasy inter-Arab equilibrium was also preferred by the Western powers, who were seeking to shore up the region against Soviet inroads.

YEARS OF TRANSITION: 1950–1954

On the surface, the first half of the 1950s was relatively calm for the Arab regional system. This was partially due to the deaths of three prime protagonists of Arab politics during the previous decades: Jordan's King `Abdallah, who was assassinated in July 1951; Egypt's King Farouk, who was deposed almost exactly a year later in a bloodless military coup and sent into Italian exile; and Saudi Arabia's elderly king `Abd al-`Aziz bin Sa`ud, the founder of the Saudi state, who died in 1953. Their departure symbolized the end of the dynastic era of inter-Arab affairs, marked by long-standing interpersonal rivalries, suspicions, and jealousies. To a lesser degree, so did the decline in status of the Iraqi Regent `Abd al-Ilah following Faysal II's reaching of maturity that same year. The new leaderships in Egypt and Jordan would have to devote their energies, at least initially, to legitimizing and consolidating their authority at home.

The ultimate impact of Farouk's deposal for inter-Arab, regional, and global affairs would be profound, but would only unfold over the next few years. `Abdallah's death, by contrast, raised an immediate question: Would the Hashimite Jordanian monarchy, and even Jordan as an entity, continue to exist, or had a vacuum been created that would create a new arena of conflict between its neighbors? `Abdallah's eldest son, Talal, assumed the kingship, but he was mentally unfit for the job and deposed a year later; his seventeen-year-old eldest son, Husayn, was officially enthroned in May 1953, as was his cousin, Faysal II, in Baghdad. Throughout the preceding two years of uncertainty, the vulnerable Jordanian ship of state was adroitly managed by the same small cohesive elite that had governed alongside `Abdallah, along with British support. This cohesion enabled them to rebuff the overtures by their Iraqi Hashimite cousins to place Jordan under their protective wing.[29]

By now, the Cold War was in full force, and its impact on inter-Arab affairs grew steadily. The main bone of contention between Arab states during the early 1950s centered on US and British efforts to establish a regional defense scheme that would serve as a bulwark against Soviet ambitions. Britain, in particular, saw the plans as a way to bypass the virulent opposition in Egypt and Iraq that had derailed efforts to renegotiate their respective bilateral treaties in 1946 and 1948. But neither the Egyptian public, nor its increasingly fragile political class, was buying it. The atmosphere in Egypt in late 1951 was highly charged, and included numerous attacks against Britain's Canal Zone base, mainly by Muslim Brotherhood militants. In December, Egyptian Prime Minister Nahhas Pasha announced the unilateral abrogation of the Anglo-Egyptian Treaty, which conferred Britain with the rights to the base, adding fuel to the fire. Nuri al-Sa`id, by contrast, hoped to bolster Iraq's status by finding a formula that would somehow reconcile Western defense needs and Egyptian sensitivities, perhaps via the Arab League's Joint Defense and Economic Cooperation that had been signed in June 1950.[30] The issue remained unresolved, and the differences between Iraq and Egypt were just an ominous foretaste of what was to come.

Interestingly, economics had very little to do with the cut and thrust of inter-Arab politics, either its cooperative or conflictual aspects during these years. The massive explosion of oil-generated wealth was a ways off, and Arab economies were still quite small in size. Moreover, Arab states were generally characterized by a low level of development and accompanying problems of health, widespread illiteracy, limited technological education, and poor infrastructure. On top of that, Arab leaders guarded their particular economic interests as closely as their political ones, and were not interested in broader regional development schemes that might adversely affect their own nascent industries. Nor was there any proper institutional framework for Arab economic complementarity, or a private sector strong enough to lead the way.[31] All of these factors militated against the forging of closer economic ties, notwithstanding that this was one of the declared goals of the Arab League Charter and the 1950 Treaty of Joint Defense and Economic Cooperation, whose economic clauses were more of a wish list than a blueprint for action. In terms of political economy, there existed neither sufficient mutual need nor a strong enough economic center to take even beginning steps toward integration.

Overall, the relative calm in inter-Arab affairs during the early 1950s was deceptive. The passing of the old guard in Arab politics militated against the status quo. The changes taking place were not just in the realm of personalities, but were societal, as new generations of increasingly urban, educated, and politicized classes asserted themselves in various ways. In particular, the military was for many the most viable path for social mobility. The Egyptian Free Officers who had overthrown Farouk belonged primarily to families from the lower middle class whose sons were given the opportunity in 1936 to enroll in the country's military academy. Ironically, here and elsewhere, the ruling elite's efforts to expand the coercive capacities of the state turned out to be a double-edged sword. In Syria, the military was the way forward for formerly marginalized minority groups, as well as those on the fringes of Sunni Arab society. This would become fully apparent in the coming years. Everywhere, younger generations of Arabs were imbibing the overlapping discourses of a more strident Arab nationalism and anti-imperialism, in the context of the shortcomings of their own ruling elites and the continued weakness of the Arab countries, epitomized by their defeat by Israel and by continued Western hegemony in the region. The growing appeal of the Syrian-based pan-Arab Ba`th Party, which championed a revolutionary socialist and unionist program, was very much a product of these processes. The ruling elites of both Jordan and Iraq would be increasingly hard-pressed to maintain their positions in the face of these developments.

In this context, 1954 witnessed a number of events that, taken together, set the stage for the tumultuous years ahead. Gamal `Abd al-Nasir emerged as the uncontested strongman of Egypt. Ironically, Egypt's relations with Britain were placed on a new and potentially more benign course, as the two countries concluded an agreement for Britain's evacuation of its Suez base within two years, in return for Egypt's conceding to Sudan's right to self-determination and independence. However, Nasir had other, more radical ideas regarding the desired regional order, ones that would swiftly lead to open confrontation with Britain. In Syria, Shishakli's overthrow and the return to civilian government marked the beginning of a renewed slide toward state collapse. As a result, the question of Syria's future status and regional and global alignments was reopened. And in conservative pro-British Iraq, Nuri al-Sa`id indicated that he was no longer willing to accept Egyptian diktats on the issue of regional security pacts. The stage was thus being set for a confrontation between Nasir and Nuri that would fundamentally alter the shape of regional politics.

5

THE RADICAL HEYDAY (1955–1967)

Radical pan-Arabism, embodied more than anyone or anything else by the charismatic Egyptian president Gamal `Abd al-Nasir, first emerged as a significant political force in 1955. Defining it has often proven elusive, but to paraphrase the American jurist Potter Stewart, one knows it when one sees it. As an idea and as a movement, radical pan-Arabism in its heyday was a dominating concept in the Arab world. Its mix of values and ideas were profoundly anti-status quo. They included genuine Arab unity in one political form or another, the overthrow of ancient regimes and their allied "old social classes,"[1] a commitment to Arab socialism, anti-imperialism, and non-alignment, with a defined tilt toward the Soviet bloc, and a view of the conflict with Israel as nothing less than a clash of destinies.[2] Taken together, these produced a powerful emotive force, for they were geared to achieve what was widely seen to have been lacking for so long—dignity, prosperity, and power. At its peak, radical pan-Arabism had the capacity to make local leaders and interests look small, insignificant, and ultimately illegitimate.[3] As such, inter-Arab politics during this period were not just struggles over material power, but also over symbolic assets. To a considerable extent, Nasir had the ability to shape Arab political discourse, namely to determine the proper content and meaning of "being Arab," which leaders and countries belonged to the "authentic" Arab camp, and which did not.[4]

However, pan-Arabism was always primarily an "expressive ideology,"[5] i.e., short on practical, concrete ideas on how to translate the dream of a powerful united Arab world into reality. Indeed, its advocates lacked the material assets to realize their vision. As far back as the mid-1930s, Iraqi Arab nationalists had championed the Prussia model of union for the Arab East, with Iraq to play the leading role, just as Prussia under Bismarck had brought about the unification of the various German principalities in 1871. Egypt under Nasir would come the closest to playing the Prussia role, but ultimately lacked Prussia's capacity to bend the others' will. Similarly, the alternative path to union—by agreement, not by coercion—would remain unrealizable.

In examining the rise and decline of the radical pan-Arab current and its supreme personification, Gamal `Abd al-Nasir, between 1955 and 1967, one may divide the period into two parts: 1955–1961, the "heroic" phase, and 1961–1967, which were bookended by two monumental failures that together sealed the fate of the radical pan-Arab vision.

THE HEROIC PHASE: 1955–1961

The Trigger: the Baghdad Pact

The conclusion of the Anglo-Egyptian agreement on July 27, 1954, stipulating the final evacuation of British troops from Egypt in 1956 after seventy-four years, seemed to have finally solved the single most vexing issue in Egyptian politics and in Anglo-Egyptian relations. It was not unreasonable for Britain and its local supporters, most notably Nuri al-Sa`id, to conclude that the agreement indicated that `Abd al-Nasir, who was now coming into his own as the leader of Egypt, would pursue pragmatic, non-ideological policies that focused primarily on domestic affairs. Indeed, in late October 1954, Nasir cracked down harshly on the Egyptian Muslim Brotherhood, two years after having received its tacit support for the coup that had overthrown Farouk.

To be sure, British officials were concerned for the future of what they liked to call the "old gang" of pro-British Iraqi leaders, particularly if Iraq's long-term development plans did not provide quick results for its young and restless rising generation. But the spurt of oil-generated revenues was sparking large development projects, giving the Iraqi leadership new confidence. Concurrently, Western insistence on establishing some kind of regional defense structure now focused on the Middle East's "Northern Tier," following Egypt's unwillingness to subordinate itself anew to the Western powers. The new American and British plan offered Nuri potential benefits that seemed too good to pass up: the replacement of the Anglo-Iraqi Treaty, which was due to expire in 1957, with a new framework promising substantial military and economic aid, integration into Western defense planning and political support. All this added up to recognition of Iraq as the major Arab power in the Arab East, an aspiration of Iraq's Sunni political class, and Nuri personally, since achieving independence in 1932. After having chafed for a decade at Egypt's domination of Arab politics, Nuri was now determined that Iraqi foreign policy not be dependent on Egyptian approval. For him, the adherence to Arab nationalist precepts and an alignment with the West were not contradictory principles. But for Nasir and his generation,[6] they were.

At the end of November 1954, the Arab League Council passed an Egyptian-sponsored resolution emphasizing that Arab foreign policies should be guided by the Arab League Charter, the 1950 Joint Defense Pact, and the UN Charter, and that other alliances would not be recognized, a clear reference to the idea of defense pacts with other non-Arab states.[7] But Nuri, perhaps misreading Nasir's intentions,[8] blatantly ignored the resolution, believing that the time was ripe for Iraq to break out of the straitjacket in which Egypt had placed it. Hence, on February 24, 1955, Iraq signed a bilateral security pact with Turkey; it was part of a series of agreements known collectively as the Baghdad Pact, involving Iran, Pakistan, and Great Britain as well, with American support. No less disturbing, from the Egyptian point of view, was that Britain and Iraq were openly keen on getting other Arab states, namely Jordan, Syria, Lebanon, and Saudi Arabia, to accede to the Pact.

The Egyptian reaction was immediate, harsh, and Manichean. Iraq, Nasir and his spokesmen proclaimed, had abandoned the Arab world in favor of those who continued to aspire to dominate it. Cairo's first counter-move on the ground came on March 6, with the proclamation of a tripartite alliance with Syria and Saudi Arabia whose official *raison d'être* was the rejection of the Baghdad Pact in favor of strengthening collective Arab defense. In practical terms, the intent was to block Syria from following in Iraq's footsteps by strengthening the anti-Iraqi, anti-Western elements within the increasingly fragmented Syrian polity.

As the Egyptians framed things, the matter was nothing short of existential. "The Arab world was at a crossroads," declared Interior Minister Salim al-Salim. "Either it will be an independent and cohesive unity with its own structures and national character or else each country will pursue its own course... [this will be] the beginning of the downfall of Arab nationhood."[9] In other words, Nasir and his associates were linking the meaning of the Baghdad Pact to both the security of the Arab states and the future of Arab nationalism, employing the symbols of Arab nationalism to mobilize Arab societies behind his particular vision.[10] In light of his background, education, and military service, Nasir's sudden conversion to Arab nationalism may have seemed surprising to some. However, given the confluence of circumstances, it was both natural and ideal for a young leader of a proud nation in need of political legitimacy.

Adeed Dawisha argues persuasively that Nasir came to Arab nationalism through the backdoor of anti-imperialism.[11] Indeed, the combination brought him an immediate dividend that boosted his prestige enormously. In April 1955, Nasir attended a weeklong conference of the leaders of twenty-nine newly independent African and Asian countries in Bandung, Indonesia. It was, in essence, the founding of the Non-Aligned movement. Those leaders present included Nehru of India, Tito of Yugoslavia, Chou En-Lai of the People's Republic of China, and the host of the conference, Indonesia's president Sukarno, all of whom had the deserved reputation of having led their countries' struggle for independence and freedom from foreign domination. Although senior representatives from six other Arab countries also attended the gathering, including Iraq's former prime minister Mohamed Fadhil al-Jamali, it was Nasir who was warmly welcomed as the representative of Arab aspirations. It was, undoubtedly, a heady experience.

The fact that the Arab-Israeli conflict was heating up further reinforced Nasir's instincts to adopt a militant Arab nationalist position. Egyptian military intelligence had been increasingly active in initiating cross-border Palestinian *fida'iyyun* (literally, "men of sacrifice") attacks from the Gaza Strip into Israel. Now, just four days after the signing of the Iraqi-Turkish agreement, a large-scale Israeli retaliatory strike against an Egyptian base in Gaza killed thirty-eight soldiers. For Nasir, the attack was a wake-up call regarding the state of his army and the need for a serious upgrade.[12] Contacts with the Soviet Union had already been initiated regarding possible arms purchases, and were now accelerated. The result was dramatic. In September 1955, it became known that Egypt had concluded an agreement with Czechoslovakia, an integral part of the Soviet-led Warsaw Pact nations, to supply it with advanced weaponry and equipment, including hundreds of combat aircraft, tanks, and artillery pieces. In doing so, Egypt had broken out of the straitjacket imposed by the Western powers' 1950 Tripartite Declaration, which had placed a severe limit on Western arms exports to the Middle East in order to preserve the existing balance of power between Arab states and Israel. From the geopolitical perspective, the Czech arms deal constituted a Soviet "leapfrogging" over the West's "Northern Tier" barrier into the heartland of the Middle East, and into a country that controlled the strategically vital Suez Canal, no less, to the dismay and consternation of Washington and London, and to Israel, as well. For Israelis, an alteration in the existing balance of power increased the likelihood of an Arab-initiated "second round" of fighting in order to roll back the results of the 1948 war. For Nuri al-Sa`id and like-minded Arab elites, the latest development set off alarm bells as well. Conversely, for Egyptians, and for much of the increasingly politicized younger generation of Arabs everywhere, the Czech arms deal seemed to provide tangible proof that Nasir's course was the right one. The fact that France's domination in North Africa was now being challenged by independence movements in Morocco, Tunisia, and Algeria, all of which included an Arab identity component in their collective self-definition, added further ingredients to the increasingly heady brew of anti-Western, anti-colonial, anti-Zionist Arab nationalist ideology and praxis pulsating back and forth across the region. The transmission of Nasir's message would be considerably aided by the latest advance in mass communication—the transistor radio, whose compact size and low cost enabled Nasir to engage in a similar kind of leapfrogging—in this case, over the heads of Arab leaders, and directly to the Arab public, via Cairo's powerful "Voice of the Arabs" radio station.

The impact of these developments was immediately felt in Jordan. In December 1955, Britain's military chief of staff, Sir Gerald Templer, arrived in Jordan offering expanded military aid to the young King Husayn in return for Jordan's accession to the Baghdad Pact. Egypt pulled out all the stops to block it, launching a vociferous propaganda campaign against the idea and calling out its supporters in Jordan for massive and violent street demonstrations. Jordan was deterred, and the episode inaugurated a lengthy period of political uncertainty in Jordan that suggested to many that the king's days were numbered.[13] Throughout 1956 and into 1957, power seemed to be passing into the hands of pro-Nasir nationalist politicians and perhaps even army officers who were chafing under British tutelage. To pacify them and curry favor with Nasir, and to bolster his own credentials, Husayn summarily dismissed the longtime commander of the Arab Legion, the retired British General John Bagot Glubb, on March 1, 1956. It was an astute move, allowing him to buy time to strengthen his position. Eventually, in April 1957, he would face down his opponents, at considerable personal risk, and reassert royal control over the kingdom. [14]

THE SUEZ EXPLOSION—NASIR'S BLESSED MOMENT [15]

The fallout from the Baghdad Pact reverberated throughout 1955 and into the first months of 1956, exacerbating the tensions between Arab states, between Nasir and the Western powers and in the Arab-Israeli arena, and further emphasizing the region's centrality to the ever-intensifying Western-Soviet Cold War. The effects of developments in each sphere on the others, both direct and indirect, would ultimately lead to the British-French-Israeli military attack on Egypt, in late October 1956. Nasir's forces in Sinai would be routed by Israel, but in political terms, the entire Suez affair would constitute a ringing victory for Nasir, confirming his "hero" status in the eyes of much of the Arab publics, and giving a further boost to the supporters of his brand of pan-Arab nationalism. Conversely, the episode constituted an ignominious defeat for Britain and France: symbolizing the end of Britain's "moment" in the Middle East. [16]

The immediate trigger to the Suez crisis came from a direction not yet addressed here: a sudden deterioration in American-Egyptian relations. Unlike Britain and France, the United States had no history in the Middle East as a colonial power. Moreover, given its own history of revolting against British rule, America's self-definition and self-image of being a beacon of hope for the world produced a strong layer of sympathy for the struggles of anti-colonial movements, first articulated in Woodrow Wilson's 14 Points emphasizing the rights of peoples to self-determination and autonomous development. Of course, in practice, as a rising great power beginning at the end of the nineteenth century, the United States often acted in contradiction to these principles, giving priority to economic, political, and military interests. The tension between American ideals and American interests, traditionally defined, would become a permanent feature of American foreign policy in the twentieth century, and remains so up until today.[17]

This tension was very much present in American-Egyptian relations during these years. As the United States gradually and reluctantly inherited Britain's role as the primary protector of Western interests in the Middle East, in the context of the region's status as a crucial arena of the Cold War, it became ever more entangled with local actors. CIA operatives had been in contact with Nasir while he was planning his coup, and apparently encouraged him to act.[18] Many US policymakers sympathized with the strivings for dignity that the younger generation of Arab nationalists articulated. Moreover, they believed that they offered the best hope of containing the spread of communism to the region.[19] Egypt's geopolitical centrality was also very much on their minds. Hence, for both idealistic and pragmatic strategic reasons, the United States had good reason to try to cultivate close ties with Nasir. But successive US administrations would be bedeviled repeatedly by Nasir's unwillingness to align Egypt unequivocally with the West, expressed in his policy of "positive neutralism" toward the Soviet-American rivalry. In practice, this meant that Egypt would try to benefit from relations with both sides. However, this became increasingly untenable as time went on, resulting in a steadily increasing tilt toward the Soviets.

American efforts were expressed in two areas: trying to broker a solution to the Arab-Israeli conflict, and fostering aid for development. Diplomatic efforts were in high gear in 1954–55, as the United States and Britain promoted Project Alpha, which envisaged an Egyptian-Israeli peace agreement in return for a solution to the Palestinian refugee issue and Israeli territorial concessions in the Negev that would enable Egypt to have a direct overland connection to Jordan and the Arab East. Western negotiators believed that doing so would properly address Arab aspirations for closer ties.[20] It is doubtful, however, that King Husayn and the Jordanian elite looked favorably upon the idea of Jordan being territorially contiguous with Nasir's Egypt. In any case, this proposal, and a subsequent effort by US President Eisenhower's personal envoy Robert Anderson to persuade Nasir to conclude a formal peace agreement with Israel, failed to gain traction,[21] as Nasir's increasingly strident pan-Arab orientation took him toward a more confrontational posture toward Israel. By now, Israel had long since been disabused of the notion, first expressed by Prime Minister David Ben-Gurion, that the new Egypt would be a more benign neighbor,[22] and adopted a more hawkish security posture toward it.

In the development field, Nasir's big-ticket project was the building of the Aswan High Dam, which promised to harness the annual Nile River floods, open up new areas for cultivation, and generate the vital electric power needed for Egypt's growth and development. The United States had committed itself in principal to providing the funding for the dam, but Secretary of State John Foster Dulles's unhappiness with Nasir's tilt to the East was palpable. The straw that broke the camel's back came on May 16, 1956, when Egypt announced that it would recognize the communist Chinese government in Peking [Beijing], in place of the US-backed Nationalist government holed up in Taiwan since its defeat in the Chinese civil war in 1949, and support a UN resolution seating it. In response, on July 19, the United States withdrew its aid offer, presuming to teach Nasir a lesson that he wouldn't forget.

Instead, Nasir upped the ante. In a dramatic speech to the nation on July 26, the anniversary of the Free Officers' coup, Nasir announced the immediate nationalization of the British-French-owned Suez Canal, long the symbol of Western domination of Egypt. The reaction of the Egyptian public and his many supporters throughout the Arab world was electric, catapulting Nasir into true hero status. Coming just six weeks after the final withdrawal of British troops from Suez, Nasir had now seemingly eliminated the very last vestige of the British presence. Britain's Prime Minister Anthony Eden viewed Nasir's action through the lens of the infamous 1938 Munich agreement, referred to him as the "new Hitler" who had blatantly violated international law, and was determined not to let the Canal's nationalization stand. He was joined by France, a junior partner in the Suez Canal Company, for one overriding reason: Nasir was seen by Paris as a crucial external supporter of the Algerian nationalists' increasingly bitter war for independence against France's 130-year rule of the country, and thus as someone who needed to be defeated at all cost. The two countries initiated preparations to retake the Canal by force, which they hoped would result in Nasir's removal from power as well. The Eisenhower Administration was nonplussed by Nasir's action, but totally opposed to a military response, and thus sought to broker an agreed-upon diplomatic solution involving the international community, albeit to no avail.

The war broke out on October 29, albeit from an unexpected direction: Israel attacked Egyptian forces in the Sinai Peninsula, as part of a prearranged plan that provided Britain and France with a formal, albeit utterly feeble and transparent excuse to intervene to separate the combatants and secure the Canal. Israel had observed the growth in Nasir's increasing power and prestige during the last year with trepidation, and had begun developing closer ties with France. It was the French who, in September, persuaded a reluctant Britain to invite Israel into the war plans, and Israel accepted. The Israeli part of the war went as planned, with its forces occupying the Sinai Peninsula within four days. However, the British and French part of the operation faltered, and ground to a halt after one week of fighting, in the face of widespread international opprobrium. Indeed, the Eisenhower Administration was so outraged that it caused a run on the British pound, with swift results, forcing an end to the fighting, the withdrawal of British and French forces, and the end to Eden's political career. Israeli forces would withdraw from the Sinai Peninsula by April 1957, in return for the stationing of UN troops on the Egyptian side of the border with Israel, an unwritten commitment to keep the Sinai demilitarized and the opening of the Straits of Tiran to Israeli shipping to its new southern port of Eilat, along with a US guarantee that it would remain open.

For Nasir, the war was a political triumph of the first order. In private, the Iraqi leadership had waited expectedly for the news of the Egyptian army's surrender and the toppling of Nasir from power, but in vain.[23] In public, Nasir's Arab foes had been forced to publicly toe the line in his favor, in the face of what was universally seen in the Arab world as unbridled British aggression. Indeed, the war would enter the Arab political lexicon as the "Tripartite Aggression" (*al-'udwan al-thulathi*), a "collusion" (*mu'amara*) that was, by definition, illegitimate.

Ironically, the war brought considerable benefit and respect for Israel as well. It had demonstrated that the eight years that had passed since its creation had been spent wisely, militarily speaking, and that the state was in fact a viable, going concern. The defense relationship with France would deepen over the next decade, helping give Israel a further qualitative edge that would eventually be expressed in the June 1967 War, as well as in the secret development of Israel's nuclear program.[24] No less important, the war bought a decade of relative quiet on its borders, enabling it to concentrate on internal development, particularly the absorption of a million new immigrants, resulting in a tripling of the country's population between 1948 and 1967. At the same time, Israel's collaboration with Britain and France in this "war of choice" further confirmed to Arab nationalists everywhere the already widely held image of Israel as being an implacable enemy to the Arab nation, and that the Arab-Jewish struggle was not just over Palestine but over the Arab nation's very existence.

The United States, for its part, received little credit from the Arab publics for having forced Britain and France to cease its military campaign and withdraw its troops. By contrast, the Soviet Union's condemnations of the "tripartite aggression" and blusterous threats to launch missiles at Israel if it didn't end its attack further burnished its image as a genuine supporter of Arab aspirations. Soviet prestige and influence seemed to be especially present in Syria, as the Syrian communist party grew in influence, this in the context of Syria's political order increasingly coming apart at the seams, including the progressive politicization and factionalization of the military.

The US concern with what it perceived as expanding Soviet influence in Syria was palpable. One immediate response was the propagation on January 5, 1957, of the Eisenhower Doctrine, in which the United States pledged "to secure and protect the territorial integrity and political independence of . . . nations requesting . . . aid against overt armed aggression from any nation controlled by international communism."[25] The terminology was extraordinarily vague, but it indicated that the United States would bolster its conservative pro-Western Arab allies. As the year proceeded, the United States came close to declaring Syria a country that was indeed "controlled by international communism," and thus, *ipso facto,* posed a threat to its neighbors. Extensive consultations were held with the United States's main regional allies—Turkey, Saudi Arabia, and Iraq—designed to force a confrontation with the Syrian regime and replace it with a pro-Western government.[26]

However, public opinion in both Syria and the region were distinctly supportive of Syria's anti-Western, Arab nationalist posture; hence neither Saudi Arabia's King Saud nor the Iraqi leadership was willing to take overt steps to intervene there. As a result, the United States turned to Turkey, which built up its forces along the Syrian-Turkish border in September 1957. The Soviet Union, in turn, warned Turkey not to intervene, and for a moment, a major international crisis seemed to be in the offing. But the absence of a viable pro-Western alternative in Syria, reassurances to Turkey by the Syrian leadership, and Soviet warnings led Turkey to reconsider. Overall, US actions were clumsy and unsuccessful. In mid-October, Nasir stepped in to score points, dispatching a symbolic detachment of Egyptian troops to the Syrian port of Latakia on the northern Syrian coast, ostensibly to deter "Turkish aggression." Doing so bolstered the anti-Western elements within the country and further reinforced his image as the genuine standard-bearer of Arab interests everywhere. Six months later, he would be standing on a balcony overlooking Damascus's main square, in front of a huge adoring crowd proclaiming the unification of Egypt and Syria in the United Arab Republic (UAR). It would mark the highpoint in the history of an idea—pan-Arab unity—that had captivated millions and decisively shaped the region's politics for decades, albeit not in the way that Nasir and his admirers had hoped.[27]

THE FORMATION OF THE UAR

In terms of power politics, the UAR's establishment would seem to constitute a logical consequence of Egypt's deep-rooted aspirations to be a regional hegemon, to project power into Arab Asia in order to protect and advance its interests. Doing so, of course, served Egypt's leaders well, both at home and internationally. In this regard, Nasir's embrace of the role of pan-Arab hero was instrumental, changing the specifics of how to advance Egypt's fundamental interests but not the underlying substance. However, Nasir had come to pan-Arabism through the barracks, not the university. And his preference for a united Arab world under his leadership did not necessarily entail the desire to erase existing boundaries between the different Arab entities. For Nasir, *wahdat al-hadaf* ("unity of purpose") among like-minded regimes was his distinct preference, not their wholesale swallowing up.

From this perspective, then, it was the weakness, and even potential unraveling, of the Syrian state that eventually forced Nasir's hand. Indeed, it was not Nasir who first tendered the idea of an Egyptian-Syrian union, but an Arab nationalist faction within the fragmented Syrian security and political establishment. Fearing both the communists on the left and the pro-Western, Turkish, and Iraqi factions on the right, the Arab nationalists, led by army chief of staff Gen. `Afif al-Bizri and Ba`th party leaders, sought to persuade Nasir of the utility and necessity of union. In essence, union under Egypt would "save Syria from itself," namely, impose order and stability while advancing the cherished goal of Arab unity.

At first, Nasir was hesitant, well aware of warnings that Syria was, in essence, ungovernable.[28] At the same time, he was increasingly locked into the path of union: as the widely recognized hero of the Arab nation, Nasir could hardly afford to ignore the possible consequences of inaction, namely the shift of Syria back into the conservative Western ("reactionary and imperialist") camp. It was a case of symbolic entrapment: as Barnett says, Nasir was not only a creator of the political agenda, he was also a creature of it. Were he to deny the "heroic" role in Arabic politics that he had claimed, he would be denying the very fabric of his leadership.[29]

A number of interim steps toward union were taken in late 1957 and early 1958, and Nasir eventually concluded that there was no alternative to full union. So did Syria's reluctant president Shukri al-Quwatli,[30] after being confronted with a *diktat* by Bizri, intelligence chief `Abd al-Hamid Sarraj, and like-minded officers. On January 31, 1958, Quwatli and his Cabinet were "herded like sheep" onto a plane to Cairo; the UAR was jointly proclaimed the next day by Nasir and Quwatli, confirmatory referendums were quickly organized, and Nasir and the Egyptian leadership flew to Damascus on February 24 for three weeks of celebrations with an adoring public.[31] What the celebrants did not know, of course, was that the newly proclaimed union would have a short life – just three and a half years. Nor did the Syrian Ba`th and its allies who had militated for the union understand Nasir's intentions. Having invited him to Damascus to "save Syria," i.e., to save themselves, and their vision of what Syria should be, they now presumed that, as his natural allies, they would be delegated with the task of governing the country in what would essentially be a federalist system. The Ba`th leadership's intellectual arrogance also led them to believe mistakenly that they would serve as Nasir's guide to implementing what they defined as the proper Arab nationalist tenets. But Nasir's intent was different: Having entered reluctantly into the union, he concluded that for union to succeed, it required a centralized authority, dominated by Cairo. Given Egypt's limited capacity to impose its will on the UAR's "northern province," the foundation for the UAR's breakup was thus laid at its inception.

Meanwhile, the news of the union caused great consternation among Nasir's Arab rivals, and also in Israel and Turkey. Concerned with the possible extension of Egyptian military power to its northern border with Syria, as well as with the destabilizing effect that the UAR's establishment might have on neighboring Jordan and Lebanon, Ben-Gurion forbade the Israeli media from using a literal translation of the UAR's initials into Hebrew ("R.A.M": "thunder"). Lebanon was already experiencing a mini civil war, as leftist-Muslim factions drew moral and some material support from Nasir and the Ba`th in an effort to prevent the country's conservative pro-Western president Camille Chamoun from changing the constitution so as to serve another term in office. Saudi Arabia, which up until 1957 had placed itself solidly alongside Egypt in the anti-Hashimite Arab camp, now realized where the primary threat against the regime lay: from radical pan-Arabism and its standard bearers. It thus realigned itself in what was now a clearly defined conservative camp, opposing the radical vision of anti-Western unity and social and political transformation, including the overthrow of the *ancien regimes*. These goals were shared by Arab communist parties as well.

As for the Hashimite camp itself, the original standard-bearer of Arab unity, Iraq and Jordan tried to draw the wagons, establishing an "Arab Federation" (*al-Ittihad al-`Arabi*). Formally, it was open to any Arab state wishing to join, with Kuwait, still a British protectorate but well on the way to independence, invited explicitly to join. The reasons were obvious: adding Kuwait's wealth to the federation would be a boon to impoverished Jordan, create a British-affiliated bloc of monarchies with financial clout and geo-strategic weight extending to the Persian Gulf, and provide an appropriate, albeit attenuated answer to Iraq's long-standing claim to Kuwait. Not surprisingly, however, the Al Sabah rulers of Kuwait had no interest in subordinating themselves to such a scheme, and British officials had no inclination to persuade them otherwise.

In essence, the new Arab Federation was a "family compact."[32] Iraq's King Faysal II was named president of the newly formed Federal Government, with King Husayn to preside in his absence. Its jurisdiction would include foreign and defense affairs, the establishment and management of the armed forces, diplomatic representation abroad, customs, currency, educational policy and curricula, and transportation and communications. Eighty percent of the Federal Government's budget was to be supplied by Iraq, twenty percent by Jordan. The Hashimite flag of the Hijaz would be the Federal Government's flag.[33] At the same time, each state was to preserve its independence and existing governmental structure. Moreover, in contrast to Iraq's probes in 1951–52, no mention was made of a possible unification of the two royal branches under a single crown. The new federation was an elaboration of an original proposal that had been made by King `Abdallah in 1946, which the Iraqis had brushed off. But circumstances had now changed completely: the ambitious `Abdallah was no longer on the scene, which had helped render the notion unpalatable to Baghdad; nor did there exist any potential opportunity for Iraqi aggrandizement, as had been the case after `Abdallah's death in 1951. To be sure, Nuri al-Sa`id remained unenthusiastic, viewing Jordan as an economic burden and of no help politically.[34] But the pressing defensive needs in the face of the growing threat of radical pan-Arabism made the ruling elites in both Baghdad and Amman look for ways to draw closer, in the name of the old and now threadbare banner of Hashimite leadership of a united Arab world. One practical result was the stationing of an Iraqi military detachment in northern Jordan to bolster Husayn's rule.[35] Ironically, some months later, additional troops being sent to Jordan would make a detour to Baghdad and overthrow the Iraqi monarchy.

THE ARAB COLD WAR

The rival Arab unity projects that materialized in February 1958 inaugurated what Malcolm Kerr termed the "Arab Cold War."[36] The struggle between the two rival camps was both geopolitical and ideological, as the conservative pro-Western Arab monarchies and republics (Tunisia and Lebanon) justifiably feared for their political future and physical security in the face of ascending radical pan-Arabism and its appeal to significant segments of their own societies. No less significant would be the struggle within the radical camp, with far-reaching and ultimately disastrous consequences for Arab states, societies, and what by now had become a quasi-Messianic belief in a pan-Arabism that promised something akin to redemption.

On July 14, 1958, the conservative Arab camp suddenly lost its central actor—Hashimite Iraq. Three days earlier, the Jordanians had expressed concern to the Iraqi leadership that Cols. `Abd al-Karim Qasim and `Abd al-Salam `Arif might be planning a military coup, but to no avail.[37] With stunning and brutal swiftness, their military units stormed the royal palace, executed Faysal II, his uncle Prince `Abd al-Ilah, and other family members, occupied key government buildings and media outlets, and proclaimed the establishment of a new, republican Iraq committed to the principles of pan-Arabism. Nuri al-Sa`id managed to initially elude his captors, dressed as a woman, but was found the next day and summarily shot. His body was subsequently dragged through the streets and run over repeatedly by automobiles in an act of deliberate mutilation, to the cheers of a frenzied mob. The contrast to the nonviolence of the Egyptian Free Officers' coup in 1952, the supposed model for Qasim, `Arif, and their cohorts, was striking.

In 1941, units of the British-commanded Transjordanian Arab Legion had helped restore the Iraqi monarchy after the Rashid `Ali coup. The leaders of the latest coup were concerned that King Husayn would attempt to repeat history by asserting his right of succession under the terms of the Arab Federation and rallying pro-monarchy Iraqi army units to his side. However unlikely this possibility, they nonetheless took care to withhold the news of Faysal's death for three days, during which time they consolidated their hold on the army. Indeed, King Husayn was beside himself when the news of the coup reached him, and eager to act. But there was nothing that could be done, and the task at hand was to avoid a domino effect against Hashimite Jordan.

As had been the case with Egypt, the Iraqi coup occurred in a society undergoing profound social and economic change, brought on by demographic pressures (population growth and accelerated urbanization), the expansion of the educational system, which resulted in a steadily growing politically conscious public, an economy full of distortions, due primarily in Iraq's case to the increase in oil-generated income, frustrations among the younger generation of military officers, and dysfunctional and increasingly discredited political systems. As shown in Hanna Battatu's mammoth work, the alliance between former sharifian officers, the Hashimite house, and the big landowners and tribal shaykhs, backed by Great Britain, had been sufficient to establish the Iraqi kingdom. But the "colonial state" created by Britain and run by this elite was not able, as Roger Owen says, "to create a sense that they were at the center of a single, unique coherent entity with an unchangeable claim to universal allegiance."[38] Indeed, with the bulk of the officer corps coming from the lower and middle classes, the views of the army reflected the widespread discontent in the society, while official political power remained in the hands of a narrow elite, headed by the despised "Anglo-Arab" Crown Prince `Abd al-Ilah and unpopular Nuri al-Sa`id, that had essentially lost whatever legitimacy it had had. The regime's adoption of pan-Arab ideology could not compensate for these fundamental problems. Hence, its eventual fall was probably inevitable, although the actual success of the conspirators was hardly a foregone conclusion. It was the Crown Prince's failure of nerve at the moment of truth, namely his refusal to allow the crack royal brigade at his palace to resist the plotters, that sealed his fate.[39]

In Washington and London, as well as in Amman, Beirut, Riyadh, and Jerusalem, the fear of a pan-Arab tsunami sweeping away pro-Western Arab regimes was acute. Just one day after the Iraqi coup, the United States dispatched fourteen thousand troops to Lebanon, upon the request of the embattled president Chamoun, under the terms of the Eisenhower Doctrine. In a parallel move, a small contingent of British troops was dispatched to Jordan. In both cases, the purpose was to provide encouragement to the ruling elites and signal to their foes, domestic and foreign, that the US and Britain were committed to the survival of the regimes. A year earlier, Husayn had risked his life in successfully confronting what may have developed into a military coup and had taken back full power, after a two-year period in which Arab nationalist politicians seemed to be gaining the upper hand. Now, the British presence, although it remained out of sight and confined to base, ensured Husayn's consolidation of power. Nasir, the Syrian Ba`th, and Palestinian nationalists would periodically challenge him during the next decade, even resulting in the assassination of Prime Minister Hazza` al-Majali in 1960 by Syrian (UAR) agents, but Nasir would essentially try to undermine Husayn with one hand tied behind his back, never making it a top policy priority.[40]

In Lebanon, the scene of heavily clad, battle-ready US Marines wading through the Beirut surf and sand in between swimmers and sunbathers was surreal. To his disappointment, Chamoun would not succeed in remaining in office. But the US presence certainly encouraged the quarreling Lebanese factions to settle their differences, bringing an end to civil strife and leading to the election of Gen. Fu'ad Shihab as president, inaugurating what would be a decade of relative political stability. In US institutional memory, the intervention was a ringing success, preserving a pro-Western regime without a shot being fired. This memory would contribute to the dispatch of another US military mission to Lebanon in 1982, with far different, and disastrous, results.

THE RADICAL WAVE—DREAM AND REALITY

The immediate stabilization of the Lebanese and Jordanian regimes was comforting but hardly satisfactory for Western strategists who viewed the Arab world through the prism of the Cold War. The overthrow of the Hashimite Iraqi regime, a pillar of the Baghdad Pact states, provided the Soviet Union with a new and important arena where it could exert its influence. Iraq, after all, was not only an oil-exporting state, but adjacent to the Persian Gulf, the highway of much of the world's oil exports, most of which was being produced in Iran, Saudi Arabia, and Kuwait, all pro-Western monarchies that shared borders with Iraq. From the perspective of Western interests, a pro-Soviet Iraqi state aligned with a Soviet-leaning United Arab Republic was a frightening prospect. Even if the dominos had not yet fallen, the likelihood of this happening in the future seemed high, particularly as Arab militaries grew in size and became increasingly politicized. The so-called "king's dilemma," in which autocratic rulers may undermine their basis of power by adopting reforms, but may risk the same result if they do not do so, was an acute one for pro-Western monarchs.[41] Indeed, the remaining pro-Western regimes in the Arab Middle East and North Africa would be on the defensive for the next decade, and two additional monarchies would be overthrown in military coups by officers imbued with, and inspired by, Nasir's example and vision: in Yemen, in 1962, and in Libya, in 1969. The expanding radical, anti-Western camp of Arab states would be joined by Algeria in 1962, following a bitter eight-year war of independence that brought an end to 132 years of French colonialism there and served as an inspiration to revolutionary movements throughout the world.

However, translating the radical Arab nationalist vision of Arab unity and power into reality would turn out to be a chimera. Beneath the veneer of the common vision held by Nasir, his Syrian allies, and the new rulers in Iraq lay competing interests, both personal and political, and limited capacity for successful state-building and nation-building, even within their respective territories, let alone in the region as a whole. Indeed, it was the very lack of political and social cohesion in Syria that had pushed the Syrian Arab nationalists into Nasir's reluctant arms.

For Nasir, the immediate task was how to govern this new entity, which did not even share a common border. Having decided on a highly centralized regime, Syria's fate, for all intents and purposes, was to be swallowed up by Egypt. To that end, he quickly abolished all of Syria's political parties, annulled any symbols of Syrian nationalism (e.g., cancelling Syrian national day celebrations), and appointed loyal Egyptian administrators to head the Syrian bureaucracy and Egyptian officers to senior positions in the military. Economically, he undertook steps to nationalize the Syrian economy, thus striking at the interests of the urban elites. In sum, Nasir succeeded in alienating a broad cross section of Syrian society.

Nasir's difficulties with the "northern region" of the UAR were paralleled during these years by an uncooperative Iraqi regime. Although Qasim and `Arif had initially identified themselves as belonging to the Nasirist Arab nationalist camp, Qasim, in particular, quickly made it clear that he had no intention of following the Syrian example and subsuming his new regime to Egypt's embrace. For Qasim, waving the banner of Arab regional leadership was a tool by which he hoped to consolidate his power and enhance his legitimacy at home. Ironically, it was a well-worn formula of the Hashimite monarchy and allied Sunni ruling class that he had just overthrown. But matters were more complicated for Qasim. His main domestic ally within the fractious Iraqi polity was the Iraqi Communist Party, with which he personally sympathized. The party's influence was present within the military as well, while a Nasirist faction in the army was utterly opposed to him. The result was a bloodbath, in March 1959, when an attempted coup by the Nasirite faction, based in the northern city of Mosul, was brutally suppressed. For Nasir, this was the last straw. Diplomatic relations with Iraq were severed, and Nasir's propaganda machine opened up full blast against Qasim.[42] The lines of division within the Arab radical camp were now clear to all.

Ironically, but perhaps not surprisingly, Qasim's opposition to Nasir led to a restoration of Iraqi-Jordanian relations. Ever the pragmatist, Jordan's King Husayn fully recognized the importance of good relations with neighboring Iraq, which would serve as a geopolitical counterweight to the UAR. Hence, although he would never forget the brutal murders of his Iraqi Hashimite cousins, Husayn placed his personal feelings to the side.

Qasim's activism in Arab affairs was expressed in two very different arenas. One was the Palestine question, the traditional tool for Arab leaders to bolster their credentials and diminish their rivals for alleged inaction. Hence, in December 1959, Qasim promoted, with great fanfare, the establishment of a "Palestinian Republic," designed to enable the mobilization of Palestinian and Arab energies for reviving the struggle against Israel. In doing so, he was engaging in rhetorical outbidding of Nasir, who earlier in the year had begun promoting the concept of "Palestinian entity" (*al-kiyan al-filastini*).[43] To King Husayn's satisfaction, nothing came of these rival initiatives, but it marked the revival of the Palestine "football" as a subject to be kicked around by various Arab actors[44] after almost a decade of relative somnolence, and would be a harbinger of things to come.

In June 1961, Iraq initiated a regional crisis of a very different sort, over Kuwait, which was about to be granted independence by Great Britain, after having had protectorate status since the eve of World War I. Generations of Iraqi nationalists had imbibed the official national narrative of the illegitimate truncation of Kuwait from the motherland when Iraq's borders were officially demarcated by Great Britain in the early 1920s, a claim based on the area having been a part of the Ottoman province of Basra. King Ghazi had reasserted the claim in 1938, and it was referred to by Nuri al-Sa'id on a number of subsequent occasions. Now, as Britain prepared to officially grant Kuwait independence and withdraw its small military presence, Qasim seized on the issue and threatened to move Iraqi troops into Kuwait in order to right a historical wrong. Geo-strategically, holding Kuwait would give Iraq unfettered access to the Persian Gulf, not to mention control over Kuwait's oil riches.

Was Qasim just blustering, as was often his style? There is no concrete evidence that Iraq actually moved its troops into position to seize Kuwait. But his rhetoric was strident enough so as to induce a sense of crisis among British officials and in the Kuwaiti royal family. Hence, on July 1, a naval task force was deployed to the area and troops, eventually numbering seven thousand, took up positions near Kuwait's border with Iraq to serve as a tripwire to deter Qasim from any sort of military adventurism.[45] They were immediately joined by a small Saudi contingent.

For Riyadh, Qasim's verbal aggressiveness was extremely unnerving. The specter of a powerful Iraq on its northern border had always been nightmarish; the fact that the Ottoman province of Basra extended into Saudi Arabian territory south of Kuwait gave the Saudis additional reason to fear Qasim's maneuvers.[46]

For Nasir, Qasim's initial threats had posed a conundrum. Preventing Iraqi aggrandizement was a top priority. But British intervention, and in support of a "reactionary" Arab monarchy, no less, contradicted the fundamental tenets of Nasirist Arab nationalism. Nasir sought to solve the problem by blaming Qasim for serving as an unwitting tool of imperialism, as well as failing to consult the Kuwaiti people regarding their desired future. The proposed "Arab solution" to the problem, i.e., the replacement of Britain's forces in Kuwait with an Arab deterrent force sanctioned by the Arab League, posed new problems. For Nasir, the idea of placing his troops alongside those of the conservative monarchies whom he detested and was seeking to replace was extremely distasteful.

Conversely, the possibility that a large share of the force would be Egyptian was unacceptable to the conservative Arab monarchies. In Jordanian eyes, it was Nasir who posed the main regional threat, not Qasim. As for the Kuwaitis, said a Jordanian official, they would need to learn to share their wealth with their poorer Arab brothers if they expected to be able to live in peace and security in the long run.[47] This resentment of Kuwaiti wealth by less fortunate Arab societies would reappear forcefully during the 1990–91 Gulf crisis and war.

Eventually, the Arab League mechanism was successfully employed, establishing an approximately three-thousand-man force, composed mainly of Saudi and Jordanian troops, that replaced British forces. Egypt's small contingent would be withdrawn almost immediately in response to Syria's secession from the UAR, for which Cairo blamed Saudi meddling. Kuwait would be officially admitted to the Arab League two years later, when Iraq rescinded its objection and officially recognized Kuwait's independence after Qasim's overthrow by another group of Arab nationalist officers. The entire episode would enter the annals of inter-Arab conflict mediation as a ringing success, a rarity indeed.[48]

THE DOWNTURN—1961–1967

On September 28, 1961, anti-unionist officers seized key positions in Damascus, proclaimed the dissolution of the three-year-old UAR, and sent the Egyptians home. Nasir could do little but rant against the "secessionists" for having betrayed the sacred ideal of Arab unity. He reserved his most scathing comments for his supposed ideological soul mates—the Ba'th. In retrospect, the failure of the three-year-old experiment in Arab unity between these two large Arab states would be one of the definitive markers of modern Arab political history.

Between the Syrian secession and the necessity of supporting monarchical Kuwait's independence against Qasim's Iraq, Nasir's image as the sole legitimate standard-bearer of Arab unity was now seriously tarnished. Nonetheless, he would continue to serve as the central pole of Arab politics, around which domestic and regional politics spun. Policywise, Nasir was fated to incessantly maneuver between two worlds: that of pragmatic politics and that of the vision of Arab unity and power under his charismatic leadership. His confidante and mouthpiece, Mohammed Hassenein Heikal, expressed Nasir's dilemma, and his strategy for coping with it, thusly: Egypt, he wrote, was both a "state" and a "revolution."As a state, it was natural and appropriate for it to pursue its interests and conduct itself according to established norms, thus necessitating relations with other states regardless of their ideological orientations. As a "revolution," on the other hand, Egypt embodied the hopes of the Arab "masses" everywhere, who longed for a new order based on the supreme values of Arab unity, social justice, and anti-imperialism. [49]

At home, Nasir's response to the Syrian secession was to double down, adopting more systematic and far-reaching policies of state socialism, as well as to brutally crush all dissenters, particularly the Muslim Brotherhood. A corollary to Nasir's enhanced "scientific socialism" was a further deepening of military and economic ties with the Soviet Union. And in the region, Egyptian geopolitical and ideological interests came together in Yemen, in what would prove to be a disastrous military adventure.

On September 25, 1962, Yemen, heretofore remote from the wider currents of Arab affairs, was thrust into the center of Arab politics, when a group of army officers overthrew Yemen's new ruler, Imam Muhammad al-Badr (he had assumed power only one week earlier following the death of his father, Ahmad). The background to the coup included a mix of domestic and foreign policy factors. Under Ahmed's father, Yahya (who was assassinated in 1948), the Yemeni monarchy (imamate), which was underpinned by the Zaydi branch of Shi`i Islam, was renewed, while maintaining a rigid policy of isolation from the outside world and without creating modern administrative institutions. Discontent among urban intellectuals grew, as well as among the non-Zaydi populace in general, in response to Yahya's attempt to extend his rule southward, where they were concentrated. In the 1950s, Imam Ahmed, whose succession was not universally welcomed by the Zaydi elite families, and his son Crown Prince Badr tried to initiate domestic reforms and ease the country's isolation. It also sought powerful patrons, even at the risk of opening up the country to foreign influences, to help them rid southern Yemen of the British presence (the Red Sea Port of Aden was a British Crown Colony, and other adjacent areas in the south were under British tutelage). To that end, he sent Yemeni officers to Egypt to train and sought to align his foreign policy with Egypt. Yemen even declared a federal affiliation with the newly established UAR in March 1958. The overall result was that Soviet and Egyptian protégés soon sought to undermine the existing order.[50]

Indeed, the coup-makers modeled themselves after the Egyptian Free Officers and publicly identified with the dominant radical Arab nationalist current of the time.[51] Within days, Nasir dispatched Egyptian troops to San`a to bolster the new rulers, upon the request of their leader, Col. Muhammad al-Sallal. In doing so, he placed Egyptian troops on the Arabian Peninsula for the first time since the forces of Ottoman Egypt's increasingly independent viceroy, Muhammad 'Ali, had sacked Mecca in 1813, and ultimately destroyed the kingdom of Saudi Arabia's Wahhabi forbears. For the Saudis, a republican Arab nationalist Yemen that was essentially being run by Egyptians[52] posed a direct and immediate threat, and they swiftly mobilized to meet the challenge. Fortunately for them, the Imam had escaped capture and fled to the hills. There, his royalist forces regrouped, inaugurating a five-year civil war that was, in essence, a proxy war between Egypt, representing the radical Arab nationalist and pro-Soviet camp, and Saudi Arabia, representing the monarchical, conservative pro-Western camp. For Egypt the adventure would prove to be costly: 150,000 of its best troops would be rotated through Yemen for five years, at least ten percent of whom were killed or maimed.[53] Egyptian military historians would refer to the five-year war as Egypt's Vietnam.[54]

Less than six months after the Yemen coup came two more developments that were in line with the ascending Arab radical current and, ostensibly, with the vision of Egypt as leader of the Arab revolution. Army officers in Syria and Iraq, both identified with the Ba'th party, seized power in Damascus and Baghdad. On the surface, the ground seemed eminently favorable for the revival of the Arab unity project under Nasir's leadership. Indeed, the two new ruling cliques were eager to legitimize their actions, and thus quickly turned to Nasir for support. High-level delegations from both countries, including Syrian Ba'th leaders Michel 'Aflaq and Salah al-din Bitar, hastened to Cairo for unity talks that were conducted during mid-March and mid-April 1963. But Nasir had no intention of repeating his bitter experience with the UAR. Instead he used the talks to demonstratively chastise the Ba'th leaders for supporting Syrian secession in 1961. The meetings concluded with a ringing declaration of plans to establish an Egyptian-Syrian-Iraqi federation, but there was no actual intent to do so.[55] Within months, Egyptian-Syrian relations were more poisoned than ever. By contrast, the Ba'this in Iraq were ousted from power in November 1963 by 'Abd al-Salam 'Arif, who was more inclined to avoid confrontation with Egypt. They would return to power only in 1968.

By the end of 1963, the Arab Cold War was anything but cold. Within the radical camp, Syria's new ruling clique, in acute need of legitimacy, adopted a militant pan-Arab position vis-à-vis Israel and the West. In practice, this entailed strident attacks against Nasir for shying away from confrontation with Israel. From the other side of the spectrum, the Saudis viewed the presence of Egyptian troops in Yemen as a direct threat and did everything they could to support the Yemeni royalists. Egyptian air force bombing raids against Yemeni royalist bases in Saudi territory and the use of chemical weapons against Yemeni opponents highlighted the combustible nature of the conflict.[56] The Saudis also provided shelter for Egyptian Muslim Brotherhood exiles. Jordanian leaders, for their part, continued to view Nasir as the primary threat to the regime's survival.

It was at this moment that the Arab-Israeli conflict became newly relevant to inter-Arab affairs. Israel's big-ticket National Water Carrier project, carrying water from the Sea of Galilee and feeder streams southward for development, was about to come online. For the new and vulner-

able Syrian regime, the Israeli project promised to widen the gaps between it and Israel, this in the context of ongoing tensions over the Syrian-Israeli demilitarized zones and attendant water resources. For Syria,
the only way to mobilize Arab support was to tap into the widely held
sentiment that Israel was a threat to the whole Arab nation. This in turn
placed Nasir in an extremely difficult position, as he could hardly justify
inaction, while knowing full well that the military balance of power was
decisively in Israel's favor.

Nasir's strategy at this juncture was astute. On January 13–16, 1964,
he convened an all-Arab summit conference of Arab heads of state in
Cairo to address the Israeli challenge. In doing so, he provided the Jordanians, Saudis, and other conservative regimes—those he had witheringly
branded as the forces of "reaction" that were doomed to removal—with
an important measure of legitimacy, for he was now willing to sit with
them as equals, more or less. The summit thus served as a formal marker
in the evolution of the norms of Arabism that were consistent with state
sovereignty. With the growing recognition that real Arab unity was off
the table, the summit also meant Arabism was being increasingly defined
in terms of one's commitment to the cause of Palestine. This would
render Arab leaders increasingly vulnerable to symbolic sanctions, and
inaugurate what would eventually be a deadly game of outbidding (*mu-
zayada*) and symbolic entrapment.[57]

The summit's focus on the conflict with Israel included the question of
Palestinian representation. Throughout the 1950s and into the 1960s, Palestinian political activism had generally been subsumed in larger Arab
nationalist frameworks. According to this line of thinking, which was
especially prominent among the younger generation, achieving Arab
unity and social transformation was a prerequisite for restoring Arab
Palestine. Now however, with the Palestine question playing an ever
more important role in defining a "good" Arab nationalist, Arab leaders
had little choice but to follow Nasir's lead in declaring their support for
the creation of a Palestinian organization that would contribute to the
cause. Four months later, the Palestine Liberation Organization (PLO)
was officially born, headed by Ahmad Shuqayri, a lawyer and activist
who had previously served as a diplomat at the UN for Syria and Saudi
Arabia, and as assistant secretary-general of the Arab League. For Nasir,
extending Egypt's patronage over the PLO was another piece of his strategy of maintaining his preeminent position on Arab affairs. Ironically, the

PLO's founding conference was held in Jordanian Jerusalem, under the patronage of King Husayn, who hoped to demonstrate his solidarity with the Palestinian cause while ensuring that the PLO didn't pose a challenge to Jordanian sovereignty in the West Bank. However, Shuqayri took his job of mobilizing support among the Palestinian public seriously, particularly among refugees living in the West Bank, and Husayn quickly understood that the Egyptian-supported PLO did pose a threat to his rule there.

So did a previously unknown Palestinian actor from a different direction. On January 1, 1965, a Palestinian squad based in Syria carried out a sabotage operation against Israel's National Water Carrier. On its way back to Syria, via Jordan, it was confronted by a Jordanian patrol, which shot and killed one of the members. The squad belonged to al-Fatah,[58] which had first been established in 1959 by a small group of Palestinians in Kuwait, led by Yasir 'Arafat. Tired of waiting for an Arab revolution that would enable the restoration of Arab Palestine, and imbued with the ideals of armed struggle by revolutionary, anti-colonial movements, Fatah hoped to stimulate a general Arab-Israeli war through guerilla operations. Given its subsequent status as the largest Palestinian faction and primary advocate of Palestinian independence vis-à-vis the neighboring Arab states, there is no small irony in the fact that its main patron at this stage was radical pan-Arabist Syria, which in subsequent years would incessantly seek to subsume Fatah to Syria's own agenda. At this stage, however, they found common cause in embarrassing Nasir for his inaction, as well as provoking Israeli retaliatory military operations against Jordan.

The spirit of inter-Arab cooperation embodied by the first Arab summit was thus short-lived. Two more summits would be held during 1964–65 that sought to both maintain a semblance of unity vis-à-vis Israel and broker an end to the Yemen war, but to no avail. Regarding Israel, efforts were made to establish a united Arab military command on the eastern front, and undertake the diversion of Syrian waters flowing into Israeli territory. However, Israeli military action put a stop to the diversion project, and no serious progress was made in establishing a common military strategy. At the same time, steadily escalating Palestinian guerilla attacks from both Syria and Jordan were generating Israeli responses.

By the end of 1965, then, the Arab Cold War was back in full swing, with Nasir perched uneasily at the top of a quarrelsome collection of Arab states and rival Palestinian factions. With some of the best units of his army bogged down in Yemen, Nasir repeatedly explained to his critics that he would indeed confront Israel, but only when he and the rest of the Arab world had properly mobilized their forces—military, economic, and political. The battle, he explained, was long-term, and would only be won on that basis.[59] His rivals in the radical camp, however, viewed these explanations as an excuse for inaction. Meanwhile, Saudi Arabia and Jordan had joined with two non-Arab states, monarchical Iran and Pakistan, in an "Islamic alliance" designed to combat radical leftist, pro-Soviet forces, i.e., `Abd al-Nasir and his supporters.

Yet another Syrian coup in February 1966 turned out to be a fateful development. The coup makers were predominantly `Alawi[60] Ba`thists, who quickly sent the veteran civilian Ba`athist leadership packing. Party founder Michel `Aflaq took up residence in Iraq. Faced with an acute legitimacy deficit, the new Syrian leadership wrapped itself in the mantle of a radical Arab nationalist vision that promoted socialist revolution at home and armed struggle against Israel in order to achieve the liberation of Palestine. On the ground, this entailed support for increasing Palestinian guerrilla attacks against Israel, efforts to destabilize Jordan's conservative monarchy, and incessant attacks against Nasir for his "crime" of inaction. As cross-border violence between Israel and its eastern neighbors escalated, Nasir concluded a mutual defense pact with Syria in November 1966, in which he pledged to come to Syria's aid in the event of Israeli "aggression."[61] Intended to place a brake on Syria's strident actions, it instead resulted in Egypt's symbolic entrapment in a disastrous war that Nasir had up until then studiously avoided being dragged into.

CRISIS AND WAR: MAY–JUNE 1967

The three-week crisis that led up to the June 1967 Arab-Israeli war[62] had been preceded by an escalation of fighting and accompanying war of words on the Syrian-Israeli front. On May 13, the Soviet Union, the patron of both Syria and Egypt, deliberately conveyed false information to Egypt that Israeli forces were being mobilized for a large-scale military operation against Syria. The Egyptians quickly and correctly concluded that the information was false. Nonetheless, on May 15, Nasir sent a hundred thousand troops into the Sinai Peninsula opposite the border with

Israel, in order to "deter Israeli aggression" against Syria. Israel responded with a general mobilization of its mostly reserve army, and the countdown to war began, although at this point, it is clear that Nasir was seeking not war but a political victory by seemingly preventing Israel from attacking Syria, and thus proving to his critics that he remained the undisputed leader of the Arab nation.

But the very public militarization of the Sinai created new political challenges. What was supposed to happen next? King Husayn, long the target of Arab radicals, had repeatedly sought to score propaganda points of his own during the previous months, scorning Nasir for "hiding behind the UN's skirts." If he was really serious about confronting Israel, Husayn said, he would insist on the removal of the 4,500 UNEF troops that had been stationed along the ceasefire line with Israel since 1957. On May 17, Nasir did just that, and UN Secretary-General U Thant quickly acceded to the request. Five days later, on May 22, Nasir moved again, announcing the closure of the Straits of Tiran to Israeli shipping. Within one week's time, the pre-Suez War status quo had been restored. The Egyptian and Arab publics were ecstatic, while the Israeli public became extremely nervous and Israeli decision-makers debated heatedly whether to strike quickly before Egypt's forces in Sinai were fully dug in or, alternatively, to give more time to American-led diplomatic efforts to peacefully resolve the crisis. In choosing the latter option, it gave further encouragement to Nasir, and to his hawkish Defense Minister and brother-in-law `Abd al-Hakim `Amr. But it also helped legitimize its actions when it did eventually go to war.

Meanwhile, however, it appeared to Nasir that almost overnight, the balance of power had shifted in his favor, and that he could indeed successfully confront Israel. A broad Arab coalition was forming behind him, backed by Egyptian and Arab public opinion, and no less importantly, by the Soviet Union, which promised to neutralize any US intervention on behalf of Israel. Reviewing his armored formations impressively arrayed at the Bir Gafgafa air base in Sinai on May 25, Nasir may well have concluded that his own forces were now ready for battle. If Israel wanted war, he declared, "it was welcome."[63] And on May 29, Nasser told the Egyptian National Assembly that the issue at hand was "the aggression which took place in 1948 . . . , the expulsion of the Arabs from Palestine, the usurpation of their rights and the plunder of their property."[64] The very next day, King Husayn reluctantly flew to Cairo to align with Nasir, placing his troops under Egyptian command and publicly reconciling with his arch foe and rival, the PLO's Shuqayri. And on May 31, Iraq announced that it would be sending forces westward to join the fight. The noose around Israel was apparently being tightened with great effect.

On June 5, with no diplomatic solution to the crisis in sight, Israel struck. Within hours, the Egyptian air force had been largely obliterated by waves of Israeli air attacks on Egyptian bases, and Iraqi, Jordanian, and Syrian air bases were similarly hit hard. Egyptian forces in the Sinai were decimated, with Israeli troops reaching the Suez Canal on day four of the fighting. At the end of six days of war, Israel had also conquered the West Bank and Old Jerusalem from Jordan, and the Syrian Golan Heights overlooking northern Israel. Unlike the 1948 war, Israel had now conquered territories belonging to sovereign Arab states, which would substantially change the political calculus. Moreover, it marked the Waterloo for the radical pan-Arab current.

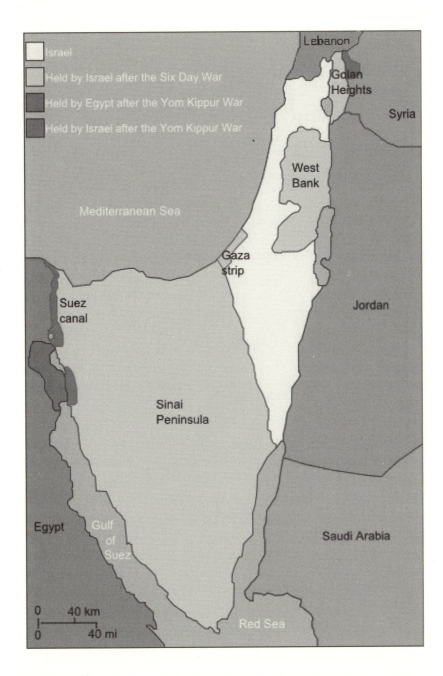

Figure 5.1.   The June 11, 1967, and October 24, 1973, Arab-Israeli ceasefire lines. By Yom_Kippur_War_map.svg: Raul654 derivative work: Supreme Deliciousness (Yom_Kippur_War_map.svg) [CC BY-SA 2.5 (http://creativecommons.org/licenses/by-sa/2.5)], via Wikimedia Commons.

II

From Order to Disorder:
The Triumph and Decline of Arab States

6

AFTER THE JUNE 1967 DEBACLE

Picking Up the Pieces (1967–1970)

While the breakup of the UAR six years earlier was a clear indication that the pan-Arab unity vision was beyond realization, the catastrophic military defeat by Israel exposed the larger shortcomings of the radical Arab nationalist project that had dominated Arab politics for more than a decade. The military and political failure in 1948 had been laid squarely at the feet of the old social classes, and that war had helped catalyze the subsequent political upheavals that brought revolutionary regimes to power. The 1967 war, by contrast, was entirely the product of these same revolutionary regimes. The pan-Arabist promise of Arab power had been proven to be divorced from reality, and the quasi-messianic fervor that the meshing of ideology and Nasir's charismatic personality had unleashed came crashing down. The impact on Arab societies, states, and inter-Arab alignments was immediate, profound, and far-reaching.

This chapter surveys the political, intellectual, and cultural responses to the defeat in the June 1967–September 1970 period. Two elements stand out in the political sphere: the end of Egypt's decade-long confrontation with Saudi Arabia and Jordan, and the renewal of Palestinian agency, via a transformed PLO now made up of guerrilla groups and attracting thousands of young Palestinians and other Arabs to their ranks. In the intellectual-cultural sphere, the defeat spawned sharp critiques of Arab societies and elites from both the secular left and conservative Muslim circles. For much of the Arab Muslim publics, it was the critique of the latter that resonated loudest, contributing over time to the increasing Islamization of Arab identity.

In a nationwide television address on June 11, Nasir acknowledged the dimensions of the military disaster and announced his resignation.[1] Thousands of anguished people immediately poured into Egyptian streets, calling on him to rescind his decision and not to abandon them in their hour of need. Whether orchestrated or not, it had the desired effect, and Nasir would remain in power until his death three years later. In an effort to control the postwar discourse, Nasir and his supporters characterized the 1967 war as a *naksa* ("setback"), in obvious contrast to the 1948 *nakba*. The message was clear: the defeat was not irrevocable, the conflict was not over, and the task at hand was to rebuild, rearm, and not succumb to despair. In practice, this was translated into a major shift in Egypt's inter-Arab alignments toward the conservative pro-Western camp and more pragmatic policies while also, ironically, binding Egypt more tightly to the Soviet Union, its main patron.

The new collective Arab landscape was consecrated at the Khartoum Arab summit conference, on August 30–September 1, eleven weeks after the guns of the June war had fallen silent. The summit is best known for reasserting the long-standing collective Arab norms that had undergirded official policies toward Israel, namely the "3 No's": no peace, no negotiation, and no recognition of Israel, as well as the insistence on attaining "the rights of the Palestinian people in their own country," i.e., the wholesale right of return of Palestinian refugees to their homes and lands lost in 1948. But the summit also marked the end of Nasir's decade-long challenge to the Saudi-led conservative camp. In return for massive aid from Riyadh, and from Kuwait as well, Nasir agreed to withdraw Egyptian troops from Yemen (the Saudi-backed royalists would not regain power, but what was important for the Saudis was that the Egyptian troops were gone); the embargo on oil sales to Western countries that had been imposed at the start of the war was now officially lifted, in the name of accumulating wealth to serve the collective Arab interest; and Nasir now ceased his efforts to delegitimize the conservative, pro-Western regimes.[2] However painful it must have been for him to effect a rapprochement with Saudi Arabia in the aftermath of the June 1967 war, the acute need for financial aid from the increasingly wealthy Gulf Arab states overrode all other considerations. Heikel pithily expressed the new reality of Arab politics, stating that the guiding theme of the previous decade, *thawra* ("revolution"), was now being replaced by *tharwa* ("wealth").[3] As Barnett explains, the war served as a ruinous reminder that the promise of radical pan-Arabism had outstripped its payoff, and the power conferred by the symbolic capital of the radical pan-Arab vision was gradually replaced by the economic capital being generated by oil production in the Gulf. For their part, the conservative Gulf Arab states were willing to pay handsomely in return for the promotion of a more statist Arab environment, i.e., one which did not call the legitimacy of their existence into question.[4] In the coming decades, their unprecedented wealth would give them powerful tools to mediate inter-Arab disputes. Active mediation would not only prove their fidelity to still-potent collective Arab norms, but also, and even more importantly, help prevent conflicts in neighboring states from spilling over into their own vulnerable territories. Their wealth would also enable them to energetically promote Islamic values in the region through charitable and educational institutions, a central part of the Saudi legitimacy formula. Doing so was a vital tool for coping with the country's own Islamic radicals, in whose eyes the Saudi regime had become irrevocably corrupted by its wealth and association with Western powers.

Nasir's decision to cease trying to subvert conservative Arab monarchies and begin redefining the specifics of Egyptian leadership of the Arab world was especially important for Jordan's beleaguered King Husayn. Jordan had reluctantly initiated hostilities with Israel on the first day of the war, and repositioned its troops in line with the Egyptian command's instructions only to have Syria fail to fulfill its commitment to dispatch units to fill the void.[5] It unsuccessfully sought a cease-fire with Israel at the end of the second day, and ended up losing all of the territory west of the Jordan River that it had it worked so hard to acquire in 1948, including the *Haram al-Sharif* ("Noble Sanctuary"; Jerusalem's Temple Mount), the third holiest site in Islam. But by lining up with Nasir, however reluctantly, and with his forces fighting hard on the battlefield, Husayn won a measure of legitimacy in the Arab public's eyes, and may well have saved his throne. Indeed, other language in the Khartoum resolutions also essentially legitimized Husayn's postwar diplomacy, which sought to recover the territories it had lost, even if the price would be making peace with Israel. The contradiction between this Egyptian-Jordanian understanding and the "Three No's" was never put to the test, as Israel was not willing to agree to Jordan's insistence on a complete and total withdrawal to the June 4, 1967, armistice line, and Jordan could not accept anything less. But the emphasis on diplomacy also enabled both Egypt and Jordan to engage in indirect negotiations with Israel sponsored by the UN, on the basis of UN Security Council Resolution 242.[6] Overall, it appears that the discussions and resulting resolutions of the Khartoum summit marked the beginning of a shift in Arab perceptions of the conflict, with the focus now increasingly on the issue of territories and boundaries. But it would take another major Arab-Israeli war and Nasir's successor to consummate the shift.[7]

In addition to Jordan's inherent vulnerability, which prevented it from adopting positions that were overtly at odds with the official Arab consensus on Israel, there was now a new factor at work: the renewed centrality of the Palestinian dimension to the Arab-Israeli conflict. As the armies of the Arab states lay prostrate on the battlefield, Palestinian guerrilla groups filled the vacuum, and quickly recruited thousands of enthusiastic young Palestinians, mainly from refugee camps in Jordan, Lebanon, and Syria, as well as other Arabs. This would be consecrated in a rejuvenated PLO, which was transformed from an organization of civilian activists to a coalition of guerrilla groups committed to the liberation of Palestine through armed struggle, in line with the doctrines of third-world revolutionary warfare made popular by Mao Tse-Tung, Algeria's FLN, Che Guevara, and the Vietnamese communists. To be sure, there were serious differences within the PLO. Its dominant group, Yasir `Arafat's al-Fatah, was primarily focused on the liberation of Palestine, and preferred to avoid entanglement in inter-Arab rivalries. Marxist-oriented groups like George Habash's Popular Front for the Liberation of Palestine and Na'if Hawatmeh's Democratic Front, on the other hand, were more ideologically committed to promoting revolutionary change in Arab states as an integral part of the struggle, and viewed the road to Jerusalem as passing through Amman. Either way, the growing strength of Palestinian guerrilla groups on Jordanian soil posed what became a fundamental challenge to the Jordanian regime's sovereign existence, as Palestinian armed groups established their own authority in the Palestinian refugee camps that ringed Amman. At the end of the day, in September 1970, Husayn chose to put an end to the situation, ordering his forces to crush all opposition, in what became known as "Black September."

The inter-Arab and larger regional and global aspects to the "Black September" events illustrated the complexity of the situation. Armored units of the weak but still militant Syrian Ba'th regime briefly penetrated into northern Jordan in support of the Palestinian guerrillas, but were driven back by the newly confident Jordanians, who had received assurances from Israel that it would not stand idly by in the face of a Syrian advance, backed by the mobilization of Israeli troops on the Israeli side of the border. The US, for its part, had assured Israel that it would intervene to block Soviet military moves on behalf of its client Syria, were that to occur. The degree of Syrian dysfunction was highlighted by the failure of Syria's air force to participate in the fighting. Its unwilling commander, Defense Minister Hafiz al-Asad, would seize power in a bloodless coup two months later.[8]

For Nasir, the emergence of a militant and popular Palestinian movement had presented a conundrum. He himself had midwifed the birth of the PLO in 1964, as part of his efforts to both renew his all-Arab legitimacy and contain the stirrings in the radical camp. In tilting toward the conservative Arab camp after 1967, he demonstrated an acute awareness of the damage that excess pan-Arab fervor had caused, and a determination not to be symbolically entrapped again. However, he also genuinely sympathized with this new generation of Palestinian fighters and could hardly ignore their popularity. Hence, in September 1970, he found himself in what was nearly an impossible situation, opposed to the destruction of the Jordanian state but committed to preventing the crushing of the Palestinian resistance. His intensive mediation between the warring sides, preceded by the spiriting of the besieged Yasir 'Arafat out of Amman to Cairo, culminated in an agreement on September 27 to end the fighting. The Jordanian state authorities had restored their control and ensured the country's survival. The PLO's expulsion from Jordan would be completed in June 1971, and Lebanon now became its prime base of operations.

It was Nasir's last act. Already suffering from diabetes, his intensive and stress-filled diplomatic efforts proved to be fatal to his health: the very next day, he died of a massive heart attack. His funeral in Cairo was an extraordinary outpouring of collective grief as millions of people mobbed the city. With the death of its revered champion, the era of radical pan-Arabism was now officially over.

INTELLECTUAL AND SOCIAL RESPONSES TO THE DEFEAT

The trauma of the sudden and catastrophic military defeat by Israel generated trenchant criticism of the state of the Arab world and the pan-Arab nationalist vision that had attained hegemonic status during the preceding decade. Two diametrically opposed critiques were cogently identified by Fouad Ajami: one from the radical secular intelligentsia, the other from the Islamist camp.[9] For the secular radicals such as philosophy professor Sadiq al-`Azm and the poets Adonis and Nizar Qabbani, the defeat came like a sudden cloudburst on a clear day. In his seminal critique, "Self-Criticism after the Defeat" (*Naqd al-Dhati Ba`ad al-Hazima*), published one year after the war, `Azm related the excitement that gripped him and his university friends in the Beirut cafes prior to the war, and their utter shock at the result. `Azm's conclusion was that the social transformation that the radical pan-Arab leadership had been trumpeting was just so much talk. Arab societies, he said, remained imprisoned by hidebound traditional and religious modes of thought, and underpinned by familial and tribal allegiances and values. Social ties to institutions, organizations, and political parties, the sine qua non for forging a modern and cohesive state, were largely absent. Arab leaders and religious elites had avoided an honest and unvarnished analysis of what had happened and why, or any semblance of assuming responsibility for it. Blame for the defeat was shifted elsewhere. How else, `Azm said, could one explain the gap between the feverish prewar rhetoric and the utter lack of preparedness of the Arab armies once the war came, highlighted by the destruction of their air forces in the first hours of the war before they even got off the ground? How else could one understand the complaints in the Arab media after the war that the Israeli enemy hadn't "fought fair," that instead of engaging in hand-to-hand combat in which the bravery and superiority of Arab soldiers would have been amply demonstrated, Israel bombarded Arab armies from afar? How else could one interpret the hysteria that gripped Cairo ten months after the war when an image of the Virgin Mary weeping for her children was widely reported to have appeared at a Cairo church? And how else should one explain the official discourse that branded the war as merely a "setback" (*naksa*), instead of the utter and total "defeat" (*hazima*) that it actually was? The only solution, `Azm declared, was a true revolution in every aspect of life, accompanied by a complete and total mobilization of society for the struggle with Israel. Only by taking a long-term perspective, and following the examples of the Vietnamese and Algerian revolutions, could Israel, a modern Sparta equipped with the tools of Western modernity, be overcome. [10]

However insightful `Azm's critique may have been, the prospects of his prescription being adopted were nil, and the Arab Left, a prominent feature of political life in Arab states during the 1950s and 1960s, would be reduced to insignificance. [11] More often than not, major collective traumas generate a search for the comforting tenets of faith, and the post-1967 period in the Arab world was no exception. For many believing Arab Muslims, the failure was not due to excessive tradition and religion but not enough of it. After all, it was the radical and essentially secular pan-Arabs, led by Nasir, who had repressed, tortured, and executed members of the Muslim Brotherhood, including its leading ideologue in the mid-1960s, Sayyid Qutb, in the name of building a secular-national and revolutionary-socialist Arab order. [12] Its failure, epitomized by the June war and the internecine bloodletting among competing Ba`thi and other pan-Arab factions in Syria and Iraq, offered seemingly ample proof that the fundamentals of the vision were flawed. The logical conclusion, then, was more piety and attention to Islamic precepts, not less. And indeed, political Islam, in both radical and conservative varieties, would become an increasingly important feature of post-1967 Arab and Middle Eastern political life.

7

DIMINISHED LEADERSHIP

Egypt and the Arab Order in the Sadat-Mubarak Era
(1970–2010)

Beginning in the mid-1930s, leadership of the Arab world had been an integral part of Egypt's collective self-definition. `Abd al-Nasir had radically altered the content of Egypt's Arabism, but even before his death was returning to the long-held formula of *primus inter pares*. His successors, Anwar al-Sadat (1970–1981) and Husni Mubarak (1981–2011), would faithfully continue on that course. Egypt's achievements in the Arab and regional arenas were not inconsiderable, particularly in the first half of this forty-year period. But the second half was a different story. Cairo's regional weight steadily declined, mirroring the decline of Arab collective power and cohesion as a whole. For all of Egypt's successes vis-à-vis its Arab rivals, the institutionalization of a stable and cohesive Arab regional order remained out of reach, thanks primarily to the utter absence of political will among ruling Arab elites.

Underpinning Egypt's shrinking influence was its political and economic stagnation. Having roughly tripled its population between 1967 and 2011 (from 27 million to 81 million), Egypt's authoritarian "deep state," controlled by a military-economic-bureaucratic oligarchy, decisively dominated society but was unable to establish a productive, internationally competitive economy, effectively address the deep problems of poverty and inequality, or widen the bases of political participation, all of which were essential for effective governance, political stability, and remaining a first-rank regional power.

This chapter focuses on Egypt's efforts to maintain its leadership of the Arab world in the post-Nasir era, and the difficulties in translating that leadership into concrete achievements. Under Sadat, these would be expressed largely within the context of the conflict with Israel. During Mubarak's three decades in power, Egypt's efforts to play a counterbalancing and stabilizing role, first vis-à-vis Iran, than Iraq, and then Iran again, would be paramount. Egypt would also continue seeking to play the role of primary patron of the Palestinian movement, and pay special attention to its immediate problematic neighbors, the mercurial Mu`ammar al-Qaddafi of Libya and (as of 1989) Islamist Sudan.

Anwar al-Sadat's emergence in 1971 as `Abd al-Nasir's unrivaled successor fit in neatly with the broader trend of declining pan-Arabism and renewed emphasis on both the preeminence of Arab state sovereignty and the conservative-Islamic features of Arab identity. Sadat had been the Free Officers' liaison to the Muslim Brotherhood back in the early 1950s, and had been utterly marginalized in the years after the revolution. Appointed for a second time to the vice presidency in 1969, he assumed the office of president after Nasir's death, as was required by the Egyptian constitution. Most analysts assumed that his tenure would be short-lived. However, in May 1971, Sadat consolidated his control of the levers of state power by purging leftist pro-Soviet elements, headed by his vice president and former prime minister under Nasir, `Ali Sabri. For Sadat, an outwardly pious man, draping himself in the cloak of Islamic legitimacy came naturally. So did his recalibration of the symbolic and ideological balance between "Egyptianism" and "Arabism." To be sure, Nasir had already moved in this direction in his last years, but Sadat took it to a new level: in 1971, "Egypt" was restored to the country's official name. The "United Arab Republic," which had been maintained even after the breakup of the UAR in 1961, was now the "Arab Republic of Egypt." In essence, Egypt's Arab policy would now officially return to what it had been in the monarchical era, i.e., one that emphasized Egypt's natural and rightful leadership of the Arab state system and advancing the norms of Arab solidarity and cooperation between sovereign and independent Arab states. This fit in well with the increasingly vocal views of Egyptian commentators and intellectuals who criticized Nasir for placing Egypt's destiny in the hands of unstable radical Arab regimes.[1] The proclamation of the short-lived Federation of Arab Republics in late 1971, involving Egypt, Sudan, and Libya. in no way contradicted this, but was rather a desultory Egyptian attempt to control developments in its immediate geographic sphere, following political upheavals in Libya and Sudan: Qaddafi, the last of the unreconstructed Nasirite pan-Arabs, had led the overthrow of the conservative Libyan monarchy in September 1969, three months after a military junta led by Col. Ja`far al-Numayri had seized power in Sudan.

LEADING THE ARAB STATES TO WAR: OCTOBER 1973

Sadat had assumed office less than two months after a US-brokered cease-fire had brought an end to the bitter Israeli-Egyptian War of Attrition across the Suez Canal, which Nasir had officially launched in March 1969 after having reequipped his armed forces thanks to Soviet support and Saudi largesse. Sadat understood from the outset that an indefinite continuation of the status quo, in which Israeli troops sat on the east bank of the Suez Canal, which Egypt had closed to international shipping since the June 1967 war, would render his rule untenable. Conversely, pushing Israel out of sovereign Egyptian territory would ensure his place in Egyptian history and renew Egypt's position as the unchallenged leader of the Arab world.

By early 1973, Sadat sought to quietly convince US National Security Adviser Henry Kissinger that he would not tolerate the status quo for much longer, and that he was in fact contemplating war. The messages were relayed both directly, via Sadat's secret envoy to Washington, Hafiz Isma`il, and through Saudi Arabia's Foreign Minister Sa`ud al-Faysal. But the warnings fell on deaf ears.[2]

On October 6, 1973, which that year fell on the holiest day of the year in the Jewish calendar, Yom Kippur, Egyptian and Syrian armed forces mounted a massive assault across the cease-fire lines, beginning at exactly two p.m. The plans for the war had been many months in the making, with Saudi Arabia playing an integral part, as the Saudis promised to exert their economic and political clout in the international arena, including the use of oil as a weapon. By contrast, Jordan, which had also lost territory in 1967, had no intention of taking part in the war, and Sadat and Asad did not expect otherwise from Husayn. A three-way meeting between them in Cairo on September 10 most certainly resulted in Hussain's understanding that war preparations were in an advanced state. Two weeks later, he made a secret visit to Jerusalem to warn the Israelis that the continued diplomatic stalemate was untenable, but his cryptic warnings were not properly understood.[3]

From the wider Arab perspective, the 1973 war (October 6–24) constituted an unprecedented expression of solidarity and coordination. From the Atlantic Ocean (adjoining North Africa) to the (Persian/Arab) Gulf (*min al-muhit ila al-khalij*; the Arab "space," as defined by generations of Arab nationalists), Arab states rushed to support the war effort. Ba`thi Iraq temporarily put aside its antipathy toward its Syrian twin and dispatched two armored divisions to the Syrian front; Jordan was not expected to open up a third front against Israel, but King Husayn did feel it necessary to dispatch two armored brigades to bolster the Syrian forces, notwithstanding the fact that Syrian forces had invaded Jordan only three years earlier. Two Moroccan battalions had been stationed in Syria since March 1973 and participated in the fighting as well. Algeria, Libya, Saudi Arabia, Tunisia, Kuwait, and Sudan also made symbolic troop commitments. Arab solidarity was also registered in the economic realm: led by Saudi Arabia, Arab oil producers successfully employed the "oil weapon" against Western countries, displaying a degree of economic clout never before witnessed, and thus significantly altering the diplomatic landscape in the Arabs' favor.

To be sure, the euphoria of the initial days of the war, in which Israeli troops were being killed and captured in large numbers and Egyptian and Syrian troops were on the offensive, slowly shifted. Indeed, Egypt's 6th of October War Panorama Museum commemorates the "heroic" crossing of the Canal and the first days of fighting in which Egypt consolidated its foothold on the Sinai Peninsula, but refrains from narrating the unfolding of the rest of the war. By the end of the fighting, Israel had regained the initiative, pushing Syrian forces back beyond their initial positions and crossing into Egypt proper, registering significant territorial gains, and cutting off the Egyptian Third Army in Sinai from its supply lines. The high-stakes international diplomacy that resulted in the cease-fire included Soviet threats to intervene to stop Israel's advances and an American nuclear alert.

At bottom, although Israel had achieved the upper hand, its victory was bitter and partial. For Sadat, the high-stakes gambler, the war had achieved what it set out to do—breaking the diplomatic stalemate, demonstrating collective Arab power under his leadership, and making him an unchallenged "hero of the crossing" at home. With extraordinary acumen, he also combined postwar diplomacy with a progressive shift away from Egypt's traditional Soviet patron and into the arms of an eager United States. The ultimate goal, a comprehensive settlement according to the principles laid out by UN Security Council Resolution 242, interpreted by Sadat as necessitating full withdrawal from the territories conquered by Israel in the 1967 war, did not preclude making concessions to Israel, including ending the state of war with it. For Syrian president Hafiz al-Asad, on the other hand, diplomacy was permissible, but the struggle with Israel was a zero-sum game that needed to be continued until Arab rights were restored.[4] It was against this background that the war's results were more problematic for Asad. As the junior partner to the fighting, Syria was suspicious from the outset that Egypt's battlefield intentions were more limited, and that Syria would be left to face Israel alone. These suspicions reached a peak as the Egyptian army failed to capitalize on its initial gains and race toward two strategic passes, the control of which was vital if Israel was to be pushed out of the Sinai entirely and threatened with total defeat. The Egyptian pause enabled Israel to concentrate its forces on repelling the Syrian thrusts and pushing the combined Arab forces back toward Damascus. But Asad avoided overt confrontation with his wartime ally at this stage.[5]

PEACE-MAKING AND THE UNRAVELING OF THE ARAB CONSENSUS: 1973–1978

One month after the war's end, Arab leaders convened in Algiers to assess the war's outcome. For Sadat, it was vital to have a collective Arab legitimation as he prepared for an open-ended diplomatic process that would not tie his hands to the demands of Arab radicals. Both Iraq and Libya boycotted the summit, recognizing that their pure anti-Zionist and anti-Western ideological principles were not going to carry the day in the face of Egypt's pressing need to translate the war's outcome into substantive political and economic gains, and Saudi Arabia's support for the Egyptian position, particularly the beginning of Sadat's tilt toward the US. Host Algeria, and more importantly Syria, were willing to be prag-

matic about the next steps, but remained committed to preventing anything that smacked of recognition of Israel's legitimacy and existence, a
central facet of their own Arab nationalist and anti-imperialist credentials.
To that end, they insisted that the PLO be an integral part of the collective
Arab response, thus rejecting the reframing of the Arab-Israeli conflict as
one that could be resolved by addressing the consequences of the June
1967 war. Only Jordan's opposition to the resolution rendered it nonbind-
ing.

One year later, the scenario would be repeated, but with different
results, thanks to Egypt. In July 1974, Sadat had expressed his support for
Jordan's efforts to regain West Bank territory, which would have provided Jordan with crucial backing against Arab radicals. Once that possibility receded, however, Sadat switched his position, leaving Jordan
little choice but to accede to the general consensus. Hence, the 7th Arab
Summit conference, held in Morocco's capital Rabat on October 28–29,
unanimously recognized the PLO as the "sole legitimate representative of
the Palestinian people."[6]

Sadat's siding with the PLO was in one sense natural, in line with
Egypt's traditional support for Palestinian rights and its well-defined regional leadership role. Less well understood at the time was that the Arab
League's endorsement of the PLO at Rabat was part of Sadat's ongoing
pursuit of a diplomatic resolution of the Arab-Israeli conflict that would
enable him to recover all of the territory Egypt had lost in 1967. In raising
the PLO's status, Sadat was essentially giving it primary responsibility
for the Palestinians' future, thus enabling Egypt to take a step back from
the matter and preserve its own freedom to pursue the diplomatic avenues
being opened up by Sadat's "good friend Henry" Kissinger.

Less than a year later, Sadat's strategy bore fruit. On September 4,
1975, after months of negotiations, Egypt and Israel signed the Sinai II
disengagement agreement. It was a watershed moment in the history of
the Arab-Israeli conflict and, in retrospect, was a major way-station on
the road to the 1979 Israeli-Egyptian peace treaty.[7]

For the Syrian leadership, the agreement was tantamount to betrayal.
Egypt was clearly willing to take far-reaching steps toward peace without
conditioning them on Syria's agreement, let alone on parallel measures
on other fronts vis-à-vis Israel. Syria's nightmare scenario of seeing
Egypt withdraw from the struggle, and thus leaving Israel with a decisive
military edge, appeared significantly closer to becoming reality. Given

the escalating civil war in Lebanon, the Egyptian-Israeli agreement could not have come at a worse time. A full year would pass before the Lebanese civil war would be damped down, and with them Egyptian-Syrian mutual animosities and mistrust, albeit temporarily (for details, see chapter 9).

Taking office in January 1977, the Carter Administration in Washington immediately gave high priority to Arab-Israeli diplomacy. The eventual outcome would be a historic breakthrough. Ironically, though, events did not unfold according to the US blueprint, but in opposition to it. This was due largely to Sadat, with an assist from Israel's prime minister Menahem Begin (elected in May 1977), thus demonstrating anew the decisive weight that local actors in the region can bring to bear on a particular issue in the face of their Great Power patrons' reluctance, and even opposition.

The prevailing concept in Washington was that it was time to resolve the remaining outstanding issues in a comprehensive matter, and that a reconvening of the Geneva Conference, co-chaired by the US and the Soviet Union, was the appropriate way to begin. (A single opening session of the Conference had been held in December 1973 to legitimize the subsequent bilateral negotiations for interim agreements between Israel and its wartime adversaries.) But the obstacles were formidable, beginning with the question of Palestinian representation. The PLO's official status as "the sole legitimate representative of the Palestinians" could hardly be ignored, but neither could the PLO's rejection of UNSC resolutions 242 and 338, which stipulated the recognition of "all states in the region" (i.e., including Israel), and served as the agreed-on foundation of the Geneva conference and all other internationally recognized diplomatic efforts over the previous decade. For Syria, a proposed united Arab delegation, in which Palestinians not overtly identified with the PLO would participate, was a useful approach: as always, Damascus's main concern was that Egypt be held back by the Arab collective from pursuing an independent policy. Of course, this was exactly what Anwar al-Sadat feared. Hence, on November 9, 1977, in front of a cheering Egyptian national assembly session and with a stunned Yasir `Arafat in the front row as guest of honor, Sadat announced that he would even "go to the Knesset" (Israel's parliament) to talk peace.[8] As the plans for the visit gathered steam in the following days, Sadat journeyed to Damascus to invite Asad to go to Jerusalem with him, but could hardly have been surprised when Asad angrily declined the offer.[9] Two days later, on the evening of November 19, Sadat's plane landed in Israel. It was a dramatic event, televised around the world, with far-reaching consequences.

SUSPENSION AND RETURN, 1978–1989

From the perspective of the Arab system, Sadat's visit broke the ultimate taboo: recognition of Israel was symbolically and verbally conferred by Sadat's speech to the Israeli Knesset, even before peace negotiations had begun and without prior consultation and coordination with Egypt's fellow Arab states. Sadat's visit was a political earthquake, in every sense, and Arab states scrambled to respond. Initially, he was supported by Morocco, Sudan, Oman, and Tunisia; his opponents in the Arab radical camp—Iraq, Syria, Algeria, Libya, South Yemen (PDRY), and the PLO as well—sought, but failed, to form a coherent opposition bloc, owing to Iraq's unbridled and vituperative attacks on Syria's alleged softness regarding the conflict with Israel, a constant Iraqi refrain since the end of the 1973 war. Without Iraq to provide Syria with military reinforcement and real strategic depth, Syria could only join the other three countries and the PLO in a less weighty "Steadfastness Front" (*jabhat al-sumud wa al-tasaddi*) bloc. For Saudi Arabia, the dilemma was acute: Sadat had decisively broken with long-standing Arab "rules of the game," and the resulting opposition from the radical camp could well destabilize the Arab arena as a whole. On the other hand, were Sadat to fail and be overthrown, the consequences for regional stability were likely to be no less severe. Hence, throughout the next ten months of intensive stop-and-go Egyptian-Israeli diplomacy, the Saudis searched incessantly for a way to preserve at least a minimal degree of Arab consensus. In this, they were joined by an anxious Jordan: while supportive of the idea of peace with Israel, King Husayn could not afford to risk openly supporting Sadat at this stage and thus expose himself to Palestinian and Syrian anger.

The conclusion of the US-brokered Israeli-Egyptian Camp David Accords on September 17, 1978, brought matters to a head. For Sadat, the challenge throughout the previous ten months had been to achieve a linkage between the bilateral aspects of his negotiations with Israel and those concerned with the future of the Palestinian question. Doing so would enable him to both regain the rest of Egyptian sovereign territory in the Sinai Peninsula and demonstrate that he was not abandoning his responsibilities as leader of the Arab world. The accords, painstakingly and often acrimoniously negotiated with deep and sustained American involvement, from President Jimmy Carter on down, addressed both of those matters. The bilateral aspect, stipulating full Israeli withdrawal for full peace, was relatively straightforward and detailed. By contrast, Part 2 of the Camp David Accords was far less firm: it envisaged an interim five-year agreement for Palestinian autonomy in the West Bank and Gaza, during which time negotiations would be held to determine the area's final status. Egypt hoped that Jordanian and Palestinian representatives would join it in fleshing out and implementing the agreement. However, this did not happen, and Egypt ended up negotiating unsuccessfully with Israel on the subject for the next three years. [10]

By signing the Camp David Accords, Sadat had essentially crossed the Rubicon. Whatever hopes the Saudis and Jordanians had entertained of avoiding choosing sides between Egypt and the radical Arab camp and maintaining at least a thin veneer of consensus had been dashed. To make matters even more difficult, Iraqi strongman Saddam Husayn now jumped at the opportunity to make a leadership bid of his own, convening an emergency Arab summit conference in Baghdad in November 1978 and a follow-up ministerial conference in March 1979 to impose collective sanctions on Cairo. Egypt was suspended from the Arab League, and its headquarters transferred to Tunis. Other sanctions included the withdrawal of Arab ambassadors from Cairo, a halt in all financial and technical aid, and an agreement to not provide Egypt with oil and oil derivatives. The Arab boycott of Israel was to be extended to all Egyptian organizations dealing directly or indirectly with Israel, whether commercial, artistic, or cultural in nature. Egypt was also suspended from a host of inter-Arab organizations. For all intents and purposes, Egypt was now formally outside of the Arab fold.

To be sure, Egypt's isolation, while significant both practically and psychologically, was far from total. Some countries, e.g., Jordan, officially broke off diplomatic relations, but preserved normal ties through the interest section of the Pakistani embassy. EgyptAir resumed regular flights to a number of countries after a brief suspension. Deposits from Arab countries in Egyptian banks were never withdrawn, nor were any obstacles placed in the way of the millions of Egyptian workers in Arab countries, whose remittances continued to provide a major source of income for Egypt.

From the outset, Egyptian officials from Sadat on down scornfully insisted that the rest of the Arab world needed Egypt more than Egypt needed it. Indeed, the Saudi-led grouping, although angry with Sadat, feared the consequences of Egypt's forced absence from regional affairs and thus did not fully implement the Arab League-mandated sanctions. At bottom, the Baghdad consensus against Egypt was significant but short-lived. Ironically, Egypt's way back to the Arab fold during the 1980s would be paved by Iraq.

Shortly after the outbreak of the Iran-Iraq war in September 1980, Sadat branded Iraq as the "aggressor," reflecting an initial assessment that it might emerge victorious, thus enabling Saddam to play an outsized role in Arab affairs, particularly in the Gulf, as the proven defender of the Arab homeland. This quickly proved to be inaccurate, and as a result, Egyptian and Iraqi interests began to converge. Within months, Egypt sold Iraq a quantity of Soviet-made arms, which Egypt had begun to phase out in any case, as it reequipped itself with US-made weaponry. By the end of the eight-year war, billions of dollars' worth of Egyptian assistance would be sold to Iraq, and include a gamut of heavy weapons and supplies, and even military experts to assist in training Iraqis in missile defense. No less significant was Egypt's demographic weight. Egyptian manpower became increasingly crucial for Iraq as the war dragged on and it was compelled to mobilize more and more of its male population for military service. At the war's end in July 1988, approximately two million Egyptians were working in Iraq, in both unskilled agricultural and factory jobs and white-collar positions. By propping up the Iraqi state against Iranian pressure, Egypt also played an essential role in maintaining Gulf security and protecting the Arab Gulf regimes. As such, Egypt's preeminent role in Arab affairs was renewed and taken to a new level.

To be sure, the formal confirmation of Egypt's status, as expressed through the restoration of diplomatic relations and reentry in the Arab League, would come only gradually, and not be completed until May 1989 at the Casablanca Arab Summit conference. But the trend had become clearer much earlier. In addition, Sadat's assassination in October 1981 and replacement by his vice president, Husni Mubarak, removed the personal element from the equation: Mubarak's low-key style of leadership contrasted sharply with Sadat's flamboyance, which had resulted in bitter exchanges with Arab leaders in his last years. In addition, Mubarak made a calculated decision to keep Israel at arm's length, maintaining their peace treaty but keeping it "cold," i.e., keeping economic, cultural, and societal ties to a minimum. This came almost naturally, in any case, as the failure to produce an interim regime for the West Bank and Gaza, as stipulated by the Camp David accords, essentially froze the peace process.

With Egypt's readmission to the Arab League, League headquarters were quickly returned to Cairo after a decade in Tunis. Most importantly, Egypt had been readmitted on its terms, maintaining its peace treaty with Israel, while proving to all and sundry that a collective Arab framework without Egypt playing a leading role was simply not viable, and even dangerous. Even Qaddafi, the last pan-Arab true believer and purist when it came to advocating Arab unity and opposing a political settlement to the Arab-Israeli conflict, was willing to put aside his criticism of Egypt, meet with Mubarak, and improve bilateral ties.

EGYPT VERSUS IRAQ—AGAIN

In February 1989, Egypt, Iraq, Jordan, and the Yemen Arab Republic joined together in a new sub-regional grouping, the Arab Cooperation Council (ACC). Its establishment raised more than a few eyebrows, for the four countries lacked geographical contiguity (apart from Iraq and Jordan), similarities in regime types, economies, social structures, and ideological orientations. In essence, this group of four had decided to try to institutionalize their alliance during the Iran-Iraq war (in addition to Egypt's vital assistance, Jordan and Yemen had provided symbolic contingents of volunteer soldiers and unwavering political support; the Gulf Arab states, by contrast, had aided Iraq with enormous sums of money, but had never backed Iraq unreservedly).

The ACC's primary emphasis was supposedly on economic development and cooperation, but the situation was hardly propitious. As an authoritative Western source wrote at the time, "the potential for flourishing economic interdependence is retarded by the shortage of productive investment in the member countries, exacerbated by their combined debts."[11] The only area of real economic complementarity between Iraq and Egypt had been in the realm of Egyptian manpower, but the end of the Iran-Iraq war lessened Iraq's need for Egyptian labor. Indeed, as Iraqi troops began to be demobilized and search for work, reports of violence against Egyptians began filtering back to Egypt.

From the moment of the ACC's inception, in fact, it was clear that Egypt and Iraq did not view it in the same way. Mubarak insisted it had no purpose other than promoting economic integration and growth, while Iraqi officials emphasized the need for a common political strategy on the major regional issues facing them: the Palestinian question, relations with Iran, the Lebanese crisis, and the need to bolster "pan-Arab security," an extremely nebulous concept open to all kinds of interpretations. Iraqi rhetoric became progressively more aggressive over time, emphasizing what Saddam called a Western-Zionist conspiracy to prevent Iraq, and the Arab nation as a whole, from advancing in the technological, scientific, and military fields. Iraq and Jordan pushed ACC leaders to advocate the establishment of a large-scale fund to channel Gulf state money to poorer Arab states, and also tried to introduce a military dimension into the ACC framework. Mubarak, though, would have no part of it, and even informed Saudi Arabia's King Fahd of what had transpired, creating consternation in Riyadh.[12] For Saddam, this was essentially a cover for his immediate ambitions, directed at Kuwait, which he said was conducting economic warfare against Iraq by pumping oil in excess of agreed-on OPEC quotas, thus driving down its price and thus costing Iraq billions of much-needed dollars.

In mid-July 1990, Iraq's threat to Kuwait now became more tangible. Together with Saudi Arabia, Egypt undertook high-level mediation between the two countries. However, Cairo both overestimated its own weight and influence and underestimated the severity of the crisis, and particularly Saddam's determination not to return to the status quo ante. Its operating assumption—that the long-prevailing pan-Arab norms that had acted as an effective restraint on actors from going too far in seeking to advance their particular agendas were still operative—proved to be sorely mistaken. As Yezid Sayigh cogently argues, these norms had already been fatally compromised, hence Saddam was no longer constrained by them.[13]

While the personalities of individual leaders are important for politics everywhere, in the Arab world this is especially the case, particularly in the realm of foreign policy. In this instance, a meeting between Mubarak and Saddam in Baghdad on July 26 turned out to be crucial. Mubarak left it believing that Saddam had promised him he would not use force to resolve Iraq's dispute with Kuwait, and encouraged that Saddam had agreed to send his deputy, `Izzat Ibrahim ad-Duri, to Jeddah for a meeting on July 31 with Kuwait's Crown Prince Sa`d `Abdallah, in the presence of the Egyptians and the host Saudis.[14] But rather than damping down the conflict, the meeting exacerbated it by contributing to Kuwaiti complacency.

On August 2, within a matter of hours, Iraqi forces occupied Kuwait, and the Kuwaiti Amir and his family fled to Saudi Arabia. For Mubarak, the invasion was not only a dangerous and unacceptable act, but also a personal humiliation and embarrassment. He quickly grasped that the long-standing inter-Arab rules of the game were no longer operative, and that Arab states were incapable of resolving the crisis on their own. In stark contrast, Jordan's King Husayn desperately sought an Arab solution, pleading with Mubarak and Saudi Arabia's King Fahd not to push Saddam into a corner, and rushing to Baghdad to urge Saddam to be flexible, albeit to no avail.

On August 10, Cairo hosted an emergency Arab summit conference. Originally planned for November, what was to have been a consensual celebration of Egypt's renewed pride of place in the Arab firmament turned into an Egyptian-led effort to block Iraq's bid for regional hegemony. Ironically, Saddam Husayn was concurrently draping himself in the mantle of Gamal `Abd al-Nasir as he sought to appeal over the heads of Arab governments to the "Arab masses."

Befitting the gravity of the occasion, fifteen of the twenty-one delegations to the summit were led by their heads of state. Iraq was not one of them, being represented by first deputy prime minister Taha Yasin Ramadan. Not surprisingly, the level of mutual invective was extraordinarily high, and various efforts by `Arafat and Qaddafi to forestall anti-Iraqi measures came to naught. With a bare majority of twelve votes, Saudi Arabia and Egypt pushed through a resolution condemning Iraq, calling for the restoration of Kuwaiti sovereignty, and most importantly: a) supporting Saudi Arabia's actions taken on behalf of its "right of legitimate defense" (i.e., inviting in foreign troops, which were already arriving); and b) declaring the intent to favorably answer Saudi Arabia's request for Arab forces to help defend its territory. Never had such a controversial resolution been adopted against the active or passive opposition of almost half of the League's member states. Those supporting the resolution were Egypt, the six Gulf Cooperation Council (GCC) states led by Saudi Arabia (for its establishment in 1981, see chapter 8), Morocco, Somalia, Djibouti, Lebanon, and, most importantly, Syria. Not since the October 1973 war had the Egyptian-Saudi-Syrian triangle acted together on an issue of such overriding importance. Syria's joining the conservative, pro-Western camp of states was a crucial component of the legitimacy formula now being provided by the Arab League to the Saudis and the Western powers.

Mubarak wasted no time in dispatching forces to Saudi Arabia. The first of what would eventually amount to thirty thousand troops began arriving on August 11. By the end of the year, Arab military forces gathered in Saudi Arabia would also include seventeen thousand Syrian troops, three thousand to five thousand Kuwaitis, a total of thirty-one hundred from the other four Gulf principalities, and one thousand to twelve hundred from Morocco. Token Egyptian, Moroccan, and Syrian contingents were also deployed in the United Arab Emirates (UAE). Altogether, including Saudi Arabia's forty-five-thousand-man army, the number of Arab troops participating in the anti-Iraq coalition was approximately one hundred thousand.

By the end of 1990, the Arab world, along with the international community as a whole, was holding its collective breath in anticipation of the UN Security Council's January 15, 1991, deadline for an unconditional Iraqi withdrawal. Mubarak, Fahd, and their Arab partners in the anti-Saddam coalition feared that Iraq would spring a "January surprise," i.e., show enough flexibility, including perhaps carrying out a partial pullback of its forces, to derail the coalition's military plans, and thus leave Iraqi power undamaged and astride the Gulf. They were also concerned that Saddam's incessant linking of any resolution of the Gulf crisis to the achievement of Palestinian rights would appeal to Arab public opinion, as well as his promise to attack Israel in the event of war, and thus enable Saddam to cast himself as a latter-day Nasir, standing up for Arab rights against Western and Zionist aggression as well as perfidious Arab regimes who would be fighting on the same side as Israel. Hence, the foreign ministers of Egypt, Syria, and Saudi Arabia issued a joint statement on January 5, 1991, promising to redouble their efforts to achieve an Arab-Israeli settlement based on the withdrawal of Israeli forces from the West Bank and Gaza, and the establishment of a Palestinian state.[15] The statement, and their accompanying concerns, illustrated that the perennial unsolved question of Palestine still resonated in the Arab universe.

The US-led coalition began a massive aerial bombardment on January 17, 1991. Five weeks later, a swift ground campaign completed the mission.[16] For Cairo and Riyadh, the results were all that they had hoped for: Saddam's army was smashed, the status quo ante in Kuwait was restored, and even Israel was not drawn into the conflict, despite Iraq's launching of SCUD missiles against it.

A NEW ARAB ORDER?

The crushing defeat of Iraq and the imposition of strict UN-mandated sanctions against Saddam Husayn's regime neutralized Iraq's ability to be a serious actor in Arab politics. The victorious Six Plus Two coalition (the Saudi-led GCC states, Egypt, and Syria) could now, in theory, fashion an Arab order according to a common vision, without encountering significant resistance.

On March 5, 1991, they attempted to do just that. Meeting in Damascus, the foreign ministers of the Six Plus Two group moved to institutionalize their wartime alliance and thus defy the legacy of past failures in forging durable multilateral frameworks. To that end, they issued the "Damascus Declaration," spelling out their vision of the postwar Arab and regional order. Not surprisingly, it was to be based on the principles embodied in the UN and Arab League charters, emphasizing respect for the sovereignty and territorial integrity of every state, nonintervention in another country's domestic affairs, and a commitment to settle disputes by peaceful means. Reflecting the imminent economic union among European Community countries, one of the declaration's objectives was the establishment of an Arab economic grouping. More immediately, the GCC states reportedly pledged $5 billion in economic assistance to Egypt and Syria, with more to come.

The declaration's security component was significant. Egypt's and Syria's participation in the anti-Saddam coalition was not considered to be a one-time event. Rather, the two countries' presence in the Gulf was defined as "a nucleus for an Arab peace force" that would safeguard the security of the Gulf Arab states.[17] The declaration's principles were implicitly endorsed by the United States at a joint meeting of the Six Plus

Two foreign ministers with US Secretary of State James Baker on March 10. The group's willingness to advertise its pro-American tilt was unprecedented in modern Arab history, and a sign of the times.

By May 1991, however, it was clear that a multilateral Arab military force in the Gulf was not going to be established, as Egypt began withdrawing its troops, and Syria followed suit. A revised Damascus Declaration, issued on July 16, made no mention of the force. What had happened? At bottom, the failure to implement the original plan was political: the Gulf states had preferred to resume their traditional balancing act between stronger regional powers—in this case, between Egypt and Iran, which had objected to the whole notion of an US-endorsed exclusively Arab Gulf security plan. For the Gulf states, there was actually little value to having standing Arab forces on their territory. During the crisis, their presence had had important symbolic value, but now that it was over, considerations of *realpolitik* took precedence. In addition, their aversion to the stationing of Egyptian and Syrian forces in their territories also reflected a lingering wariness of more powerful Arab states. Egypt, for its part, while angry about Iran's interference and the GCC's perceived ingratitude, quickly understood the signals emanating from the Gulf and preempted what would be an embarrassing request for the withdrawal of its troops. For its part, Syria had no wish to do anything to antagonize its Iranian ally, and thus quickly pulled out its troops as well.

Discussions on how to revitalize collective Arab institutions and promote a better future for Arab states and societies would continue during the coming years. For the time being, though, ruling Arab elites were concerned with the immediate geopolitical ramifications of the Gulf War—the severe weakening of Iraq, the concomitant strengthening of non-Arab Iran, the progressive dissolving of the Soviet Union (made official on December 26, 1991), and the ramifications of a major new American diplomatic initiative to resolve the Arab-Israeli conflict.

In any event, the failure in the spring of 1991 to establish a viable institutional framework with a regional security component indicated that a common vision was in fact lacking, and that ruling Arab elites remained highly suspicious of one another. This was true even among the Gulf Cooperation Council states, who constituted the most cohesive and like-minded bloc of Arab entities. For example, Qatar, Oman, and the UAE favored as much normalization with Iran as possible, while Bahrain, Saudi Arabia, and Kuwait were much more suspicious of Tehran's regional aspirations. Iran's consolidation of control over three Gulf islands, Abu Musa and Greater and Lesser Tunbs, which are generally accepted as belonging to the UAE, was a permanent subject on the GCC's agenda. The UAE repeatedly, albeit futilely sought to mobilize support for its claims while preferring to avoid a direct confrontation with Tehran and maintain strong economic links with it. During the latter part of the 1990s, a majority of the Gulf states also came to favor a gradual easing of Iraq's regional isolation and of sanctions, but Kuwait and Saudi Arabia insisted that they continue to toe a hardline. A bilateral territorial dispute between Qatar and Bahrain remained unresolved and toxic. Economic integration, one of the GCC's declared goals, proceeded at a snail's pace. And on the issue of collective security, Oman's efforts to transform existing token collective units ("Peninsula Shield") into a robust one of a hundred-thousand-man GCC defense force gained no traction, as GCC states relied ever more openly on individual bilateral security arrangements with Western powers.

A further blow to the very notion of an Arab order was the emergence of a nascent Kurdish autonomous entity in northern Iraq, undermining the unitary Arabness that had been the conceptual basis of the Iraqi state since its establishment. And in North Africa, the momentary hopes for a new era of regional cooperation, stability, and development that had been raised by the creation in February 1989 of the five-nation Arab Maghrib Union (*ittihad al-maghrib al-`arabi*, AMU) were dashed: Algeria was plunged into a decade of horrific violent strife between an Islamist opposition and the regime, the historically bad Moroccan-Algerian relations again deteriorated, and Libya found itself isolated from its neighbors by tough UN-imposed sanctions owing to its involvement in the bombing of a US commercial airliner over Lockerbie, Scotland in December 1988, and a French airliner over the Sahara in 1989.

Parallel to these geo-strategic developments was the triumph of the principle of *raison d'état* over *raison de la nation Arabe*, accompanied by the growth in the degree of "stateness," measured by Arab states' bureaucratic expansion, increased means of coercion, control over national economies, comprehensive educational systems, and the cultivation of particular national-territorial symbols and history. However, this did not mean that states had truly become "strong," in the sense used by Joel Migdal, namely having acquired the requisite degree of social control that enabled them to overcome existing social forces resistant to centralizing policies aimed at transforming social and political realities to the state's benefit.[18] This distinction is especially useful when thinking about Egypt.

Migdal's ideal type is an entity that is both a strong state and a strong society, in which a healthy balance is maintained between the two. The reality of most Arab states was far removed from that. They had become too powerful in their domination of other social and political forces— "overstated," in Nazih Ayubi's words, but were not truly powerful, lacking the requisite degree of social cohesion and social control necessary for achieving long-term success and regime legitimacy. Instead, Arab regimes relied on excessive coercion by the top-heavy national security apparatuses, making them not "strong" but "fierce."[19] The imbalance between state and society served as a drag on state performance at a time when domestic social and economic reforms were vital to adapt properly to international trends and cope with the growing challenges at home. Entering the 1990s, Arab states were far from being ready to join the "third wave" of democratizing states concurrently manifesting itself in Latin America and Eastern Europe.[20] They were instead characterized by unproductive and noncompetitive economies, excessive state control, large-scale indebtedness, large, youthful, partially educated populations suffering from high rates of unemployment and underemployment, and authoritarian political systems.

EGYPT AND THE ARAB-ISRAELI SPHERE

In mid-1993, a Norwegian-hosted diplomatic back-channel between Israel and the PLO produced a dramatic agreement, the Oslo Accords (for details, see chapter 10). Egypt quickly endorsed it and moved to solidify its traditional position as the patron of the Palestinian cause. But its leadership of the Arab bloc was fraying. Over the next year, the PLO-Israeli agreement opened the door to the establishment of various forms of aboveboard diplomatic ties between a number of Arab states and Israel, led by a full-fledged peace treaty between Jordan and Israel. Significantly, the GCC states formally removed the secondary and tertiary aspects of the boycott of Israel, and a series of annual regional economic summits were inaugurated in 1994 in Casablanca, where Israel adopted a high profile, giving rise to many critical remarks in the Arab media regarding Israel's alleged hegemonic aspirations in the region.

All of this did not sit well in Cairo, for it was occurring without prior coordination with it, and thus implicitly undercutting its leadership status. Speaking at a 1995 economic summit conference in Amman, Egyptian Foreign Minister `Amr Musa criticized (unnamed) Arab parties who were acting in haste (*harwala*) to normalize ties with Israel.[21] Egyptian unhappiness also derived in part from a widespread view of Israel as a geostrategic adversary, the peace treaty notwithstanding. In addition, the bulk of the intellectual class in the Arab world, a product of the Nasirist and Ba`thist era, had been overwhelmingly opposed to Sadat's peace with Israel, while hoping that what they called "the Pharaoh's peace" would collapse under its own weight. Most secular Arab intellectuals viewed the 1993 Israeli-PLO agreement as surrender to an American-backed Israeli *diktat*, a "Palestinian Versailles," in Edward Said's words.[22] To be sure, a minority of intellectuals, including the Egyptian Nobel Prize-winning author Naguib Mahfouz, playwright 'Ali Salem, and sociologist Saad Eddin Ibrahim, favored engagement with Israeli society and its achievements instead of boycott and utterly ignoring the country. However, as Arab rulers moved forward in establishing diplomatic and economic ties with Israel, opposition to *tatbi`* ("normalization") became the last refuge for many, and those writers, artists, and businessmen who did buck the trend risked ostracism, sanctions, and worse.[23]

NEW ISSUES FOR THE NEW MILLENNIUM

Broader and partially overlapping regional trends during the first decade of the new millennium starkly illustrated the gap between Egypt's self-image as a naturally entitled regional leader and the extant realities, in which it lacked the capabilities to shape events. These included the collapse of the Oslo process in September 2000 and reigniting of a Palestinian-Israeli violent confrontation, the American war in Iraq, which toppled the Ba`th regime, the increased power of two non-state actors—Hizballah and Hamas—and resulting rounds of violent conflict with Israel, persistent efforts by Qatar to play a significant role in the region, the growing salience of the Sunni-Shi`i divide, and the enhanced power of non-Arab regional powers, namely Iran and Turkey.

During the Nasir era, Egypt and Iran had been on opposite sides of regional and global fault lines. Iran's membership in the Baghdad Pact in the mid-1950s placed it alongside of Iraq, the main rival of Nasir's Egypt. Throughout the 1960s, Iran paid close attention to Iraq's shift into the radical Arab camp and to Nasir's support for Arab revolutionary groups in Yemen and the Gulf, supporting Yemeni royalists, helping suppress the Dhofar rebellion in Oman, and developing a close relationship with Israel in both the security and economic realms. With Egypt's turn westward under Sadat, Iran and Egypt briefly constituted two important pillars of America's regional strategy. Just how close was demonstrated by Sadat's granting the Shah asylum after his overthrow in February 1979. His death in July 1980 occasioned a state funeral and burial near King Farouk and other Egyptian monarchs in Cairo's al-Rifa'i Mosque.

Everything changed in the aftermath of the Islamic Revolution. Diplomatic relations were broken off and never fully restored. Iran and Egypt were again on opposing sides of the geostrategic and political fence and, as mentioned, Egypt played a crucial role in bolstering Iraq against Iran during their eight-year war. Iranian authorities, for their part, named a street after Sadat's assassin.

However problematic Saddam Husayn's regime had been, in the eyes of Sunni Arab governments it served as a vital buffer against Persian Shi`i, hegemonic-minded, and revolutionary Islamic Iran. Its toppling in 2003 and replacement by a Shi`i-led government removed that buffer and the geopolitical ramifications were profound. Mubarak and Jordan's King `Abdallah II openly voiced their concern about an emerging "Shi`i Crescent," stretching from Tehran to Beirut, including Iraq, Iran's main regional ally Syria (whose ruling 'Alawi core was not authentically Shi`i, but this hardly mattered), and its Hizballah client in Lebanon. The steady extension of Iranian military and political influence into Lebanon during the first decade of the twenty-first century was deeply disturbing to both Cairo and Riyadh. Official Egypt was even more perturbed by Iran's efforts to extend its influence over Palestinian groups, Egypt's traditional bailiwick, beginning with Israel's interdiction of an Iranian shipment of arms to Yasir `Arafat forces during the early days of the Second Intifada, and expanding into strategic backing for Hamas, with Hizballah providing crucial logistical support. The 2006 Israel-Hizballah war and 2009 Israel-Hamas war in Gaza exposed Arab regimes to harsh criticism from their publics for their inability to prevent the Israeli onslaught. The fact that reliable public opinion polls showed broad support among Arab publics, including their own, for Iranian President Mahmoud Ahmadinejad and Hizballah's leader Hassan Nasrallah, owing to their populist message of defiance of Western and Israeli policies, was disquieting as well, for it indicated widespread dissatisfaction with their own leaderships.[24] Most disturbing for Egypt was the apparent penetration of Iranian-sponsored Hizballah smuggling and sabotage rings into the Sinai, Egyptian sovereign territory, coupled with Nasrallah's intolerable calls for the Egyptian public to insist on the lifting of the siege of Gaza.

Similarly, Turkey's Sunni Islamist government, having gradually consolidated its power since first being elected in 2003 and guided by a neo-Ottoman vision promoting the restoration of the country's preeminent influence, became increasingly assertive in regional affairs. This included an embrace of the Palestinian Islamist Hamas, which as of 2007 exclusively ruled the Gaza region. Turkey's new patronage of the Palestinian cause was highlighted by the Mevi Marmara incident in 2009, in which a Turkish civilian ship demonstratively seeking to break Israel's blockade of Gaza and bring humanitarian aid to its residents was interdicted by the Israeli navy. In the resulting confrontation, nine Turkish citizens died and a major crisis in Turkish-Israeli relations ensued. Understandably, Egypt strongly disapproved of Turkey's assertiveness in Palestinian affairs, but there was little that it could do to prevent it.

Overall, then, Egypt's influence in regional affairs had declined precipitously in the two decades since its central symbolic role in the 1990–1991 anti-Saddam coalition, mirroring the sorry state of the Arab system as a whole, and contrasting sharply with the increased power of the three non-Arab states in the region: Turkey, Iran, and Israel.

8

FAILED ASPIRATIONS, FAILED STATE

Iraq Under Saddam, and Beyond (1968–2010)

During the last three decades of the twentieth century, Iraq and Syria would come to be the epitome of totalitarian-like *duwal mukhabarat* ("fierce" or "national security states").[1] If Syria under the Asad dynasty was "fierce," Iraq, its perpetually adversarial Ba`thi twin, was even more so. The Ba`th regime had returned to power in May 1968 in a military coup, and under the brutal hand of regime strongman Saddam Husayn, it worked assiduously during the next decade to physically eliminate its domestic enemies, real and imagined. Over time, it would truly become a "republic of fear," an Arab totalitarian state that eerily resembled Stalin's USSR and Hitler's Germany, in its conception and *modus operandi*, if not in its capabilities.[2] Iraq's vast oil resources and fertile soil had always conferred it with the potential of being a regional power. But the very nature of the post-World War I monarchical state fashioned by Great Britain had placed serious limitations on its efforts to dominate the Arab Fertile Crescent. The overthrow of the monarchy in 1958 then inaugurated two decades of chronic instability and weakness, substantially marginalizing Iraq's influence in regional and Arab affairs. Moreover, in addition to hunting down its enemies at home, the Ba`th regime would be utterly preoccupied with a full-scale armed revolt from its Kurdish minority (c. 20 percent of the population) between 1970 and 1975.[3] It was only toward the end of the 1970s that Iraq would emerge as a major player in inter-Arab politics, one with outsized ambitions, but without the requisite capacity to realize them. In 1980 and again in 1990, Saddam would play havoc with the regional order, first by invading Iran and then Kuwait. The consequences were ultimately catastrophic for Iraq, and the coup de grace for the Ba'thi regime would be delivered by the US in 2003. Power now passed into the hands of the long-marginalized Shi'i majority, ending the historic domination of the Iraqi state by its Sunni Arab minority, opening the door for Iran to extend its influence via its Shi'a coreligionists, and creating new possibilities for Iraq's Kurds. In other words, Iraq's existence as a coherent state within its recognized boundaries came to hang in the balance, and its self-definition as an "Arab" state that aspired to play a leading role in Arab affairs was now being consigned to the history books. In that sense, the fate of Iraq served as a metaphor for the idea of modern Arabism and the Arab state system as whole.

OPPORTUNITY AND THREAT: SADAT AND KHOMEINI

In March 1975, Saddam Husayn had been compelled to agree to a humiliating border demarcation agreement with Iran as a quid pro quo for the cessation of Iranian support for the ongoing Kurdish revolt in northern Iraq, enabling him to crush it. In the ensuing three years, awash in post-1973 oil revenues (Iraq was one of the OPEC "hawks" regarding pricing and the use of oil as a political weapon), he brutally consolidated his control over the Iraqi state, still officially headed by Ahmad Hasan al-Bakr.

Autumn 1978 was a crucial time, as next door to Iraq, a Shi'ite Islamic revolt against the Shah of Iran's pro-Western monarchical regime gathered steam. Hence, Egypt's concurrent decision to pursue the peace process with Israel to its conclusion was for Saddam a golden opportunity to promote himself, and Iraq, as the new leader of the Arab world at a crucial moment for the entire region.

Saddam's primary tool for doing so, at this stage, was the Arab Summit Conference, which convened in emergency session in Baghdad on November 2–5, 1978. At this point, Iraqi president Bakr told the assembled leaders, "there will be no scope for being neutral"; either one was opposed to Sadat's actions or supportive of them.[4] The not-so-veiled warning to the Saudis, who were angry with Sadat but reluctant to fully align themselves with Arab radicals, was clear. At the same time, Iraq was interested in having Saudi Arabia within the fold, and thus showed tactical flexibility in deference to the Saudis' desire not to burn bridges with Egypt.

On March 27, 1979, the very next day after Sadat and Begin signed the peace treaty on the White House lawn in Carter's presence, Arab foreign and economy ministers convened in Baghdad to decide on the exact implementation of the Baghdad summit resolutions. At issue was the severity and application of the sanctions, and the gathering was extremely acrimonious. Saddam Husayn repeated Bakr's statement that Iraq would oppose without compromise anyone aligning with Sadat. The Saudis and most of the other Gulf monarchies struggled to somehow keep the door open to Egypt by softening the severity of the sanctions, while Jordan was primarily keen on ensconcing itself within as broad an Arab consensus as possible. After incessant Iraqi media attacks, Jordanian persuasion, Kuwaiti advocacy, and PLO pressures, the Saudis and the other Gulf Arab states acceded to a serious set of anti-Egyptian sanctions.

Iraq's bid for all-Arab leadership at this juncture also included an unprecedented, albeit brief thaw with Syria. The two countries had been at swords drawn since the mid-1960s, as their narrowly based leaderships sought to legitimize their increasingly harsh and totalitarian regimes by claiming exclusive right to the mantle of Ba'thi Arab nationalism. The flight from Syria to Iraq during the mid-1960s of some of the Ba'th's founders, notably Michel 'Aflaq, gave the Iraqi Ba'th some added credibility in the competition. More importantly, Iraq, unlike Syria, was not a direct party to the conflict with Israel, and thus didn't have to make the same kind of pragmatic compromises that Syria did, enabling it to remain ideologically pure. In this, there was continuity with Iraq's verbal militancy toward the question of Palestine in the 1940s.

At this point in time, however, the two countries needed each other. Syria, in particular, was keen on bolstering its overall security posture now that Egypt had officially withdrawn from the conflict. It was thus willing to explore the establishment of closer ties with Iraq, and the Iraqis were eager to engage them on the idea, as they had been since the 1930s, in fact, and as part of their overall leadership bid. The rapprochement was inaugurated during the preparations for the Baghdad summit, which included Asad's first presidential visit to Baghdad. At its conclusion, on October 26, 1978, he and Bakr signed a "Charter for Joint National Action," outlining steps for the institutionalization of a union between the two countries, the long-held vision of generations of Arab nationalists, and particularly the Ba'th Party. To be sure, at this stage the Charter was a declaration of intent for union, not a prescription for implementation. But given the decade of almost continuous unbridled hostility that had preceded it, the sudden turnabout was dramatic.[5]

Subsequent high-level meetings in the winter and spring of 1978–79 sought to flesh out the details. However, behind the continued declarations of intent to unify their foreign, defense, and economic policies, the process was doomed to failure. Given the singular role of the ruling Ba'th Party in both countries, party unification was a sine qua non for achieving the Charter's goals. But overcoming the years of rancor and mistrust, not to mention the questions related to the distribution of power in the future unified entity, was impossible. On July 28, 1979, the efforts ground to a halt. Saddam Husayn, who had officially assumed the presidency twelve days earlier after forcing Bakr into retirement, announced the uncovering of a "plot" against the regime and carried out a brutal wholesale purge of the leadership echelon. The plotters, he said, had been in contact with a "foreign government," i.e., Syria, and the unity talks were consigned to oblivion, Syria's persistent denials of culpability notwithstanding.[6]

The reasons for the failure were both multiple and familiar. Syria, the weaker and needier party, wanted the strategic depth vis-à-vis Israel that Iraq would provide, but was unwilling to repeat the mistake of the UAR experience, which Egypt had utterly dominated. For Iraq, its initiative was a take-it or leave-it matter. Without being able to station troops in Damascus and dominate a unified Ba'th Party, the very things that the Asad regime adamantly rejected, there was no point in Iraq pursuing the matter any further. Instead, Baghdad turned its attentions eastward, toward the new regime in Tehran.

From the outset, the Islamic Republic of Iran posed a sizeable potential threat, combining the power of a large state with a revolutionary Islamic message directly aimed at Iraq's large, disenfranchised, and increasingly restive Shi'i community. Iraqi-Iranian relations steadily deteriorated during the eighteen months after the overthrow of the Pahlavi monarchy. For Iraq, Iran's new and explicitly Shi'i regime posed a clear and present danger, providing a potential pole of attraction to its own disaffected Shi'i majority, which, while ethnically Arab, did have strong ties to Iranian Shi'i, particularly in the shrine cities of Najaf and Karbala. As was its wont, Saddam's regime used extreme repression of any signs of dissent, executing the country's leading Shi'i cleric, Ayatollah Muhammad Baqir al-Sadr, in April 1980. Throughout the year, Baghdad and Tehran conducted an increasingly harsh war of words, and by September unresolved border issues were generating regular exchanges of fire.

To build up a regional counterweight to Iran at this stage, Iraq moved to improve ties with its neighboring conservative Sunni Arab monarchies, Saudi Arabia and Jordan. In doing so, it began moving away from its traditional "odd man out" Arab orientation, even as it continued to attack Syria from the "left" for its insufficiently militant position toward Israel. Following the collapse of the rapprochement efforts in July 1979, Syrian-Iraqi relations deteriorated significantly, with each side accusing the other, often with justification, of subversive actions. Syria's support for the new regime in Tehran certainly didn't help matters either. For Asad, the fall of the Shah, a pillar of American influence in the region and tacit ally of Israel as well, was a strategic boon of major proportions. The new Iranian order, headed by the Supreme Guide, Grand Ayatollah Ruhollah Khomeini, was a declared enemy of both the US and Israel and committed to supporting Arab and Palestinian rights, and thus a natural ally. Saddam, of course, viewed the Tehran regime through an entirely different set of lenses.

Eventually, Saddam Husayn's outsized ambitions, desire to roll back the 1975 Algiers agreement that enabled Iran to hamper Iraq's already minimal access to the open waters of the Persian Gulf, concerns about Iran's revolutionary appeal, and belief that Iran's domestic chaos offered him a tremendous opportunity led him to take a historic gamble. On September 17, Saddam announced that the Algiers agreement was null and void. Five days later, on September 22, 1980, Iraqi troops poured across the border in a full-scale military offensive. Iraq hoped for a quick and decisive victory, one that would deal a mortal blow to the Iranian geopolitical and religious-communal threat, expand Iraq's territory to include Iran's predominantly ethnic Arab Khuzistan region in the southwest of the country, and confirm its domination of the Gulf region. However, this quickly proved unrealizable. In fact, the war generated a tide of Iranian patriotism, enabling the new regime to consolidate its authority and mobilize the country's resources to resist. Saddam's gamble would quickly prove to be a failure, and what he had envisaged as a three-week operation would evolve into a brutal and costly eight-year war. And almost immediately, the Iran-Iraq war would become a bone of contention in Arab affairs no less toxic than the Arab-Israeli cluster of issues. (For details on the November 1980 Amman Arab summit conference that starkly highlighted the deep rifts that had opened up, see chapter 9.) From this point on, and throughout the decade, the Arab collective would be adrift, lacking in even a minimal semblance of cohesion and common sense of purpose, with Egypt suspended and isolated, Iraq being both newly assertive and entangled in a war with Iran, Syria doggedly standing firm in opposition to the Arab majority on key issues, and Saudi Arabia discovering anew that its vast wealth was not easily translatable into successful political leadership.

SAUDI ARABIA AND THE GULF COOPERATION COUNCIL

The idea of establishing a framework to promote cooperation among the Arab Gulf states was floated from the time of the British withdrawal in 1971 and the establishment of the independent states of Bahrain, Qatar,

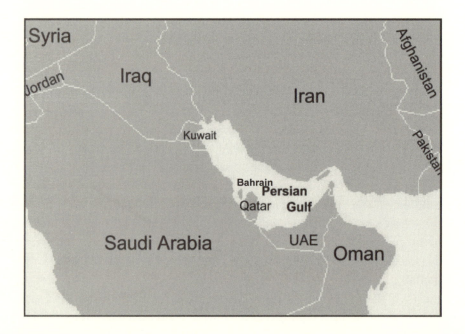

Figure 8.1.   The Persian Gulf–Kuwait, Iraq, Iran. By Edbrown05 at en.wikinews [Public domain], via Wikimedia Commons.

and the United Arab Emirates, but only gained momentum in 1979 with the fall of the Shah and the Soviet invasion of Afghanistan. The outbreak of the Iran-Iraq war in September 1980 gave Gulf leaders the final impetus to act on the idea.

For the Saudis, the previous two years had been extremely difficult: they had been forced to favor its long-standing adversarial neighbor, Iraq, over its long-standing ally, Egypt; they watched their neighbor and fellow US client-ally Iran be transformed into a militant anti-Western Shi`i adversary; the Soviet invasion of Afghanistan constituted an additional unexpected threat to the regional order; and its own internal vulnerability had been put on full display in November 1979 when a militant Sunni group took over the Ka`ba complex in Mecca—Islam's holiest site. It would take more than two weeks to dislodge them. Hence, for the Saudis, establishing a regional Gulf organization, under its leadership, was a useful way to consolidate its leadership in its immediate environs and project an image of resoluteness.

After months of preparatory meetings, the six-member Gulf Cooperation Council (GCC; *majlis al-ta'awun li duwal al-khalij al-`arabiyya*; literally "the Council for Cooperation among States of the Arab Gulf"), composed of Saudi Arabia, Kuwait, the UAE, Bahrain, Qatar, and Oman, was established in May 1981, with its headquarters in Riyadh. Pointedly, Iraq, which was also technically a Gulf power, by virtue of its 58 kilometers of coastline at the head of the Gulf, was not invited to join, partly because Ba`thi Iraq had often sought to undermine the Gulf principalities through subversion, and partly because the GCC states were keen not to antagonize Iran. The Iraqis were openly bitter about their exclusion, but their need for Saudi and Kuwaiti aid in the already extremely costly war with Iran outweighed any instinct to try to punish them for being excluded. Unlike Iraq, the Syrian-led Steadfastness Front countries didn't spare their criticism of the GCC as an oil-rich club subservient to US and Egyptian interests. Indeed, Oman had already restored diplomatic relations with Egypt and was developing closer military ties with it; and Cairo was increasingly vocal about playing a role in maintaining Gulf security.

At bottom, the GCC was a like-minded club, one with similar regimes, social structures, economies, and political cultures. Answering criticisms that the GCC's establishment came at the expense of the Arab League and collective Arab norms, Gulf analysts and officials emphasized that the opposite was the case, that smaller regional bodies based on cultural affinities, political homogeneity, and geographical proximity would form the ideal building blocks for achieving the still officially sacred goal of comprehensive Arab unity, albeit at a much later stage. In so doing, they hearkened back to the "kernel" concepts of Arab politics that had been widespread in the 1940s, promoted by Nuri al-Sa'id, among others, such as "the Unity of the Fertile Crescent," "Greater Syria," and "the Unity of the Nile Valley." By implication, advocates of this approach dismissed unity schemes based solely on ideology, without the necessary geographic and social components, e.g., the UAR (1958–61), the still-born Federation of Arab Republics (1971), and a recently proclaimed (1980) Syrian-Libyan unity scheme.

The GCC's declared goal was to "achieve coordination, integration, and cooperation among the member-states in all fields in order to bring about their unity."[7] In particular, much discussion, albeit little action would take place in the years ahead about the need to establish a substantially sized joint military force ("Peninsula Shield"). Achieving these goals would remain elusive, and as shown in 1990–1991, the United States would remain the ultimate protector of Saudi Arabia and Kuwait. Nonetheless, the GCC framework and attendant institutions would prove to be durable and a generally useful arm of Saudi foreign policy.

IRAQ ON THE DEFENSIVE

On June 7, 1981, Iraq suffered a blow to its prestige when an Israeli air strike destroyed its Osirak nuclear reactor, which was on the verge of coming online. The reaction in the region, and internationally, for that matter, was one of shock and public condemnation. Behind the scenes however, neither Iran, which had tried to bomb the reactor in the early days of the war, nor Iraq's Arab neighbors from across the spectrum, could have been anything but satisfied by Israel's action.

Iraq's power was waning on the battlefield as well. Iranian troops broke the siege of the city of Abadan in late September 1981, and nervous tremors went up and down the Gulf as nearby Kuwaiti oil installations were bombed, accidentally or not, by the Iranian air force. A successful Iranian offensive in Khuzistan, and an Iranian-sponsored coup attempt in Bahrain, whose majority Shi'i populace was both alienated from the regime and possessed considerable links to Iran, provided further cause for alarm among the Gulf Arabs. Iran had claimed Bahrain, which would be joined by a causeway to Saudi Arabia in 1986, as part of its national patrimony since the eighteenth century. By the spring of 1982, Iraq's troops were clearly on the defensive, and the specter of Iranian troops rolling into Iraq, and possibly Kuwait as well, seemed all too real. For Syria, which counted Iran as a strategic ally and Iraq as an unbridled enemy of both Syria and "true" all-Arab principles, it was a moment of truth. Whose side was it on?

Syrian-Iraqi relations had reached a new low by March 1982, as each faced a significant crisis—Iraq on the battlefield, the Syrian regime in its violent confrontation with the opposition Muslim Brotherhood, especially in the city of Hama, where a whole quarter would be leveled by Syrian artillery, causing the deaths of thousands. Each regime blamed the other for its troubles, sponsoring opposition groups, propaganda broadcasts, and sabotage activities, and carrying the conflict beyond their borders into other countries.

Hence, for Damascus, the choice between Iran and Iraq was clear. In mid-April 1982, Syria shut down the Iraqi oil pipeline traversing Syria to two outlets (Banyas and Tripoli, Lebanon) on the Mediterranean, and for good measure confiscated two hundred thousand tons of Iraqi oil at the Banyas refinery. Having already lost the use of its Gulf outlet at the beginning of the war, Iraq was now left with only a single operational pipeline by which to export its oil, through Turkey. Whereas Iraq had exported an average of 2.5 million barrels of oil a day before the onset of the war, earning more than $25 billion, in 1982 it barely averaged 600,000 barrels per day, earning a total of $6–$8 billion. In foregoing the $20–$40 million in annual transit fees, and the supply of Iraqi oil to Syrian refineries, Iran agreed to supply Syria with 8.7 million tons of oil for the coming year at discounted prices, and would continue to do so for many years afterward.[8] The Syrian-Iranian alliance had thus moved beyond the level of political support to open economic warfare against Saddam Husayn's regime. For Syria, the opprobrium of the Saudi-led Arab majority, which increased in tandem with Iran's military offensive, was deemed worth incurring. For the next six years, Damascus would stubbornly resist Saudi-led efforts to pry it away from Tehran. Indeed, the Syrian-Iranian alliance, commonly characterized as "unholy" due to the utterly contrasting nature of their regimes—one explicitly Shi`i Islamic, underpinned by Persian ethnic nationalism, and one explicitly secular, based on Arab nationalism—would prove to be the most durable of all Middle Eastern bilateral alliances, enduring until this day.

With the handwriting on the wall, Saddam Husayn realized it was time to try and cut his losses. Hence, on June 20, 1982, he announced that all Iraqi troops were being withdrawn from Iran, apart from enclaves that it claimed to be part of its national territory and had seized in the weeks prior to the war's outbreak. The withdrawal was completed in ten days, and a UN Security Council resolution calling for a cease-fire was adopted a fortnight later. However, while accepted by Iraq, it was rejected by Iran, which insisted that the war would not end until Saddam was appropriately punished for unleashing it in the first place.

Six more years of fighting would ensue, at an enormous cost in blood and treasure. For most of the other Arab states, the mission now became one of ensuring Iraq's survival as a bulwark against Iran. Ironically, it was the Saudi-led GCC—the objects of Iraq's ambition—and Egypt—its traditional rival, which it had consigned to pariah status just three years earlier—who came to Iraq's rescue: the Gulf states, with $60 billion of aid, and Egypt, with surplus Soviet-made weaponry and manpower. In doing so, they acted not in the name of an overarching principle of defending "the eastern flank of the Arab homeland," as Saddam liked to call Iraq, but simply to prevent Shi`i Iran from becoming the new regional hegemon. Eventually, they succeeded. Iraq's successes on the battlefield, particularly the retaking of the Fao peninsula in April 1988, and the accompanying international and regional pressure on Iran, brought the Ayatollah Khomeini to the bitter realization that Iran's ultimate aim, the punishment and overthrow of Saddam, was out of reach, and that further fighting would only work against Iran. Hence, on July 20, 1988, Khomeini announced to the nation that he was compelled to accept a cease-fire, as stipulated by UNSC Resolution 598, a decision that he likened to "drinking the poison chalice."[9] The costs of the war had been gargantuan: an estimated one million casualties and more than a trillion dollars. For the GCC states, the outcome of the war—a return to the territorial status quo ante, with no victor and no vanquished, thus preserving the existing geostrategic balance in the region—was the optimal one. Moreover, they momentarily breathed a sigh of relief, assuming that having been bloodied by the long and costly conflict, both countries would direct their energies to internal reconstruction for years to come, and not pose threats to their neighbors. However, Saddam Husayn had other ideas.

"ARAB QUAKE": THE GUNS OF AUGUST 1990

Iraq's forcible swallowing up of Kuwait, a fellow Arab League member state, on August 2, 1990, provoked the worst crisis in the history of the Arab state system. Although collective Arab norms had repeatedly been found wanting in the past, Iraq's invasion and swift refashioning of Kuwait as Iraq's "nineteenth province" constituted an unprecedentedly brazen violation of every principle and tenet contained in the Arab League Charter, not to mention the Charter of the United Nations. The response was equally unprecedented, as a small majority of Arab states joined together to participate in a US-led international war coalition that forced Iraq out of Kuwait. It was the first post-Cold War crisis, coming just after the "Soviet quake," i.e., the fall of the Berlin Wall that symbolized the end of Soviet hegemony in Eastern Europe. For the Arab system, it was the ultimate earthquake. [10]

Although no one could have predicted that Kuwait would become the prime target of his ambitions, Saddam Husayn's disquiet with the existing state of affairs, domestically and regionally, was visible from the outset of 1990. Eight years of inconclusive war with Iran had left Iraq without improved access to the Persian Gulf and with huge debts, up to $90 billion, more than a third of which it owed to the Gulf Arab states. Saddam's suggestion that they forgive the debts on the grounds that Iraq had incurred them by defending them against Iran fell on deaf ears. Budget austerity measures resulted in serious shortages of basic consumer commodities and the decline of living standards. Internationally, the crumbling of the Soviet bloc, which had provided Iraq with vital military support over the years, the emergence of the United States as the world's sole superpower, and the wave of democratization in Eastern Europe, including the demise of long-standing dictators such as Romania's Nicolae Ceauşescu, all gave Saddam pause. His responses quickly put paid to the hopes that the Arab world was entering into a more sober and cooperative era.

Saddam first mentioned Iraq's "Kuwaiti problem" to other Arabs at the May 1990 Baghdad Arab summit conference. However, neither Ku-

wait nor the other Arab states took Saddam's implied threats too seriously, believing that his bellicose rhetoric was merely a prelude to expected
Arab mediation to damp down the crisis, according to long-established
inter-Arab praxis.

However, in mid-July, Iraq made it clear that more than routine matters were at stake. On July 16, Foreign Minister Tariq ʿAziz dispatched a
long memorandum to Arab League Secretary-General Chedli Klibi detailing the alleged crimes committed against Iraq by Kuwait and the UAE,
ranging from border encroachments to a continued glutting of the oil
market. Moreover, he said, some of the surplus oil being dumped had
been stolen from Iraq's Rumayla oil field astride the Iraqi-Kuwaiti border. Lastly, Kuwait continued to insist on the repayment of aid given to
Iraq during the war with Iran, even though Iraq had been defending
Kuwait's "territory, honor, and wealth."[11] Not mentioned, but very much
present in Iraqi thinking, was the long-standing desire to improve Iraq's
access to the Persian Gulf, and thus its strategic position vis-à-vis Iran, by
leasing or annexing Kuwait's Bubiyan Island. And this in turn was underpinned by Iraq's historical claim on Kuwait, based on it having been a
part of the Ottoman province of Basra, and its unhappiness with the
British-delineated boundaries that separated Mandated Iraq from Britain's Kuwaiti protectorate.

Between Iraq's harsh words and reports of large-scale Iraqi troop
movements southward toward the Iraqi-Kuwaiti border, Kuwait was now
shaken out of its previous equanimity. It responded to Iraq's accusations
with blistering ones of its own, and encouraged Saudi Arabia to take the
lead in mediating the brewing crisis. Egypt joined in as well.

Saddam, for his part, seems to have been engaged in an elaborate
deception to mask his true intention, even as he offered Kuwait one last
chance to make major concessions. At a meeting in Jeddah under Saudi
and Egyptian auspices on July 31–August 1, the Kuwaitis were apparently now willing to cancel Iraq's $14 billion debt and lease Iraq a smaller
island at the head of the Gulf. But the Jeddah talks went nowhere, and
Saddam's deputy, ʿIzzat Ibrahim ad-Duri, quickly left for home. Contrary
to expectations, Arab mediation efforts had contributed to a further exac-
erbation of the crisis, as each side understood the outcome of the Jeddah
meeting in diametrically opposed fashion: the Kuwaitis believed that
negotiations would continue indefinitely, in the time-honored tradition of
inter-Arab conflict mediation, and without fear of an Iraqi attack, while

the Iraqis saw the others' attitude as nothing more than stonewalling.[12] Fatally, Saddam also underestimated the determination of the Western powers to stand by the principles of international law and defend their strategic interests. As a result, he concluded that the consequences of a military attack would be politically manageable. Just over twenty-four hours later, in the early hours of August 2, Iraqi helicopter units flew into Kuwait City, spearheading the lightning occupation of the country.

Ruling Arab elites were universally shocked by Iraq's invasion of Kuwait. But they were sharply divided as to the appropriate response. Two camps quickly emerged: the first, led by Saudi Arabia and Egypt, advocated unequivocal condemnation in all Arab and international forums, and support for international efforts to roll back the invasion; the second, spearheaded by Jordan, Yemen, and the PLO, tried to contain the crisis through the promotion of "an Arab solution," i.e., pacification by means of a continuous bargaining process that treated all parties' claims as negotiable, while excluding the involvement of non-Arab parties.

The Saudis were stunned by what had happened. Overnight, a new status quo had been created that, if left in place, promised to alter the Gulf region's political and military balance of power. There was also the possibility that the Iraqi army intended to occupy Saudi oilfields in northeastern Saudi Arabia. The fact that the Ottoman province of Basra, the basis of Iraq's historical claim on Kuwait, extended into this area of Saudi Arabia was not absent from Saudi thinking either. Hence, for King Fahd, the time for Arab mediation had passed, and he thus rebuffed the frantic efforts of Jordan's King Husayn. Once he became persuaded that the United States was genuinely committed to defending the kingdom and rolling back Iraqi gains by whatever means were necessary, he decided on August 6 to invite an American-led multinational force to deploy on Saudi soil. They would be joined by a coalition of Arab states led by Egypt, cobbled together at an emergency Arab summit conference held in Cairo on August 10 (for details, see chapter 7). Militarily, the Arab contribution to the eventual war in early 1991 to oust Iraqi forces from Kuwait would be insignificant, but politically, it was crucial. Syria's participation was particularly meaningful, given the fact that it had been ranged against the United States and the majority of Arab states for more than a decade. For Syria, opposing Saddam was essentially payback for having launched a war against its ally Iran, at the expense of maintaining the anti-Egyptian post-Camp David front, as well as a unique opportunity to be aligned with the Arab majority, this at a time when its long-standing superpower patron, the Soviet Union, was breaking apart.

In stark contrast, Jordan's King Husayn desperately sought an Arab solution, pleading with Mubarak and Fahd not to push Saddam into a corner, and rushing to Baghdad to urge Saddam to be flexible. Not only were Husayn's efforts unsuccessful, they created a crisis in Jordan's relations with Saudi Arabia and Kuwait that would take many years to heal.

Jordan's behavior during the crisis requires explanation. Jordan had grown increasingly close to Iraq in recent years. Economically, it had served as a crucial economic lifeline for Iraq during the Iran-Iraq War.[13] On the political-strategic side, Jordan was extremely concerned over the possible spillover of the Palestinian *intifada*, now more than eighteen months old (see chapter 10), including the expulsion of large numbers of West Bank Palestinians to Jordan: This was Jordan's nightmare scenario, one in which Israel adopted a "Jordan is Palestine" solution to its Palestinian problem at Jordan's expense. By way of response, Jordan conducted joint patrols with Iraqi air force jets near its border with Israel, a clear signal to Israel that Jordan would not stand by idly in the event of an Israeli-generated outflow of Palestinians. Moreover, Husayn's own public, particularly Jordan's large Palestinian population, was instinctively supportive of Saddam. Saddam's harsh anti-Israeli rhetoric, including threats to "burn half of Israel" in the event of a confrontation with it, resonated widely, particularly in the midst of the intifada. As for the subject of Kuwait, the wealth of the Gulf Arabs had always been a sore spot for the have-nots in the Arab world, including the Jordanians and Palestinians, Yemenis, most Egyptians, and many Moroccans as well. Saddam's rhetoric played this to the hilt, appealing to the "Arab masses" against the "rapacious oil sheikhs."[14] Hence, there was little sympathy for the Kuwaitis among Arab publics, and a widespread feeling that they had received their comeuppance. With Jordan having experienced a major economic crisis and considerable public unrest only a year earlier, King Husayn's number one priority was ensuring the stability of his regime. His conclusion was that he should swim with the tide of pan-Arab, anti-Western, and pro-Palestinian fervor, notwithstanding his own personal predilections in favor of the pro-Western, pragmatic, and legalistic orientations of the GCC states and the Egyptian authorities. This is not to say that he was part of Saddam's grand design to reorder the region, or that Husayn viewed Saddam's actions with favor after the fact, but simply that he felt compelled to maneuver in this fashion between a whirlwind of competing regional and domestic currents.[15]

The Saudis wasted no time in punishing Jordan, Yemen, and the PLO for their failure to line up behind them. As far as Riyadh was concerned, King Husayn's actions were being done at Saddam's behest. Its financial commitments to Jordan, as laid out by the 1978 Baghdad summit, and constituting 15 percent of Jordan's annual budget, ceased entirely, as did Saudi shipments of oil to Jordan. A number of Jordanian diplomats were expelled from Riyadh, and the Saudis also reportedly stepped up covert support for major tribes and clans in southern Jordan contiguous to the Saudi border. Concurrently, King Husayn's directive to the Jordanian media that he be referred to as a sharif, a descendant of the Prophet Muhammad, touched a raw Saudi nerve, as it served as a reminder of the expulsion of the Hashimites from the Hijaz by the Saudis in 1926, and this at a time when Iraqi propaganda was insisting that the Al Saud had forfeited its religious legitimacy as "protector of the two holy shrines" (*Khadim al-Haramayn*; Mecca and Madina) by inviting in "infidels" to desecrate sacred Islamic ground. The theme would be picked up by Osama bin Laden and like-minded jihadis in subsequent years, with deadly consequences.

Yemen had found itself in a similar dilemma to Jordan, having also benefitted from Iraqi aid, and now torn between Western and Arab pressures to toe the line, and Iraqi blandishments not to. Moreover, as the holder of the rotating Arab seat on the UN Security Council, Yemen was especially exposed. For the Saudis, though, there could be no shades of gray, hence Yemen's efforts to remain neutral were seen as pro-Iraqi. The consequences were harsh. Saudi Arabia imposed strict residency requirements on the more than one million Yemenis working in Saudi Arabia, resulting in a swift mass exodus of up to eight hundred thousand Yemenis, with all the attendant economic damage and personal hardship. The Saudis also renewed their time-honored tactic of supporting anti-government tribes adjacent to the Saudi border.

THE DENOUEMENT AND BEYOND

Throughout the five-month military buildup of the anti-Saddam coalition, Saddam sought to drape himself in the mantle of ʿAbd al-Nasir, present-

ing himself as a hero of the Arab masses standing against Western imperial powers, Israeli-Zionist colonialists, and mendacious Arab leaders,
particularly the oil-rich sheikhs of the Gulf. He may have also had the
1956 Suez war in mind, which conferred a great political victory on Nasir
at the expense of Britain and France. But this was not 1956, popularity in
the "Arab street" did not translate into the destabilization of opposing
regimes, and Saddam was not Nasir.

Operation Desert Storm, the six-week US-led military campaign to
evict Iraq from Kuwait, achieved its goal of forcing Iraqi forces to withdraw from Kuwait, after suffering heavy losses. The crushing defeat of
Iraq and the imposition of strict UN-mandated sanctions against Saddam
Hussein's regime permanently neutralized Iraq's ability to be a serious
actor in Arab politics.

To be sure, Saddam was able to quickly regroup his forces and survive
the debacle wrought by his brazen adventurism. In the days and weeks
after the war's end, the Iraqi army brutally beat back a Shi`i rebellion in
Iraq's south and a similar Kurdish rebellion in the north. In the latter case,
however, Iraq lost effective control over a portion of its sovereign territory, thanks to the belated establishment of an Allied-protected Kurdish
zone beyond the reach of the Baghdad authorities. This outcome undermined the conceptual basis of the Iraqi state since its establishment, and
gave a historic boost to Kurdish national aspirations. In retrospect, it was
the beginning of the end for the Sunni Arab-dominated Iraqi state that had
been created after World War I.

THE KURDISH PHOENIX

In contrast to the other main ethnic groups in the Near East and Mesopotamia—Turks, Arabs, and Iranians, all of which acquired or strengthened
their existing territorial bases in the post-World War I settlement—the
region's large Kurdish-speaking populations were complete losers. The
1920 Treaty of Sevrès had included a provision for Kurdish national
expression, but the treaty became a dead letter in light of Turkish national
reassertion under Mustafa Kemal Attatürk. The resulting Treaty of Lausanne (1923) established the borders of the independent Turkish Republic. Greater Kurdistan was divided among four main neighboring states—
Turkey, Syria, Iraq, and Iran (with a small number in the Soviet Union's

territories as well)—none of which were willing to widen their collective national self-definitions to include ethnic Kurds. Republican Turkey, which contained by far the largest concentration of Kurds (constituting 20 percent of the country's population), would brook absolutely no manifestation of collective Kurdish identity, to the point where the word "Kurd" was banned from the official lexicon, being replaced by "mountain Turks." The result of decades of repression and neglect of the mostly Kurdish southeast region of Turkey would be a sustained and violent revolt by the Kurdish Workers Party (PKK), beginning in 1984 and claiming over thirty thousand lives.[16] Syria's much smaller Kurdish community in the northeast region, constituting less than ten percent of the population, would be similarly neglected, and even deprived of Syrian citizenship in many cases. In Iraq, where the problematic nation-building and state-building processes were led by the minority Sunni Arab community, Kurds were in an almost continuous state of rebellion. In 1970, the Ba`th Party regime sought to buy time to consolidate its hold on power and remove more threatening political enemies, and thus announced a far-reaching autonomy plan for the Iraqi Kurdistan region. However, this quickly proved to be a dead letter, and the Kurds rose in revolt, with the support of Iran, Israel, and the United States, only to lose out in 1975 as part of the Iranian-Iraqi deal consecrated in Algiers. Throughout the 1980s, Iraqi Kurds were subjected to the extreme brutalization of the regime's Anfal campaign, involving the eradication of hundreds of villages and the forcible transfer of their population to remote areas, resulting in an estimated one hundred thousand deaths.[17] The single most infamous episode was the use of poison gas against the village of Halabja, which was suspected of supporting Iranian armed units who had penetrated into the area, resulting in over five thousand fatalities. No wonder then that the Kurds rose up again in March 1991, simultaneously with the Shi`i south, as the Iraqi regime appeared to be tottering. As Saddam's army retaliated, more than one million persons fled to the mountains. Many died from the extreme weather conditions they encountered, before the US belatedly set up a protected region where authority would be uneasily shared by the two rival parties, the Kurdish Democratic Party (KDP) and the Patriotic Union of Kurdistan (PUK).

In essence, the establishment of the American-protected Kurdish autonomous region was the first crack in the territorial state system in the Arab Middle East that had been laid out at the end of World War I but only recently consolidated with the fading of the pan-Arab dream. The fledgling Kurdish entity would experience a major crisis in 1996, with Saddam Husayn momentarily regaining some influence as the KDP and PUK came to blows and the KDP reestablished ties with Baghdad as part of its struggle. But this episode passed, and the two groups agreed on certain power-sharing arrangements. Although the strident opposition of all of the surrounding countries to the idea of an independent Kurdish state made it premature for Kurds to speak openly of secession, Iraq's already frayed cohesion and territorial unity was being further eroded daily as the Kurdish entity took on a life of its own. Nation-building efforts included the foregrounding of Kurdish identity and history, and emphasis on the teaching of the Kurdish language at the expense of Arabic, thus reversing decades of state policies of Arabization.

IRAQ AND ARABISM: THE END OF AN ERA

By the beginning of the new century, most other Arab states were keen on bringing Iraq back into the Arab fold. The steady erosion of support in the Arab street and among many Arab governments for the international sanctions regime, and the widespread sympathy with the sufferings of the Iraqi people, attributed to the sanctions, had weakened the Kuwaiti-Saudi insistence on holding Iraq accountable for its actions in 1990–1991 and as a price for Iraq's reentry into the Arab system as a member in good standing. Iraq's continuing weakness and isolation was also understood by Sunni Arab elites to be Shi`i Persian Iran's gain, strategically speaking. However, the United States had other ideas.

The 2003 US War in Iraq

The September 11, 2001, bombings of US targets by al-Qa`ida operatives fundamentally altered American thinking about the region. Although the US quickly brought its military might to bear in Afghanistan against al-Qa`ida and its host, the Taliban regime, American officials, from the president and vice president on down, quickly concluded that an opportunity to conclude America's unfinished business with Iraq was at hand, and the countdown to war began. Over the next eighteen months, the United States prepared a case for war that centered on Iraq's alleged continuing clandestine programs to develop nuclear, chemical, and bio-logical weapons and failure to cooperate with UN inspectors whose job it was to unearth and destroy them. But beyond the declared goal of remov-ing the threat posed by Saddam's alleged arsenal, senior US administra-tion officials were guided by a larger agenda, one that saw regime change in Iraq as a first step toward reforming and democratizing the Arab world. According to their logic, the rise of Islamic extremism and terrorism, so shockingly manifested in the 9/11 bombings, and supported by Iraq and Iran, members of what President George W. Bush called the "Axis of Evil," was the unwanted outcome of decades of repressive authoritarian rule, often supported by the US. Guided by the models of the reconstruc-tion of post-war Germany and Japan, a new Iraq could be fashioned under American tutelage—one that would be genuinely representative of its variegated population, governed by the rule of law. The new Iraqi order would serve as an example for the rest of the Arab world, the "swamp of extremism" would gradually be drained, and the Middle East members of the "axis of evil"—Iraq, Iran, and Libya—would be contained and even-tually toppled, and replaced by more benign and liberal-democratic re-gimes. It was a uniquely American approach, meshing the country's deep-rooted ideals and extraordinary military power along with, in the case of President Bush, a sincere and powerful evangelical Christian faith. It would turn out to be a fundamentally flawed vision, radically out of touch with the realities on the ground.

By March 2003, an American-led coalition of forces was ready to do what the 1991 Western-Arab military coalition had studiously refrained from doing, namely marching to Baghdad and overthrowing the regime.

The powerlessness of Arab states to prevent such an occurrence was obvious to all. So was the resignation of most to its inevitability, the ambivalence of some, and quiet support by others, for the forthcoming American operation, even in the absence of an authorizing UN Security Council resolution. A last-minute Arab summit conference in Egypt's Sharm al-Shaykh called for nonparticipation in the expected war, but also for Saddam to comply fully with all UN resolutions, which would prevent the war from taking place. UN inspectors, they said, should be given more time to complete their work. Arab League Secretary-General `Amr Musa expressed the prevailing mood, asking: "What's the hurry to con-duct a war that is extremely unpopular in the region, in the world, and unjustified? We don't understand why." While Qaddafi blamed Saudi

Arabia for originally introducing US troops into the region, and Asad warned Arab leaders that they too would become victims of US military power, the GCC states placed the blame for the current situation on Saddam. The UAE even tendered a proposal calling on Saddam to step down in order to avert war, and for the Arab League and the UN to jointly supervise a transitional period to a new order.[18]

It was all for naught, as the die had been cast. On March 19, US-led forces launched a massive military campaign. Its Gulf Arab allies provided support in a variety of ways. But on the whole, Arab states were reduced to anxious passivity. On April 9, coalition forces occupied Baghdad, and Saddam Husayn fled into hiding. He would be eventually captured, tried along with a number of his senior officials by an Iraqi court, and executed on December 30, 2006. On May 1, 2003, President Bush made a ringing declaration of "mission accomplished."

However, the reality would be far different, and Washington's grand vision was quickly shown to be divorced from Iraqi and regional realities. The destruction of the Ba`th totalitarian regime had been straightforward, but the construction of a new Iraq under American guidance was anything but that. Iraqi Shi`is had ridden the backs of American troops to power, after having been excluded and marginalized since Iraq's establishment. Although ethnically Arab,[19] their cultural and religious ties to neighboring Iran had long made them suspect in the eyes of Iraq's Sunni Arab rulers. Now the tables were turned, and it was the Sunnis who were the sullen and defensive minority. As the remnants of Saddam's forces and Ba`thi leadership regrouped and initiated an increasingly violent insurgency against the new Shi`i-dominated government and its American patrons, they found much support among Iraq's Sunni tribes. To be sure, both the Sunni and Shi`i communities were hardly homogenous, and the power struggles within each community were not bereft of violence. But the bloodletting between the two communities over the next decade was massive. Notwithstanding Ba`thi totalitarianism (and perhaps partly because of it), Baghdad had become a mixed city in which Sunnis and Shi`is often lived as neighbors and business partners, and even married one another. The post-2003 civil war put paid to all that. Moreover, Sunni foreign fighters flocked to Iraq to join what they viewed as a *jihad* against the American occupation and its local Shi`i allies. Ironically, the Americans had spuriously linked al-Qa`ida to Saddam Husayn in an effort to justify the war, but now they were confronted with an actual al-

Qa`ida branch, established to oppose them in Iraq, and enabled by a Syrian regime that, while not Sunni, wanted to undermine the US democracy project for the region. From the other side, US troops were also targeted by the radical Shi`i militia of Moqtada al-Sadr. Over the course of the next decade, American power in the region would be severely sapped by its entanglements in Iraq and Afghanistan. Moreover, the Sunni-Shi'i divide, always present throughout the fourteen hundred years of Islamic history but not always politically salient, now became an important feature of the regional political landscape.

As for Iraq's place in the Arab firmament, it was no longer just the "odd man out" in the Arab state system. Its very identity as an Arab state was now open to question on a number of counts. Its governing elite, led by the prime minister, was a Shi`i, and patronized by Iran. Its new president, a largely ceremonial post under the new constitution, was not even an ethnic Arab, but a Kurd; the Kurdish Regional Government, whose *peshmerga* forces had participated in the Americans' march on Baghdad, was rapidly consolidating an autonomous, quasi-independent status. Iraq's new constitution, issued on January 30, 2005, and ratified in a nationwide referendum eight months later, loftily proclaimed Iraq to be "a country of multiple nationalities, religions, and sects…a founding and active member in the Arab League…committed to its charter, and… part of the Islamic world."[20] Moreover, Kurdish was recognized as an official language, along with Arabic, marking the first time that an Arab League member had given official status to a language other than Arabic. For the region's Sunni Arab states desirous of an explicitly defined "Arab" Iraq, the new constitution was hardly satisfying. And translating the lofty principles of the constitution into reality appeared to be an impossible task.

Although Iraqi Arab nationalism had been from the outset a primarily Sunni project, and in its Ba`thi version resembled Stalinist totalitarianism far more than the modernist quasi-secular values tendered by the founding Arab *nahda* generation a century earlier, post-monarchical Iraq had provided a measure of security for its mostly eastern Christian Arabic-speaking minorities, one of whom, longtime foreign minister Tariq `Aziz, was a member of the Ba`th's ruling Revolutionary Command Council. Now, however, Iraqi Christians found themselves increasingly under siege, a choice and defenseless target for Sunni jihadi insurgents. Over the ensuing decade, the community's size would be substantially denuded by emigration, raising serious questions regarding its long-term survival in the country.

THE SUNNI-SHI`I DIVIDE AND SHIFTING REGIONAL ALIGNMENTS

The question of Iraq's Arab identity was not merely theoretical or academic for its Sunni Arab neighbors. A predominantly Shi`i regime under the influence of Iran was the very antithesis, in their view, of what it meant to be an Arab state. Although Saddam Husayn had not been a member in good standing of the "club" of Arab states since his ill-fated occupation of Kuwait, at least he had stood as a buffer against Persian Shi`i hegemonic-minded and revolutionary Islamic Iran. Now the buffer had been removed, and the geopolitical ramifications were profound. Most Arab states refrained from establishing full diplomatic ties with the new rulers in Baghdad, and Arab regimes clearly sympathized with Iraq's hard-pressed Sunnis. As Iraq descended into a brutal civil war, moral and material support from wealthy Gulf Arab patrons, with at least the tacit support of their governments, helped sustain the Sunni insurgency.

An American military surge in 2007 was crucial in stabilizing the situation on the ground. But the fundamental obstacles to establishing a cohesive and legitimate political order remained. In fact, under Shi`i Prime Minister Nuri al-Maliki's heavy hand, and contrary to the repeated entreaties of his American patron, Iraq's Sunni Arab became ever more marginalized, repressed, and alienated. In December 2011, Tariq al-Hashimi, a leading Sunni Arab politician in the party opposed to Maliki, and who actually held one of the government's two vice presidential posts, fled to the safety of the Kurdish Regional Government to avoid arrest by the Baghdad authorities on trumped-up charges that included an accusation of treason. The failure to establish a viable, legitimate, and inclusive order in post-Ba`th Iraq had been obvious for years, but the sudden and dramatic loss of wide swaths of Iraqi territory in 2014 to a new Sunni-jihadi organization supported by ex-Iraqi Ba`th army leaders, the Islamic State highlighted just how fractured and dysfunctional Iraq had become (for details, see chapter 11).

9

SYRIA UNDER THE ASAD DYNASTY

From Weak State to Aspiring Regional Power
(1970–2010)

On November 13, 1970, less than two months after Nasir's death and Sadat's assumption of power, a bloodless coup in Syria brought Defense Minister Hafiz al-Asad to power. Proclaimed a "corrective movement," it was the last in the succession of military coups that had plagued Syria since 1949 and left it internally weak and vulnerable to rival Arab ambitions. From this point on, Syria would know forty years of regime continuity headed by Asad (d. 2000) and then by his son Bashar, in what essentially constituted a presidential dynasty (*gumlukiyya,* a neologism coined by the Egyptian sociologist Saad Eddin Ibrahim that combined the Arabic words for republic (*gumhuriyya*, in Egyptian Arabic) and monarchy (*malakiyya*).[1] In terms of state-building and nation-building processes and its relationship to Arabism, the Asad regimes essentially downgraded Ba`thi ideology even while maintaining the party's institutional shell as a tool for governing. It would promote, in Christopher Phillips's words, a "deliberately malleable and multi-layered identity," a Syrian territorial nationalism that incorporated pan-Arab and pan-Syrian elements.[2] No longer would the Syrian state be a candidate for merger in the name of pan-Arab unity, an option that essentially derived from its internal weakness and lack of cohesion. Rather, it would succeed, to a considerable degree, in turning the tables, projecting power outward as it sought to carve out a sphere of influence in its immediate Arab environs (Leba-

non, Jordan, and the Palestinian movement), attempting to alter the existing unfavorable balance of power with Israel, cope with its next door
Iraqi Ba'thi rival, and maintain its alliance with the Soviet Union while
opening lines of communication to the United States. Following the 1979
Iranian Islamic revolution, Syria would establish a strategic relationship
with Iran that endures to this day, and has proven crucial to the regime's
survival during the brutal civil war of the last five years. Syria's transformation from regional object to regional actor in difficult surroundings
also altered the nature of its frequently contentious relations with Turkey.

All of this would be made possible by the regime's success in consoli-
dating its authority at home, including the crushing of any and all opposition. Like Saddam's Iraq, Syria was a "fierce" state, ultimately dominated
by the intelligence and security services. Over time, the Alawi ruling core
of the regime would be surrounded by a coalition of Sunni merchants and
Christian and Druze minorities, all of whom derived material benefit
from their affiliation with it.[3] An integral part of the regime's domination
of Syrian society was the development of what Lisa Wedeen called the
"shabby cult" that venerated Asad: although it failed to produce the desired legitimacy, it was a useful disciplinary device generating public
dissimulation.[4]

More often than not during this forty-year period, Syria was in a
minority among Arab states regarding the central issues of the day—the
Arab-Israeli conflict, the Iran-Iraq war, Iran's expanding power projec-
tion in the region, Syria's heavy-handed domination of Lebanon and
similar efforts to dominate the Palestinian movement, and its close alliance with the Soviet Union and corresponding hostility toward the US.
As a pivotal state involved in many of the political crosscurrents in the
region, Syria could be neither dictated to nor ignored, hence the overall
modus operandi of other important Arab states was to try to coax Syria
into changing its policies, knowing full well that they could not force it to
do so. And when Syria did line up with the two leading conservative, pro-
Western Arab states, Egypt and Saudi Arabia—in the October 1973 War;
in bringing a halt to the Lebanese civil war in 1976; during the
1990–1991 Gulf Crisis; and in agreeing to participate in the Madrid
framework for Arab-Israeli negotiations in the 1990s—the results were
more favorable.

Some of these matters are covered in chapters 7 and 8. To avoid
excessive overlap, this chapter will focus on Syria's actions in its imme-

diate environs—Lebanon, the Arab-Israeli arena, the Palestinians, and Jordan.

LEBANON, THE ARAB-ISRAELI CONFLICT, AND ARAB SUMMITRY

Generations of Syrian Arab nationalists had viewed Lebanon as an integral part of the Syrian homeland that had been unjustly severed from it by the Western powers after World War I. Lebanon's Sunni elite initially was of the same view, but gradually forged a workable power-sharing arrangement with Lebanon's traditionally dominant Maronite Christians. In order that Lebanon's attainment of independence in 1943 would be accepted by neighboring Syria and Lebanese Sunnis, it was conditioned on Lebanon's maintaining "an Arab face," namely, that it would not act contrary to collective Arab values and orient itself in opposition to Arab interests. Although Syria accepted Lebanon's independence and inclusion as a founding member of the Arab League, Damascus continuously refrained from opening an embassy in Beirut, on the grounds that the bonds between the two "fraternal" countries were so "intimate" and "natural" that they needed no formalization of the kind that embassies signified. Beginning in 1976, this intimacy would become far more concrete and consequential.

Lebanon's "precarious republic"[5] was based on an intricate power-sharing arrangement between its numerous confessional groups whose loyalty to their respective communities continued to take precedence over loyalty to the state. The country's fragile stability would be momentarily threatened in 1958 by a mini-civil war between competing Christian and Sunni Muslim groups, the latter unhappy with the existing state of affairs and under the influence of the radical pan-Arab wave that had just established the UAR. Stability was eventually restored, which would last for approximately a decade. But following the June 1967 Arab-Israeli War, Lebanon was inexorably drawn into the Arab-Israeli conflict, as newly emergent Palestinian armed factions began using Lebanon as a base for cross-border attacks against Israel and commercial airline hijackings. In this, they were strongly supported by the large Palestinian refugee population in Lebanon. Israel's attempt to hold the Lebanese state accountable faltered in the face of the weakness of state institutions, a weakness reinforced by the sympathies the Palestinian cause evoked among a broad sector of Lebanese Sunni Muslim population, the leftist Nasirist pan-Arabist current that was prominent in Beirut's university circles, and Nasir himself. As a result, the first attempt to regulate the Palestinian presence in Lebanon, the 1969 Cairo Agreement, was an abject failure. And following the Jordanian authorities' crackdown on Palestinian armed factions in September 1970 and additional Jordanian operations against Palestinian enclaves in northern Jordan in June 1971, the PLO's operations were relocated entirely to Lebanon. Over time, the Fakhani district of West Beirut would become a de facto Palestinian political and cultural capital, eventually acquiring the moniker *al-watan al-badil* ("the alternative homeland"). For Lebanon, which had been spared the violence of the Arab-Israeli conflict between 1949 and 1967, the extension of the conflict to its territory would prove to be catastrophic.

Meanwhile, the display of Arab military and economic power in 1973–1974, a product of the Egyptian-Syrian-Saudi wartime alliance against Israel, aroused hope among some Arab pundits and within the Arab public that a fundamental breakthrough had been achieved, namely that the promise of Arab might and a redressing of the historic imbalance of power between the Arab world and the West, epitomized by Israel's establishment and subsequent military successes, was finally being achieved. However, the outbreak of civil war in Lebanon quickly put paid to that notion.[6]

By early 1975, Lebanon's fragile sociopolitical order was under profound stress on all counts—political, socioeconomic, intercommunal, and regional. Differing birth rates had resulted in a Muslim majority, but the power-sharing formula devised in 1943 remained favorable to Lebanon's Christians, and particularly its largest and most deeply rooted Christian community, the Maronites. Stirrings among Lebanon's traditionally marginalized and economically deprived Shi`is added to the tension, as did Syria's increasing power projection in Lebanon, through various Lebanese communities, the Ba`th party's Lebanese branch, and the presence of five hundred thousand Syrian laborers in the country. What finally tipped the balance was the PLO's actons: the support for the Palestinian cause among Lebanese Muslims and leftist groups and reciprocal PLO support for the anti-status quo forces placed it on a collision course with Lebanon's Maronites, and particularly its Phalange militia. As a result,

Lebanon would not only descend into intercommunal violence but become a cockpit for many of the region's cross-currents.

The violence began in earnest in April 1975 with serious clashes between Phalange and Palestinian factions in Beirut neighborhoods, who would end up providing the bulk of the anti-status quo National Front forces. Within months, the Lebanese Army, the most tangible institution of the country's fragile statehood and societal comity, had essentially collapsed, with many of its soldiers joining the militias of their respective ethno-confessional groups, or simply refusing to carry out orders to engage in combat.

As noted in chapter 7, the Syrian leadership viewed the Israeli-Egyptian Sinai II disengagement agreement, signed on September 4, 1975, in the most severe terms. Moreover, the subsequent intensification of attacks by the forces of the Maronite-led Lebanese Front forces, which Syria viewed as supported by Israel, seemed to prove Syria's complaint that Israel now had greater freedom of action in the region. Hence, Syrian anger with Egypt was expressed with a venom not witnessed since the mid-'60s. And in a further complication, the Iraqi Ba'th leadership gleefully attacked Asad from the left, mocking Syria's 1974 disengagement of forces agreement with Israel as constituting the very same defeatism and betrayal of which he was accusing Sadat. The poisoned atmosphere between Baghdad and Damascus wasn't just ideologically driven: Iraq charged that Syria's recently built Great Euphrates Dam at Tabqa was depriving downstream Iraqi peasants with vital water supplies, leading to the mobilization of Iraqi troops on Syria's border in 1975.

In January 1976, the Lebanese civil war entered a new phase, as Syria intervened militarily, albeit reluctantly, in order to stabilize the situation there and prevent any side from gaining a decisive advantage, something that was likely to impact negatively on Syria's overall strategic interests. As is so often the case with military interventions, what was intended to be a temporary action limited in scope became something far larger, lasting thirty years. Initially, Syrian-based units of the Palestine Liberation Army (PLA; established originally in 1964 as the PLO's military wing) were deployed to Lebanon to counter the gains of the Lebanese Front that seemed to augur the establishment of an independent Christian entity in Mount Lebanon. Such a scenario had been a nightmare for generations of Syrian (and Lebanese) Arab nationalists. Branded as "Christian Zionism," it suggested an alternative political model, the

autonomous rule of ethno-sectarian communities in the Levant that, if
legitimized, would pose a threat to the hegemonic status of Arab nationalism as the ideological glue holding Syria together. It also would have
immediate strategic consequences, given the likelihood of good relations
between Israel and what would be essentially a neighboring "non-Arab"
entity. Indeed, clandestine relations already existed, as Israel had begun
providing tangible military assistance to the Lebanese Front that would
increase substantially in the coming months and years, ultimately resulting in a strategic war-time alliance in 1982.

Fighting resumed in the spring of 1976, this time with the Lebanese
Front in an inferior position. Now, the primary Syrian concern was preventing the Front's defeat, and the likely establishment of a more militant, leftist Arab nationalist state in Lebanon along the lines being vocally
advocated by Syria's Ba`thi twin and rival, Iraq. The strategic implica-
tions of this outcome for Syria were no less dire, as Israel was hardly
likely to sit by idly while a militant entity bent on confrontation emerged
on its northern border. Damascus would be powerless to prevent any
resulting Israeli military action, and was likely to suffer from it as well.
Ironically, Syria now found itself in a position similar to the one it had
placed Nasir in the mid-1960s, torn between ideology and *raison d'état*.
The matter was resolved by reluctant but tangible support for the Lebanese Front against PLO and Lebanese Muslim forces, highlighted by the
Front's lengthy siege of the Palestinian Tel al-Za`tar refugee camp out-
side of Beirut, which resulted in up to three thousand Palestinian deaths,
mostly civilians. In an extraordinary turn of events, Syria and Israel were
now both supporting the same side in the conflict, and they quietly
worked out an understanding in which Israel would not challenge the
entry of Syrian troops into Lebanon as long as they kept their distance
from the Israeli-Lebanese border. (The agreement would last for approximately five years before unraveling.) Syria's actions were so at odds with
its ideological principles that Asad came in for extraordinary criticism
within the Ba`th leadership, compelling him to address the issue at length
in a July 22, 1976, speech to the Ba`th party congress.[7]

By mid-October 1976, Asad had basically achieved his aims of ensuring a "no victor, no vanquished" outcome of the fighting under a Syrian
umbrella, and was now ready to start repairing relations with his Arab
neighbors. His desire was made more acute by the fact that a US presidential election was only weeks away, heralding the imminent renewal of

US-led Arab-Israeli diplomacy, which for Syria would require maximum inter-Arab coordination in order to safeguard and advance its interests. Egypt and Saudi Arabia, each for its own reasons, were of a similar mind. Hence, Saudi and Kuwaiti urgings for reconciliation now bore fruit. A restricted summit conference hosted by Saudi Arabia's King Khalid in Riyadh on October 16–18[8] produced broad understandings and crucial trade-offs among the three lynchpins of the 1973 Arab war coalition regarding Lebanon and the Arab-Israeli arena. These were then endorsed in a full Arab summit conference in Cairo the following week. Syria's status as the overseer of Lebanon was confirmed, de facto: its forces in Lebanon were legitimized as peacekeepers, while being ostensibly placed under collective Arab offices. Rebranded as the Arab Deterrent Forces (*quwwat al-rida` al-`arabiyya*), they were to be joined by symbolic contingents from Saudi Arabia, the UAE, and Sudan (units of the PLA, commanded by Syria, also participated). In return, Syria agreed to cease all hostile propaganda attacks against Egypt, and Egypt's status as the principle Arab actor in the upcoming rounds of Arab-Israeli diplomacy was confirmed.

However, the renewal of the 1973 Egyptian-Saudi-Syrian alliance proved to be short-lived, thanks to Sadat's peacemaking initiative in November 1977. As recounted in previous chapters, Syria would fail in its effort to shore up its regional position through a rapprochement with Iraq in 1978–79, and had to satisfy itself with leading a less-imposing bloc of radical Arab states opposed to the Egyptian-Israeli peace agreement, the Steadfastness Front (made up of Algeria, Libya, South Yemen, and the PLO, in addition to Syria). However, it also succeeded in forging a strategic alliance with non-Arab Iran, ignoring accusations from Saddam Hussain and others that in doing so, Syria was betraying a fundamental principle of Arab solidarity. The basic principles of Arab nationalism embodied in the Arab League Charter appeared less operative than ever.

Rarely was there a less propitious moment for an Arab summit conference than the months immediately after the outbreak of the Iran-Iraq war in September 1980, but Jordan, the designated host country for the previously planned gathering, was keen on it going forward. Since 1967, King Husayn had gradually managed to place Jordan within the broad Arab consensus on most issues, and thus achieve a hard-won legitimacy for his regime and the kingdom's very existence. The original plan for the summit was that it would focus on longer-term development issues, something that was very much to Jordan's liking, given its need for large-scale aid from the oil-rich Arab countries. However, the outbreak of the Iran-Iraq war changed the context entirely. Iraq was intent on receiving a full-throated endorsement of its "defense of the Arab homeland...against the racist Persian aggressors." Jordan, having been one of only a handful of Arab countries that had lined up foursquare behind Iraq from the war's outset, was an ideal host country from Baghdad's perspective.

Syria, on the other hand, was utterly opposed to the summit's convening. All year long it had been an outlier in Arab politics, failing to condemn the December 1979 Soviet invasion of Afghanistan, opposing Iraq's regional ascent, demanding but not receiving greater support vis-à-vis Israel, and now condemning Iraq for attacking Iran. From Damascus's point of view, Iran had ceased being an American client state and become overnight a strategic regional ally against Israel, where the real priority lay. As the government newspaper *Tishrin* explained, Iraq's "fabricated war" against Iran was diverting the Arab nation's attention from "pan-Arab duties." By doing so, Iraq was objectively, and perhaps even intentionally, serving the interests of the "tripartite alliance of Camp David."[9]

Unable to achieve the summit's postponement, Syria boycotted it. Moreover, it persuaded its four fellow Steadfastness Front members to do the same, and Lebanon as well, which was now under its thumb.

In case Syria's message wasn't fully clear, namely that no meaningful summit could be held without it, Damascus also took more direct action, mobilizing its troops along the Jordanian border. The Jordanians responded in kind, and by the first week of December, thirty thousand troops from each side found themselves in a face-off. Syria's justification was that King Husayn was intending to replace the PLO as the representative of Palestinian interests, and also that it was actively supporting subversion efforts by the Syrian Muslim Brotherhood opposition, including providing them with training camps. In fact, Asad had already personally accused King Husayn of being partially responsible for the blood then being shed in Syria.[10] The early months of 1981 witnessed new verbal charges and countercharges in the wake of the kidnapping of a Jordanian diplomat in Beirut and Jordan's arrest of a Syrian hit squad allegedly planning to assassinate Jordan's prime minister, Mudar Badran. The mutual invective touched on an old, supposedly resolved issue—namely the very legitimacy of multiple Arab states, with each side marshaling the traditional theme of Arabism to attack the other: Husayn and his "illegitimate regime," said the Syrians, was the primary impediment to Arab unity; the Jordanians, in return, labeled the Syrian regime "sectarian," owing to the `Alawi core of the regime, in which it masked its "anti-Arab outlook" by propagating "false pan-Arab slogans."[11]

Meanwhile, in Lebanon, Syria continued to strive to maintain its hegemony, with mixed results. The withdrawal of the small Saudi, Sudanese, and UAE contingents from the Arab Deterrent Forces left Syria with sole Arab responsibility for maintaining the fragile order there, which was just fine with Asad. But it wasn't fine for the Lebanese Forces, and in the spring of 1981, a confrontation between them and Syria led to Israeli action on the latter's behalf against Syrian helicopters. Syria deployed SAM anti-aircraft missiles in Lebanon as a response. Israeli-PLO fighting in southern Lebanon also escalated, until a cease-fire was brokered by the US in July 1981.

THE FEZ SUMMITS

Shortly afterward, Saudi Crown Prince Fahd bin `Abd al-`Aziz issued an eight-point plan outlining the principles that he believed should form the basis of an Arab-Israeli peace agreement. While including the standard collective Arab positions regarding the need for a full and speedy Israeli withdrawal to the June 4, 1967, lines, the establishment of a Palestinian state with Jerusalem as its capital, and an "affirmation of the right of the Palestinian people to return to their homes," Point Seven of the plan also affirmed the principle that "all states in the region should be able to live in peace."[12] The plan was issued with an eye on the US Congress, which was debating the sale of advanced AWACS surveillance aircraft to Saudi Arabia, and as an alternative to Anwar al-Sadat's own concurrent diplomatic efforts in Washington. The yawning chasm between the Fahd plan and Israel's minimum requirements rendered it a non-starter in terms of operative value. But within the Arab world, the Plan, and particularly Point Seven, raised considerable hackles, for it ran directly counter to Khartoum's "Three No's" of 1967, and to the spirit of the 1978 Baghdad summit resolutions. Moreover, in an unprecedented assertion of leadership, Saudi Arabia decided to seek collective Arab support of the plan, via the upcoming November Arab Summit conference in Fez, Morocco. The Saudi leadership also hoped that the summit's endorsement of the plan would pave the way for Egypt's return to the Arab fold, following Sadat's assassination the previous month. Instead, however, the summit would be suspended after just one four-hour session, highlighting the limitations on Riyadh's capacity to exert leadership in inter-Arab affairs and the continuing salience of inter-Arab divisions. The Saudi plan had managed to temporarily reunite Iraq and Syria—the two main foes of the Sadat initiative, but also the two bitterest rivals among all of the Arab states. The plan had also placed the PLO in an even more difficult position than it had been in at the Amman summit a year earlier: caught between the Saudis, their prime political and financial backer, and Syria, their main patron on the ground in Lebanon, and on an issue which for them was existential. Iraq was uncomfortable, too, as it needed Saudi support in the war against Iran. But Point Seven was too much for Baghdad to swallow. Given the inability to fashion a broad consensus around the Saudi plan, the summit's host, Morocco's King Hasan, could only angrily suspend the summit, while criticizing Hafiz al-Asad and other Arab leaders for their "irresponsibility" by failing to personally attend the summit and delegate lower-ranking representatives in their stead.[13]

The July 1981 PLO-Israeli fighting had left Israel determined to prevent the PLO from further deepening its hold in southern Lebanon and its ability to shell northern Israeli towns and villages. Moreover, the renewal of the Lebanese civil war, and Israel's deepening support for the anti-Syrian and anti-Palestinian Christian Lebanese Front, had encouraged Israeli decision-makers, particularly Defense Minister Ariel Sharon, to think big. When a renegade Palestinian faction attempted to assassinate Israel's ambassador to London on June 3, 1982, Israel had the pretext it needed. Three days later, and just over one month after the completion of their withdrawal from Sinai, Israeli forces stormed into Lebanon in an effort to deal a mortal blow to the PLO and fundamentally alter the strategic equation in the region. Within one week, Israeli troops had conquered all of southern Lebanon up to the outskirts of Beirut, dismantling PLO positions in southern Lebanon. It also dealt a major blow to the Syrian military, destroying its missile defense system installed in Lebanon a year earlier, downing more than eighty Syrian jets while losing just one of its own, and pushing Syria back beyond the strategic Beirut-Damascus highway. In early September, a US-brokered agreement led to the departure of Yasir `Arafat and accompanying PLO officials and fighters from Beirut. With Israeli ally Bashir Gemayel newly elected to the presidency of Lebanon, Israel's larger strategic war aims momentarily seemed in reach. However, on September 14, 1982, Bashir was assassinated in a massive bomb blast that completely leveled his Phalangist party headquarters, undoubtedly by a Syrian hand. It was the first of a long series of actions by Syria that would prevent Israel from attaining its aims in Lebanon and enable Damascus to restore its hegemony there.

Before that, however, Arab leaders gathered in Fez for a summit conference. Throughout the war, the absence of a meaningful collective Arab response to Israel's military offensive against the PLO and Syria, which brought it to the gates of an Arab capital city for the first time in the history of the conflict, had highlighted the general antipathy toward Syria like never before, the gap between emotional identification with the Palestinian cause and the willingness to take concrete action that would ameliorate their plight, and overall Arab collective weakness. For some, the sense of utter powerlessness reminded them of the atmosphere at the end of the June 1967 war. It was only after the guns had fallen silent, and the PLO had exited Beirut, that the Fez Summit, suspended in November 1981, was reconvened on September 6–9, 1982.

For the Saudis, it was a propitious moment to try to "eliminate the differences" (*izalat al-khilafat*) that had brought the Arab world to such a sorry state, and to shepherd the Arab states toward a renewed consensus on major issues. The new climate produced consensual resolutions on a number of issues, the most important of which was an endorsement of a modified version of the Fahd Plan. The controversial Point Seven was replaced by a watered-down reference to Security Council guarantees for "peace for all states of the region, including the Palestinian state," and explicit references were made to the PLO's central role in any settlement, and to Palestinian "inalienable rights," i.e., the right of return of Palestinian refugees to their pre-1948 homes. In addition, a favorable reference to the "Bourguiba Plan" (advocating the acceptance of the 1947 UNGA partition resolution) left open the question of Israel's future acceptable borders, thus serving as a sop to Syria's and the PLO's refusal to explicitly accept UNSC Resolution 242 as the sole basis for any settlement.[14] Overall, the "Fez principles" constituted the lowest common denominator that could be acceptable to the broadest Arab consensus possible. They were utterly unacceptable to Israel. Nonetheless, the contrast between the Fez resolutions and the Three No's of Khartoum fifteen years earlier was substantial, as most Arab states now recognized the need to pursue a diplomatic, and not a military, resolution to the conflict, even if it meant placing core Arab principles on the sidelines for the foreseeable future.

For Damascus, moving toward the Arab consensus at the Fez Summit was a pragmatic decision born out of its weakened position at the end of the Lebanon war. But throughout most of the rest of the decade, Syria remained defiant, maintaining its alliance with Iran while focusing much of its energies on what was ultimately the successful rolling back of Israel's presence in Lebanon and restoring its domination of the fractious shell of the Lebanese polity. Its strategic alliance with Iran enabled Tehran to begin establishing its presence in Lebanon through its patronage of a new, and more militant Shi`i organization—Hizballah. Hizballah's emergence was part of a larger phenomenon—the increasing centrality of political Islam among opposition groups across the Arab world, Sunni and Shi`i alike, that had already begun manifesting itself in the wake of the 1967 war and was given new impetus by the 1979 Iranian revolution.

In 1987, Syria found itself at a crossroads, caught between its alliance with Iran and its still-vital financial and political-ideological links with the Saudi-led majority of Arab states. Following the expansion of the Iran-Iraq war into the Gulf and Iran's continuing pressure on Iraqi defenses, particularly around its second largest city, Basra, which lay 70 kilometers from Iraq's only Gulf port, the war was now firmly at the head of the collective Arab agenda. The need to pry Syria away from its unconditional support of Iran was deemed vital for forcing Iran to desist in its attacks. As had been the case at the Fez Summit in 1982, Damascus now made a tactical course correction, agreeing to the summit's condemnation of Iran, insistence on its acceptance of a UN-mandated cease-fire, and affirmation of Arab leaders' readiness to carry out their obligations toward Iraq in accordance with the Arab League Charter and the 1950 Joint Defense Pact.[15] Although the prospects of Arab military action against Iran were zero, the emphasis on the Joint Defense Pact carried symbolic importance. For Syria, the lip service was deemed necessary at this juncture and the cost (upsetting the Iranians and giving legitimacy to the Iraqis) worth incurring.

The Syrians also compromised on Egypt's status, another central item on the summit's agenda. The 1978 Baghdad summit's resolution requiring states to cut diplomatic ties with Cairo was essentially annulled, Syria would join the rest of the Arab states in restoring relations with Cairo, and Egypt's suspension from the Arab League was lifted in May 1989.

More important for Damascus were the mounting calls during 1989 for the withdrawal of Syrian forces from Lebanon, in the wake of an intensification of fighting in the Beirut environs between anti-Syrian forces and the Syrian army and its local allies, and a political-constitutional crisis preventing the selection of a new president. Collective Arab pressure on Syria, at the May 1989 Casablanca summit and months afterwards, to pull back its forces and rescind its hegemonic status was unprecedented. However, for Damascus, the matter was a zero-sum game, and even an existential one. Ultimately, the Saudi-brokered Ta'if Accords between warring Lebanese factions in October 1989 brought an official end to fourteen years of civil strife in Lebanon. Its terms did not require a complete withdrawal of Syrian forces from the country, marking another Syrian success in fending off pressures to tow the collective Arab line.[16] It would be another year before the opponents to the accords would be brought to heel. And fifteen more years would pass before Syria would be compelled to withdraw its thirty thousand troops from Lebanon, under very different circumstances. For now, though, the fighting in Lebanon had more or less ended, and in a way that was commensurate with Syrian interests.

RECALIBRATION

The collapse of the Soviet Union at the end of the 1980s left Syria bereft of its prime international patron. With few friends in the region or beyond, recalibration of its policies was in order. In that sense, Iraq's invasion of Kuwait was ideal for Damascus. In lining up with the Saudi-Egyptian–led coalition of Arab states in opposition to Saddam, Syria earned vital credit with both the Saudis and the Americans, thus reminding them both of Syria's importance. Syria accrued two very concrete benefits from its stand. The first was a $2 billion financial injection from Saudi Arabia for its strapped economy. The second, and no less important, was the tacit green light given it by both Arab states and the Western powers to forcibly subdue the heretofore defiant Lebanese general Michel 'Awn and thus reestablish Syrian hegemony in Lebanon. With his Iraqi patron in no position to provide assistance and the rest of the Arab world silent, 'Awn and his supporters were driven from the hills around Beirut in a brief and bloody battle on October 13, 1990.[17]

The Gulf crisis also benefitted Syria in another way. With Iraq now the prime enemy, the GCC states sought improved relations with Iran. In so doing, they signaled to Asad that Syria's own intimate links with Iran were acceptable. Taking advantage, Asad journeyed to Tehran with a fifty-member delegation in late September 1990 to promote closer ties, after having avoided visiting Iran throughout the Iraq-Iran war.

At the Gulf War's conclusion, Syria would host the founding conference of the Damascus Declaration states, an effort to institutionalize the wartime coalition between Egypt, Syria, Saudi Arabia, and the other GCC states (see chapter 7). In the months afterward, Syria pragmatically assented to participating in the US-initiated Madrid Conference designed to jump-start Arab-Israeli peace negotiations. Thus, after more than a decade of contrarian minority status in Arab and regional affairs, Syria was now ensconced within the proverbial tent.

However, participating in the negotiations was one thing; achieving the desired results was something else. Syria remained extremely wary that it would be left behind while other Arab states normalized their relations with Israel and thus leave it with a weak hand in negotiations. Hence, throughout the next two years, it would continuously emphasize the need for coordination among the Arab states' positions while refusing to participate in the parallel multilateral talks, which it viewed as an unwarranted reward to Israel before it had made any concessions. The Israeli-PLO agreement in 1993 awakened anew Syria's traditional fear of being left behind, thus leaving it with diminished leverage on Israel. Moreover, Syria's own desire to play the role of patron of the Palestinians, for both geostrategic and regime-legitimizing reasons, had now been effectively neutralized by the long-despised `Arafat. Adding further to Syria's discontent was the fact that Syrian-Israeli negotiations had concurrently been close to a breakthrough of their own.[18]

Indeed, the Israeli-PLO agreement had important ripple effects throughout the region, including an Israeli-Jordanian peace treaty in 1994, the beginning of normalization of relations between Israel and a number of Arab states, particularly in the Gulf, and an opening of the door to more intimate ties between Israel and rising powers such as China and India. Of most immediate concern for Syria was the emergence in 1996 of a strategic alliance between Israel and Turkey, placing Syria in a tight military squeeze. Jordan's presence as an observer of joint Turkish-Israeli naval maneuvers in the eastern Mediterranean in January 1998 added insult to injury. Jordan no longer appeared to feel bound by long-standing collective Arab restraints. Some commentators even branded the Israeli-Turkish-Jordanian alliance as a new "Baghdad Pact" (ironically, neither Jordan nor Israel had participated in the original).[19] Matters came to a head with Turkey in 1999, as Ankara threatened military action if Damascus did not cease its support for the Kurdish insurgency in south-east Turkey and expel its leader, Abdullah Öcalan, from Damascus. Having no alternative, Damascus complied. The episode was a stark example of the growing strength of non-Arab powers in the Middle East, at the expense of Arab ones.

Arab-Israeli peacemaking efforts were reenergized that same year. Israel's newly elected prime minister, Ehud Barak, was in a hurry, and so were the Americans. Intensive American-sponsored bilateral negotiations at the end of 1999 and the beginning of 2000 brought Syria and Israel close to an agreement by which Israel would fully withdraw from the territory it had captured in 1967, in return for a peace treaty and "normal" relations (language preferred by Syria, in line with its opposition to establishing a "warm" peace). However, resolving the question of whether Syrian sovereignty would extend to the shore of the Sea of Galilee, mixed in with the mutual lack of trust between the protagonists and the progressively advancing illness of Asad, resulted in the failure to consummate the negotiations. On May 24, 2000, Israel unilaterally withdrew its forces from southern Lebanon, where they had been since 1982, making them the target of periodic attacks by Hizballah.

Shortly after that, on June 10, Hafiz al-Asad died, after nearly thirty years as Head of State. The phlegmatic "Sphinx of Damascus"[20] had overseen Syria's transformation from being a weak state, an object of other countries' designs, to that of a regional actor with considerable assets and one difficult to ignore. Replaced by his son Bashar, Syria could now only sit on the sidelines and hope that a Palestinian-Israeli final status agreement would be not concluded and leave Syria in an even weaker position vis-à-vis Israel.

Bashar's wish came true. Moreover, a new and much more violent confrontation between Israel and the Palestinians ensued (the Second Intifada), and the prospects of an Israeli-Palestinian agreement receded. For Bashar, this was just fine. Like his father, he viewed support for Palestinian militancy as an integral part of his legitimizing formula at home. Just as it halfheartedly accepted a political solution to the Arab-

Israeli conflict at the 1982 Fez Summit, Syria barely accepted the 2002 Arab peace initiative adopted at the Beirut summit (see chapter 10) and dismissed its significance. Unlike his father, and much to the displeasure of the Saudi leadership, Bashar wholeheartedly embraced Hizballah's charismatic leader Hasan Nasrallah, drew even closer to Iran, and gave strong backing to Hamas. This group, he proclaimed, was the "resistance (*muqawwama*) axis," the core of firm opposition to American and Israeli plans to dominate the region. In addition, relations with Turkey were rapidly transformed for the better following the coming to power in 2002 of the Islamist AK party, led by Recep Tayyip Erdoğan. Although Syrian troops were compelled to withdraw from Lebanon in 2005 following international outrage over the killing of former Prime Minister Rafiq Hariri, Syria's hand would continue to weigh heavily on Lebanon's fractured polity. Overall, then, on the eve of the initial Arab Spring protests in late 2010–early 2011, Syria under Bashar was widely viewed as a regional actor to be reckoned with, made possible in no small part by the country's apparent domestic stability. Within a few short months, however, this evaluation proved to be profoundly mistaken.

10

SYMBOL VERSUS SUBSTANCE

The Palestinian Movement in the Arab Firmament
Since 1967

Defending Palestine's Arab character constituted a defining feature of modern Arab identity from the mid-1930s onward. However, differences between rival Arab leaders on how best to respond to the Zionist challenge and how to interact with the divided Palestinian leadership contributed significantly to the collective Arab failure in 1948. In the decades after the *nakba*, the Palestinian Arabs would gradually reemerge as an actor with a degree of hard-won agency and autonomy. But the inherent tension between the Palestinian need for Arab support and the inevitable dependence that it created would be an enduring theme. So would the yawning gap between the wall-to-wall declarative commitment of Arab states to the defense of Palestinian rights and their willingness and ability to translate that commitment into sustained and effective action. At bottom, this gap was a manifestation of two of the main themes of this study: the priority given by Arab actors to particular interests over "all-Arab" ones, and the severe deficiency of Arab state-building projects. Notwithstanding the genuine identification with Palestinian suffering among the Arab publics, tangible support from Arab states generally failed to match their verbal pledges. Ultimately, no one would become more cynical about the general Arab commitment to the cause of Palestine than the Palestinian public. This was poignantly expressed by a popular song during the Second Intifada, *"We'en al-malayeen."* ("Where are the millions" [of neighboring Arabs]?).

Ironically, the Palestinians' own experience in building governing institutions in the West Bank and Gaza territories following the Israeli-PLO accords in 1993 would mirror many of the shortcomings of neighboring Arab states, creating a legitimacy problem for the governing Fatah movement and opening the door to its Islamist rival, Hamas, which was not a part of the PLO framework and not a party to the Oslo Accords. Moreover, the nascent Palestinian entity would be severely damaged during the violent confrontation with Israel in 2000–2003, and the prospects for a final Israeli-Palestinian peace accord that would bring an end to the Israeli occupation of the West Bank and Gaza receded accordingly. In 2007, Palestinian unity, always tentative, was fractured as Hamas seized exclusive control over the Gaza region (from which Israel had unilaterally withdrawn in 2005), creating, *de facto*, an additional Palestinian entity, alongside of West Bank areas controlled by the Palestinian Authority. In essence, the Arab League's landmark 1974 resolution designating the PLO as the sole legitimate representative of the Palestinian people was no longer relevant. And as time went on, other more pressing issues crowded onto the collective Arab agenda, at the expense of the Palestinian cause.

This chapter traces the fluctuating fortunes of the Palestinian movement and its place in the post-1967 regional Arab order. Given the involvement of Arab states in the Palestinian question, earlier chapters also addressed the subject, albeit from the angle of the states themselves. This chapter concentrates on a few salient points and episodes, with emphasis on the Palestinian side of the equation.

The establishment of the Palestine Liberation Organization in 1964, under the patronage of Gamal `Abd al-Nasir, had marked the official reappearance of the Palestinians as a collective on the Arab stage, even if it was entirely dependent on Egypt. But following the June 1967 debacle, the PLO would be transformed and eventually achieve a seat at the table of the Arab League as a full member, the only such non-state in the organization.

The halting but unmistakable trend toward state and regime consolidation in the early 1970s in Syria, Jordan, and Iraq was accompanied by a parallel shift in the Palestinian nationalist discourse that placed greater emphasis on a specific Palestinian identity within the Arab family. This was already reflected in the amended Palestinian National Covenant of

1968 and in the domination of the PLO by Fatah, the least ideological and most independent minded of the Palestinian factions. Over time, Fatah would struggle mightily, albeit not often successfully, to remain aloof from inter-Arab conflicts, which were rightly understood as endangering its freedom of action and independence of decision-making. The Black September 1970 events had dealt a major blow to the PLO, both organizationally and politically (see chapter 7). In 1972, King Husayn sought to capitalize on the PLO's weakness by tendering his "United Arab Kingdom" plan, an improved version of Jordan's 1950 annexation of the West Bank, which would follow an Israeli withdrawal to the June 4, 1967, lines, including Jerusalem. However, as Israel was not willing to countenance a return to the prewar boundaries, the idea never gained traction, and Husayn's ability to reintegrate the area into his kingdom in the face of growing Palestinian nationalism was never tested. Fortunately for the PLO, Lebanon provided a convenient alternative to Jordan. It too was contiguous to Israel, rendering it a convenient place for launching attacks. It too had a large Palestinian refugee population whose younger generation was attracted to the post-1967 PLO's message of "revolution until victory." And most importantly, the Lebanese state itself was extremely weak and unable to control the Palestinian armed groups the way that Jordan ultimately did.[1]

The eviction from Jordan in 1970–71 was a low point for Palestinian nationalism, all the more so as the Palestinian fighting organizations that had sprouted up in the wake of the 1967 debacle had generated a good deal of hope among Palestinian youth and Arab revolutionaries alike. Ironically, the PLO played no part in the 1973 Arab-Israeli War, but it turned out to be one of its prime beneficiaries. In preparation for the postwar diplomacy that was about to commence, the November 1973 Arab summit, held in Algiers, adopted a "secret" resolution backing the PLO at Jordan's expense, emphasizing the Arab leaders' "commitment to restoration of the national rights of the Palestinian people, according to the decisions of the Palestine Liberation Organization, as the sole representative of the Palestinian nation."[2] Jordan indicated that it would not be bound by it. But Amman had been put on alert: The status of the West Bank and the larger question of Jordanian-Palestinian relations was being reopened by the Arab League, a quarter-century after Jordan had conquered and annexed the territory in the face of broad Arab opposition.

For the PLO and Jordan both, the next year would be momentous. The likelihood that the West Bank's future was soon going to be addressed increased as Israel and Egypt signed their first disengagement of forces interim agreement on January 18, 1974, and a similar agreement was signed between Israel and Syria four months later. The Jordanian-Israeli front was clearly next in line. Hence, in June 1974, the Palestine National Council's meeting in Cairo adopted a "strategy of phases" toward the conflict with Israel, declaring that a "fighting national authority" would be established on any liberated Palestinian land. The challenge to Jordan was clear. The Jordanians, for their part, were eager to gain a foothold on the West Bank, and in preliminary explorations with US Secretary of State Kissinger, proposed an Israeli withdrawal of a depth of 10–15 kilometers from the Jordan River, to the first line of West Bank hills. Israel, for its part, was willing to countenance a Jordanian toehold only, in an enclave centered on the town of Jericho and in the northern end of the Jordan Valley. In light of the gap in their positions, Kissinger's diplomatic efforts never really got off the ground.

One never knows how history would have unfolded. But the absence of an Israeli-Jordanian agreement opened the way for the PLO's historic breakthrough in the Arab and international arena three months later. As recounted in chapter 7, the October 1974 Rabat Arab summit conference unanimously recognized the PLO as the "sole legitimate representative of the Palestinian people." For the PLO, it was a historic breakthrough. The collective Arab stamp of legitimacy that the summit conferred would be a crucial element in the organization's tool box in the years ahead. Less than one month later, it reaped the first fruits of the endorsement, as Yasir 'Arafat addressed a rapturous session of the UN General Assembly and the PLO attained observer status at the UN. Two years later, the PLO was admitted to full membership in the Arab League.

To be sure, the PLO's recognition by the League did not fully insulate it from the influences and pressures of various Arab states, or the vicissitudes of inter-Arab relations. The "independence of decision-making" was a hallowed PLO value, but one that was often out of reach. Approximately 50 percent of Jordan's East Bank population was of Palestinian origin, and all West Bank Palestinians held Jordanian citizenship. Hence, the Palestinian issue was an immediate, even existential matter for the regime, one that directly and profoundly impacted on its survival and well-being and thus required ongoing Jordanian involvement in Palestinian affairs.

For Syria, by contrast, championing the Palestinian cause was a central facet of its ideological claim to be the champion of the Arab nation, as long as the Palestinian leadership pursued policies that were commensurate with Syrian interests. Syria had been Fatah's first patron, as part of its struggle against both `Abd al-Nasir and Jordan before the June 1967 war, but Damascus's relations with `Arafat would be more conflictual than cooperative, and often extremely hostile, over the subsequent decades. Syria's actions would include supporting Palestinian factions that actively opposed `Arafat and his Fatah organization in Lebanon, and even the founding of a Palestinian faction, Al-Sa`iqa, that was essentially an appendage of Syria's security forces. These actions were an integral part of Asad's determined effort to be a dominant actor in its immediately surrounding environs. As for Egypt, Sadat's siding with the PLO was in one sense natural, in line with Egypt's traditional support for Palestinian rights and well-defined regional leadership role. Less well understood at the time was that the Arab League's endorsement of the PLO at Rabat was part of Sadat's overall pursuit of a diplomatic resolution of the Arab-Israeli conflict that would enable him to recover all the territory Egypt had lost in 1967, to the PLO's acute distress.

The PLO had entrenched itself in Lebanon beginning in the late 1960s, and deepened its presence there further following its expulsion from Jordan in 1970–1971. Beginning in 1975, it became inextricably entangled in Lebanon's civil war, leading to bloody confrontations with Lebanese Christian forces, and at times Syrian forces as well, but unlike in Jordan, the PLO managed to maintain its presence. Sadat's peace initiative posed a new challenge to the PLO, and it responded by further building itself up as an autonomous military and political force within the fractured Lebanese entity, and periodically engaging Israel militarily in order to remain relevant. As recounted in chapter 9, all of this came crashing down in the summer of 1982, as Israeli forces marched to Beirut in an effort to deliver a mortal blow to the PLO and fundamentally alter the regional political landscape.

The mid-1980s were extremely difficult ones for Yasir `Arafat and the PLO. Having had his forces battered in war and evicted from Beirut by Israel, and then from the northern city of Tripoli by Syria a year later, he relocated his headquarters to Tunis, while some PLO units were given refuge in Yemen, far away from the front lines. For the PLO, shifting the center of its activities to the Palestinian territories occupied by Israel was now absolutely vital.[3] To do so, it needed to improve its ties with Jordan. Lengthy discussions were held about establishing a Palestinian-Jordanian confederation as a solution to the diplomatic deadlock with Israel. However, both King Husayn and `Arafat recognized that theirs was a relationship based on rivalry, not on partnership, and Husayn ultimately kept `Arafat at arm's length, preferring to try to strengthen Jordan's own links with West Bank Palestinians, explore diplomatic options with Israel, and even repair relations with Syria.

Meeting in November 1987, the Arab summit conference in Amman gave short shrift in its discussions to the cause of Palestine, the traditional centerpiece of Arab summitry, concentrating instead on the expanding threat posed by Iran in its war with Iraq. Moreover, the prestige accorded to King Husayn as summit host was widely viewed as coming at 'Arafat's and the PLO's expense. Husayn himself sought to convey the message that Jordan's role in solving the long-stalemated Palestinian question was vital, and that `Arafat and the PLO needed to adjust to their diminished status. The audience for Husayn's message was the Palestinian public, both in Jordan and just across the Jordan River in the West Bank, which was tuned in to Jordanian television. Pointedly, Husayn was not present to personally greet `Arafat upon his televised arrival at the Amman airport for the summit, delegating the task to his prime minister, `Abd al-Salam Majali. In essence, Husayn was working to undercut the 1974 Rabat resolution that had provided the PLO with crucial legitimacy, as the Syrians had been attempting to do for years.

For `Arafat and the PLO, the Amman summit was a new low point. However, less than three weeks later, violent confrontations between Palestinians and Israeli occupation forces triggered what would quickly be known as the (first) intifada. Although not initiated by the PLO, the leadership, both inside and outside the West Bank, seized the moment and reasserted the centrality of the Palestinian cause in Arab politics, and the PLO's place in it as the indisputable representative of the Palestinian people.

The intifada had immediate resonance in the Arab world. The images of stone-throwing Palestinian youth (*awlad al-hijar*, "children of stones") confronting the powerful Israeli army quickly became iconic across the Arab world, thanks to the rapid proliferation of satellite television dishes that enabled viewers to receive a multitude of both Western and Arab channels. For Arab publics increasingly alienated from their own governments and acutely aware of the continued gap between Arab ideals and realities, the unequal "heroic" confrontation evoked a gut-level response of support similar to the initial months and years after the 1967 war when Palestinian guerrillas carried the fight to Israel while Arab armies lay prostrate. Keenly aware of this, Arab regimes quickly lined up in support of the newly invigorated PLO.

In June 1988, Arab leaders convened an emergency summit in Algiers. Unlike in Amman six months previously, the Palestinian cause, and the PLO as its standard bearer, took pride of place, with the summit issuing ringing declarations of support and pledges of $400 million in aid. For Jordan, the reassertion of PLO primacy was clearly at its expense, forcing a policy reevaluation. The outcome was dramatic: On July 31, in a nationwide television address, Husayn announced that Jordan was ending its "legal and administrative responsibilities" for West Bank Palestinians, in line with the Arab consensus and PLO desires. By essentially washing Jordan's hands of the West Bank, Husayn challenged the PLO to try to do better. The response came in November, with the Palestine National Council's issuing of a Declaration of Independence, and a political program that included partial acceptance of UN Resolutions 242 and 338.[4]

Momentarily, the PLO now became a legitimate interlocutor for the US as it sought to restart diplomatic efforts against the background of the intifada. But these failed to produce results, and by mid-1990, the focus of attention in the region again shifted elsewhere.

Saddam Husayn's invasion of Kuwait in August 1990 created the worst inter-Arab crisis in modern history. The Palestinian public in Jordan, the West Bank, and Gaza were broadly sympathetic to Saddam, and 'Arafat openly tilted in his favor as well. Palestinians in Kuwait would pay a heavy price for 'Arafat's actions, and also be accused by the Kuwaitis of supporting the Iraqi invaders, resulting in a large-scale forced exodus after the 1991 war. The PLO's relations with Saudi Arabia and Kuwait would suffer accordingly. Once again, the PLO had become entangled in an inter-Arab dispute, with enormous cost.

THE OSLO YEARS

The expulsion of Iraqi forces from Kuwait cleared the way for the renewal of Arab-Israeli diplomacy, spearheaded by the United States. The Madrid Peace Conference, held on October 30–November 1, 1991, was an unprecedented diplomatic spectacle in the history of Arab-Israeli peace making. Co-sponsored by the United States and the Soviet Union, it brought together senior representatives from Israel and all four of the "ring states" (*duwal al-tawq*), as well as the secretary-generals of the six-nation GCC and five-nation AMU. The Madrid negotiating framework was extremely ambitious. Bilateral talks were to be held between Israel and Syria, Lebanon, and Jordan, respectively, for the purpose of concluding peace treaties, while Israel would negotiate with the Palestinian delegation over the terms of an interim accord for the West Bank and Gaza. Having been severely weakened by 'Arafat's perceived tilt toward Saddam Husayn during the Gulf War, the PLO had no choice but to limit its activities to a behind-the-scenes role, agreeing to have pro-PLO West Bank and Gaza representatives included within the Jordanian delegation. The subsuming of the Palestinian delegation within the Jordanian one was a tactical victory for King Husayn and Israel, but in practice, the Palestinians quickly carved out their own status as a separate group apart from Jordan in their negotiations with Israel.

The coming to power of a new government in Israel in May 1992, headed by the Labor Party's Yitzhak Rabin, eventually led to a breakthrough from an unexpected direction. A Norwegian-sponsored back-channel produced a dramatic agreement between the PLO and Israel, the Oslo Accords. They were signed and sealed on the White House lawn in September 1993 by a historic handshake between Rabin and 'Arafat. The agreement stipulated mutual recognition between the State of Israel and the PLO as the legitimate representative of the Palestinian people, and laid out a multi-stage plan to establish a five year, interim self-governing Palestinian Authority (PA) in portions of the West Bank and Gaza, during which time negotiations to determine a final status agreement were to be concluded. Eight months later, the parties concluded an implementation agreement in Cairo, 'Arafat and many of the Tunis-based PLO cadres relocated to Gaza to take charge of the PA, and stage one of the interim phase began.

The agreement caught the rest of the Arab world, including the Palestinian negotiating team in Washington, completely by surprise. Egypt quickly endorsed it; Syria and Jordan, on the other hand, looked askance at the agreement, each for its own reasons. Syria's traditional fear of being left behind, and thus with diminished leverage on Israel, seemed to be materializing. Moreover, Syria's own desire to play the role of patron of the Palestinians, for both geostrategic and regime legitimization reasons had now been effectively neutralized by the long-despised `Arafat.

Jordan, for its part, was quietly dismayed, fearing that Israel was now putting all of its eggs in the PLO basket. It was one thing for Jordan to formally concede its legal and administrative responsibilities in the West Bank to the PLO, as it did in 1988, when Israel still ruled the territory, but quite another thing if the PLO actually established a viable entity there. Such a development was deemed likely to adversely affect Jordan's long-term interests, and possibly even undermine its very existence. After contemplating the situation, Jordan's King Husayn decided that the best way to ensure his kingdom's future was to move rapidly to conclude a peace treaty of its own with Israel. The Israeli-Palestinian agreement posed a major challenge to Jordan, but also provided the necessary legitimacy to do what Husayn had always preferred in any case, but until now had never had the political security to do so.

Matters moved quickly in the summer of 1994. Husayn and Rabin appeared jointly in front of the US Congress and signed a statement of principles ending the state of war between their two countries known as the Washington Declaration. Of special importance for Jordan was a clause acknowledging Jordan's special role in safeguarding the Muslim holy sites in Jerusalem, which were to be taken into account in the final status negotiations regarding the city. Three months later, a peace treaty was concluded with a festive signing on the Jordanian-Israeli frontier just north of their respective cities of `Aqaba and Eilat at the head of the Gulf of `Aqaba. Syria's President Asad was openly perturbed, criticizing Husayn for going ahead with the agreement without prior coordination with Syria. Husayn's response to Asad was that it was "none of his business" and that Husayn's job was to protect the interests of Jordan.[5] The bluntness of Husayn's riposte spoke volumes about how far Arab political discourse had come. No longer did one have to couch one's actions in terms of the larger Arab interest at the expense of *raison d'état*, even if one was the leader of a small and vulnerable state like Jordan. Ironically, it was `Arafat who, by signing the Oslo Accords, had pushed Jordan to act accordingly.

Both on the ground and at the negotiating table, the implementation of the Oslo Accords was fraught with difficulties, tension, and violence. A sequence of terror attacks by Palestinian Islamists opposed to the Oslo Accords, a February 1994 massacre of Palestinian worshippers by an Israeli civilian, and attacks by Palestinian suicide bombers called into question the viability of the Oslo process, even as it lurched forward. In November 1995, Rabin was assassinated by an Israeli Jewish extremist; surprisingly, perhaps, the second stage of the Oslo agreement was carried out just weeks afterward, extending the Palestinian Authority's reach in the West Bank. But a new round of suicide bombings in March 1996 and a sudden escalation of fighting in southern Lebanon between Israel and the Lebanese Hizballah further undermined the Israeli public's confidence in the viability of what Shimon Peres, Rabin's successor, had been touting as the "new Middle East.. Peres was defeated in May 1996 elections and was replaced by a right-wing coalition led by Binyamin Netanyahu, prompting an emergency Arab summit conference in Cairo to reconfirm Arab states' commitment to the Palestinian cause, while also declaring their commitment to a peace agreement a "strategic choice" (*ihtiyar istratiji*) and placing the burden on Israel to realize it. The pace of implementation of the Oslo arrangements slowed precipitously during the next three years, but did not stop entirely.

The election of Ehud Barak as Israeli prime minister in May 1999 renewed the diplomatic momentum, with an initial focus on the Syrian-Israeli track. However, a peace agreement was not consummated, and the focus returned to the Palestinian track. In summer 2000, the Clinton Administration attempted to repeat Jimmy Carter's success in 1978 by hosting Barak and `Arafat at the Camp David presidential retreat for what turned out to be fifteen days of intensive diplomacy that ended without an agreement. Unlike Barak, who had strongly urged US President Clinton to convene the Camp David meetings, `Arafat was extremely reluctant from the outset, fearing that they would be subjected to heavy American pressure to sign what was expected to be an unsatisfactory agreement. The American delegation, for its part, didn't prepare adequately for the conference, and particularly for Palestinian recalcitrance. It was also counting on Egyptian, Jordanian, and Saudi encouragement to `Arafat to seriously engage the Israeli proposals at the talks, but it was not forthcoming. The Jordanians were particularly anxious regarding any possible agreement on the question of Palestinian refugees that would directly impact on Jordan, while the leaderships of all three countries were exercised over the Jerusalem question. Many Palestinians, as well as Israel's right-wing opposition, breathed a sigh of relief when the talks ended without an agreement. Indeed, `Arafat immediately journeyed to Cairo, where he was given a hero's welcome by the public for not "succumbing" to Israel.[6]

Camp David II was thus a failure. To be sure, high-level Israeli-Palestinian contacts continued to be held in the following months. However, the public atmosphere was increasingly confrontational, and in late September, another violent Israeli-Palestinian confrontation ensued, the Second Intifada (also known in the Arab political lexicon as *intifadat al-Aqsa)*, which delivered a severe blow to the prospects of an Israeli-Palestinian agreement.

THE SECOND INTIFADA AND THE ARAB PEACE INITIATIVE

The second intifada almost completely monopolized the collective Arab agenda for the next two years. Daily, real-time televised images of Palestinian casualties broadcast by Arab satellite networks across the region fed public anger and produced mass protests in nearly every Arab country, from Morocco to the Gulf, and on a scale not seen since the days of the 1991 Gulf War. Criticism from columnists and opposition figures of Arab governments and the Arab League was savage, with one columnist describing the League as the "League of the Living Dead." Fifty-five leaders and intellectuals from Islamist movements across the Arab and Muslim world banded together to issue a joint statement that denounced "Arab [governments'] submissiveness and willingness to give in," demanded that Arab and Islamic states "expel Israeli missions [and] halt all overt and covert ties of normalization with the Zionists," and called for Palestine to be liberated by mass action and armed resistance.[7]

Arab governments, for their part, were largely reduced to the status of unhappy and enfeebled spectators. The September 11, 2001, New York and Washington DC bombings by al-Qa`ida caused the image in the West of Saudi Arabia, where most of the perpetrators originated, and that of

Arabs and Muslims in generals, to sink to an unprecedented low. With the United States now reprioritizing its foreign policy to strike back at radical Islamic terrorists (as well as Saddam Husayn's regime, although this wasn't fully clear at the time), longtime allied Arab governments were now viewed in Washington through a new, more critical lens. Not only were they blamed for not doing their share in advancing the peace process and in ending the latest round of Palestinian-Israeli violence, but they were also deemed to have been insufficiently attentive, at best, to the dangerous Islamist currents spawned in their midst.

In response, the idea of a new Arab diplomatic initiative began to percolate among Saudi, Jordanian, and Egyptian officials, one that would bolster the tarnished Arab image in the West, place the onus on Israel for the continued violence, and, if possible, restart the diplomatic process on terms more favorable to Arab interests. In February 2002, Saudi Arabia's Crown Prince `Abdullah bin `Abd al-`Aziz went public with the initiative, a proposed Arab League summit conference that would call for a "full [Israeli] withdrawal from all the occupied territories, in accord with UN resolutions, including in Jerusalem, for full normalization of relations."[8] The entire episode, from the initial Saudi initiative, through the Syrian and Lebanese efforts to modify it and the eventual arrival at a consensus resolution six weeks later at the Beirut summit, was strongly reminiscent of the 1981 Fahd initiative and the eventual adoption of the Arab peace plan at Fez in 1982.

Predictably, Syrian criticism stemmed from `Abdullah's explicit use of the phrase "normalization" of relations with Israel, an old bugaboo in the Arab political lexicon. Damascus insisted on the less obligating "normal" or "normal peaceful" relations in any official communiqués, as well as on the explicit inclusion of UN General Assembly resolution 194 of December 11, 1948, which in the accepted Arab interpretation enshrined the "right of return" of Palestinian refugees. By contrast, the Jordanian monarchy, which was historically ahead of the collective Arab curve regarding the virtues of Arab-Israeli peacemaking, approached the initiative from a more conciliatory direction, one which would give, and in English, a "simple and powerful explanation" of the Arabs' position, and include an end-of-conflict clause and a commitment to full normalization, but not a specific reference to the "right of return" or resolution 194, so as not to drive Israel away from the peace table. `Abdullah, however, preferred a text in Arabic and was willing to be more accommodating to the

Syrian-Lebanese position, in line with Saudi Arabia's own traditional preference for attaining the widest possible Arab consensus on major issues. [9]

On the eve of the summit, the exact text of the initiative was still to be finalized and continued to be the subject of heated disagreement. Moreover, the overall atmosphere was anything but propitious for an Arab peace initiative. Israeli-Palestinian violence was spiking, creating widespread anger in the Arab media and on the street. Playing to the crowd, Lebanese Hizballah leader Hasan Nasrallah demanded that the Arab states arm the Palestinians instead of talking of peace with Israel. Syrian officials from Bashar al-Asad on down preferred to emphasize the Arab commitment to resistance and holding Israel accountable for its repression of the Palestinian intifada, and not prospective gestures toward it.

Concerned with the overheated and militant atmosphere surrounding the summit, Mubarak and Jordan's King 'Abdallah II (King Husayn had passed away in 1999) chose to stay away, sending lower-level representatives in their stead; the majority of other Arab leaders did so as well. Adding to the chaotic, even circus-like atmosphere of the gathering was 'Arafat's humiliation by the Lebanese authorities, who cut off the live video feed of his summit speech being delivered from his besieged Ramallah headquarters.

At the insistence of Lebanon's President Emile Lahoud, the final approved formula of the plan, reached during heated side meetings, included a separate clause in the text rejecting any "patriation" (*tawtin*) of Palestinian refugees "which conflict with the special circumstances of the Arab host countries." The Jordanians made it clear that if such a clause was to be included, it applied to them as well. Just prior to the closing session of the summit, the Libyan and Iraqi representatives tried to register their reservations to the overall initiative, but Saudi Crown Prince 'Abdullah overruled them, insisting on an up or down vote on "the Beirut Declaration" (`I'lan Beirut`), which resulted in unanimous approval.

To be sure, the meaning and value of the initiative was immediately the subject of further controversy. The summit's final statement (*al-bayan al-khitami*), which, unlike that of the declaration, was never officially translated into English, contained no reference to the Saudi plan as such, nor did it include specific language regarding the end of the conflict and the establishment of normal relations with Israel. Instead, it merely reiterated the 1996 Cairo summit's declaration that the Arab states viewed a "just and comprehensive peace" as a "strategic choice" and called on Israel to fulfill its obligations to that end. The final statement's section on the Palestinian issue included an insistence on realizing all of the Palestinian people's "inalienable rights," including the "right of return," and the complete refusal by Arab leaders to resettle the refugees outside of their specific ancestral homes (*diyarihim*).[10] Clearly, this was a far cry from an "agreed-on" understanding of resolution 194 to which Israel could accede.[11]

At the moment of its birth, the Arab Peace Initiative appeared to be stillborn. Inter-Arab wrangling over its specifics and the poor reception it received from both Arab commentators and the Arab street seriously limited its value. Moreover, a string of Palestinian suicide bombings, the most serious one at a Passover holiday celebration at an Israeli hotel on the evening of the first day of the Beirut summit, left Israeli public opinion both traumatized and dismissive of any purported Arab-initiated peace plan. In response to the bombings, Israel launched its most extensive military operation in the West Bank since June 1967. The second intifada would leave both sides scarred and brutalized, and although diplomatic efforts would never cease, the prospects for an Israeli-Palestinian peace agreement receded. Nonetheless, the Arab peace initiative would come to be considered to be a valid part of the foundations upon which a permanent Arab-Israeli peace was to be built, along with "the Madrid Conference, the principle of land for peace, UNSCRs 242, 338, and 1397,[12] and agreements previously reached by the parties." It would also be a marker determining the shaky parameters of acceptable, collective Arab action on the subject.

In 2005–2006, the parameters of the Israeli-Palestinian conflict were significantly altered by Israel's unilateral withdrawal from the Gaza Strip, and by the victory of Hamas in Palestinian elections in the West Bank and Gaza five months later. Hamas's unwillingness to embrace the Arab Peace Initiative and internationally recognized principles for an end to the Israeli-Palestinian conflict rendered it unacceptable to Israel, which clamped down tighter on Hamas-dominated Gaza. This, along with unbridgeable internal divisions between Hamas and the Fatah movement that dominated the Palestinian Authority, resulted in the de facto emergence in 2007 of two Palestinian entities—one in Gaza, controlled by Hamas, and one in the West Bank, controlled by the PA. While Hamas controlled Gaza, Israel controlled access to it, resulting in endless tension, frequent rocket fire from Gaza into Israel, and Israeli retaliations. In December–January 2008–09, this always-combustible situation exploded, as Israel undertook a major military operation in an effort to silence the rocket fire and reestablish deterrence. The scenario would repeat itself in November 2012 and again in July–August 2014, bringing untoward misery to the Gaza population. Overall, the end of Israel's occupation of the West Bank, nearly fifty years old, was nowhere in sight, and the Palestinian plight in Gaza was steadily worsening, exacerbated further by the confrontation between Hamas and the Sisi government in Egypt (see chapter 11). And beginning in 2012, the residents of the Palestinian refugee camp of Yarmouk, in the environs of Damascus, found themselves being brutally battered by opposing forces in the Syrian civil war, making them the latest symbol of Palestinian marginalization and abandonment.

11

THE ARAB SPRING
Disorder and Disintegration

BACKGROUND TO THE UPHEAVALS

The inter-Arab system had entered the new millennium with a bevy of question marks. The implications for the Arab world of accelerating globalization (`awlama`) was a favorite topic of commentators and scholars, with most agreeing that Arab governments and societies had failed to develop policies that would benefit the general Arab interest, and that they were being left further and further behind the globalizing train.[1] At the same time, at least three factors militated against the likelihood of significant change in the near term: a) the apparent staying power of authoritarian regimes; b) the absence of a robust civil society and genuine pluralism; and c) the uncertainties surrounding the assumption to power of a younger generation of leaders, which dictated cautious approaches to policy issues. The political economy of Arab states was in a state of equilibrium, namely one in which "self-seeking agents learn nothing new and so their behavior becomes routinized." Continuity in performance was the watchword, notwithstanding changes in policy, ownership and control, ideology, and even political rule.[2]

Regional difficulties, which were both symptoms and causes of collective Arab weakness, compounded matters further: (1) the decade-long unfinished business of the Gulf War, which left Iraq an embittered pariah state, albeit with considerable mischief-making ability and growing sympathy among Arab populations; (2) the halting, unconcluded Arab-Israeli peace process, and the resulting uncertainty throughout the region; (3) the growing strength of regional, non-Arab powers (Turkey, Israel, and Iran); and (4) the failure to develop concrete collective policies toward regional issues and build more formal collective mechanisms to manage inter-Arab disputes. Given the absence of a common regional agenda, the "Arab world" seemed to be increasingly a misnomer, in political terms, masking the reality of a series of zones of conflict and concern (the Maghrib, the Nile Valley, the Levant, the Fertile Crescent, the Arabian peninsula, and the Gulf) in which states pursued their particular agendas with scant reference to wider, common goals.

Hasan Naf'a of the al-Ahram Center for Strategic and Political Studies aptly captured the prevailing mood among committed Arab nationalists: "Unlike other regions in the world, the new Arab millennium appears very ominous indeed. . . . The Arab world," he wrote, "seems like a paralyzed wreck badly in need of a complete new nervous system."[3]

Evidence to this difficult state of affairs abounded. The 1998 Unified Arab Economic Report—a joint analysis of the Arab Monetary Fund, the Organization of Arab Petroleum Export Countries (OAPEC), the Arab League, and the Arab Fund for Economic and Social Development—emphasized the continued socioeconomic difficulties as measured by most macro-indicators in the Arab region as a whole. Population growth, while down from an annual growth rate of more than 3.5 percent in 1980 to 2.5 percent in 1997, still outstripped economic growth: 60 percent population growth (from 165 million to 264 million), to 37 percent total GDP. Excessive dependence on oil export revenues, high food imports, and low levels of revenue derived from taxation—29 percent, with only 8 percent derived from direct taxation—provided tangible evidence that Arab states were not truly becoming "strong" in the sense meant by Joel Migdal that was referred to earlier.[4]

The fragmented, conflictual character of the inter-Arab system was a common theme of the critiques of Arab policymakers and intellectuals. Jordan's then-Crown Prince Hasan bemoaned the absence of "a code of honor for bilateral and multilateral relations…and a methodology for dealing objectively with crises and resolving disputes," thus making it easier for foreign intervention in Arab affairs. The biggest danger the Arab world faced, he stated, was "Balkanization and Lebanonization. . . . If we fail to open a dialogue within the framework of civil society and the state of law within the regimes of these countries, it would be difficult to expect the Arab regime to last."⁵ Like Hassan, the Palestinian-American intellectual luminary Hisham Sharabi was blunt in his analysis: "The present generation of patriarchal leaders is bankrupt," he wrote, "incapable of halting the disintegration of the Arab order that was built over the past half century. People feel an urgent need for new approaches and methods to transform the prevailing social and state orders, halt the deterioration, and avoid disaster."⁶ In light of the subsequent upheavals across the region, their words were especially prescient.

Arab leaders were not unaware of the criticism, while maintaining the traditional discourse of prioritizing a common Arab identity over all other ones. Arab League Secretary-General 'Ismat 'Abd al-Magid claimed that fruitful "joint Arab action" was occurring in a variety of social and economic spheres. Although constitutional unity was a far-off matter, the Arab League, he insisted, would oppose the propagation of alternative ideas for collective identity that had been raised by a number of liberal Arab intellectuals in recent years—"Middle Easternism" (*sharq awsatiyya*), and "Mediterraneanism" (*mutawasatiyya*). Such ideas were both more inclusive (leaving room for Israel to be a legitimate and "normal" member of a regional order), and gave encouragement to other ethnocommunal forms of identity, e.g., among Kurds, Berbers, Maronites, Copts, etc. As such, said 'Abd al-Magid, they were damaging to "Arab identity and its fate."⁷

Among the most passionate and poetic articulators of that identity, Nizar Qabbani, died in London on April 30, 1998, at the age of seventy-five. In the words of a Lebanese literary journal, Qabbani was the "supreme conscience of the Arab nation in a time of ugliness and hate." Like other noted Syrian poets who had left the repressive atmosphere of Syria for the more open environment of Beirut, he was eventually awarded Lebanese citizenship (he left Beirut in 1982 following the Israeli invasion, and eventually settled in London). Politicized by the 1967 Arab-Israeli war, his poems throbbed with rage and defiance toward the perceived oppressors of the Arabs. Nor did he spare Arab leaders from his rage, particularly in the last years of his life, railing against the *jahililyya* ("darkness"; a powerful term evoking the alleged age of ignorance of pre-Islamic Arabia) of contemporary Arab reality. "When Will They Announce the Death of the Arabs?" was the title of one poem. He was proud to have distanced himself from Arab authority (*sulta*) in the last decades of his life: "I have never dined at the table of any sultan or any general or any emir or minister. My sixth sense always warned me that to dine with such company would be my last supper." However, his passionate opposition to the "treasonous" Oslo accords and resulting Arab-Israeli peace process led to a convergence in death of his own personal interests—his wish to be buried in his native Damascus—and those of the *sulta*, Syria's President Hafiz al-Asad, who dispatched a special plane to bring his body home.[8]

Qabbani's death also symbolized the withering away of politically meaningful secular opposition forces during the last decades of the twentieth century. Consequently, Islamist movements had become the opposition of choice for many.[9] Algeria's chaotic experiment in sudden democratization in 1989–1991 had brought the Islamic Salvation Front (FIS, in its French acronym) to the brink of power, before the military intervened in early 1992. The situation quickly deteriorated into a lengthy and bloody civil war for most of the decade between ever more militant and brutal Islamist elements and a regime grimly determined to survive at all costs, which it eventually did.[10] The Algerian events served to guide other Arab regimes dealing with Islamists opponents. While aware of the need for change, they preferred only limited reforms designed primarily to shore up their hold on power. For this they needed time and Western support. In this context, participating in an American-led Arab-Israeli peace process, and even supporting a diplomatic resolution to the conflict, had become an integral part of their policies.

The year 2009 marked the twentieth anniversary of the 1989 collapse of the East Bloc and the end of the Cold War. Symbolically, the breaching and dismantling of the Berlin Wall by throngs of ordinary German citizens had been the single most powerful image of that event-filled year. But for Middle Eastern rulers and publics alike, the sight of Romania's long-ruling dictator Nicolae Ceauşescu lying dead in a roadside ditch had been no less poignant. Was this, as many in the region hoped at the time, the inevitable fate of its dictators? Would civil society reemerge as a significant force, after decades of domination by repressive authorities, as many Western academics theorized? Would the Arab world belatedly join the "third wave" of democratization witnessed in Europe and Latin America two decades earlier?[11]

Very little is inevitable in history, in part because it is heavily contingent on the actions of individuals. Prior to the Arab Spring upheavals in

2011, Iraq was the only Arab country to undergo regime change in the previous three decades, and not thanks to its own public, for that matter.[12] Most regimes used the tools of power more wisely than he, enabling them to survive turbulent times. As for the reemergence of civil society, this had proven to have been a pious wish. Genuinely democratic civil society, i.e., the existence of a strong network of voluntary civic and social organizations and institutions outside the realm of the state, requires the rule of law, alternative centers of economic power, and self-restraint by the authorities, all of which were in short supply in the Arab world.

This is not to say, however, that the Arab societies were entirely stagnant. Issues related to women's status and the environment were now squarely on the public agenda. Governments no longer had a complete monopoly in the information sphere, thanks to satellite TV dishes and the Internet. NGOs had proliferated, often in cooperation with, and support from, Western institutions and organizations. Still, the balance between state authorities and non-state forces remained decisively in favor of the former, and Islamist movements, hardly the standard-bearers of democratic values, remained the only viable political opposition in most places.

The Arab world had badly lagged behind much of the rest of the world in economic and social development, even prior to the latest post-Cold War wave of globalization. Part of the problem was that even just speaking frankly about these matters had never been a simple task. Ruling Arab elites generally viewed nonofficial intellectual endeavor with suspicion and acted to co-opt, corrupt, or repress independent voices that might delegitimize their authority and thus threaten their monopoly on power. This is at least one of the reasons that Arab political and intellectual life over the preceding half-century had been severely stunted, characterized by a dearth of public self-criticism, with the preponderance of blame for Arab societies' shortcomings and the failure to enact meaningful political and economic reforms often being ascribed to pernicious foreign forces. However, this was no longer entirely the case, thanks in part to the series of Arab Human Development Reports (AHDRs) crafted by a cross section of Arab academicians from the region and beyond, in cooperation with the United Nations Development Program.

Five lengthy reports were issued between 2002 and 2009.[13] They pointed to "deficits" in such areas as political freedom, knowledge, human rights, basic security, and gender as being the underlying causes for tepid Arab economic development, particularly in comparison to East Asia and Latin America. For example, the fifth Report, titled "Challenges to Human Security in the Arab Countries," painted a sobering portrait of contemporary Arab social and political realities. The threats to human security were analyzed according to seven categories: (1) pressures on environmental resources; (2) the performance of the state in guaranteeing or undermining human security; (3) the personal insecurity of vulnerable groups; (4) economic vulnerability, poverty, and unemployment; (5) food security and nutrition; (6) health and welfare; and (7) the systemic insecurity of occupation and foreign military intervention. The problems were daunting, to say the least. Each section was extremely sobering. For example, with regard to the environment, the total population of Arab countries was scheduled to increase from 150 million in 1980 to 395 million in 2015, while renewable water reserves were being depleted faster than they could be replenished, water pollution and desertification was expanding, and access to clean water declining, thus exposing children, in particular, to a range of diseases.

With regard to the prototypical Arab State, the 2009 Report suggested that it was a major part of the problem, pointing to its authoritarian ways, the absence of democratic governance, representative institutions and the rule of law, and a failure to respect cultural, ethnic, religious, and linguistic diversity. Women were deemed among the most vulnerable of groups, and the report pulled no punches in detailing the myriad ways in which women were continuously exposed to family and institutionalized violence, not only physically but also as victims of cultural and social practices, such as female genital mutilation and child marriage, as well as human trafficking.

The Arab countries' "fabled oil wealth," the Report said, masked and in fact caused serious structural weaknesses of many Arab economies. Hunger and malnutrition rates were rising, according to the Report; the only other region where this was the case is sub-Saharan Africa. In the health sphere, despite improvements, health-care systems available to most Arabs were inadequate, with wide disparities in quality both within and between countries. Moreover, HIV/AIDS "represent[ed] a stubborn, proximate, and misunderstood danger."

As for the role of occupation and military intervention, the Report detailed the damage to all spheres of human security, particularly in Iraq, the West Bank and Gaza, and Somalia (a nominal member of the Arab

League). Interestingly, it noted how both extremist groups and Arab governments exploited these situations to their own ends and thus perpetuated cycles of destruction and oppressive rule.

Not surprisingly, the 2009 Report's findings generated controversy. Its lead author, Cairo University professor Mustafa Kamel El-Sayed, actually disassociated himself from it, declaring that his final draft had been substantially altered by its United Nations publishers so as to emphasize domestic factors at the expense of external causes, in order to appease the United States and Israel. Samir Radwan, a former International Labor Organization official, chimed in, calling the Report's emphasis on issues like female genital mutilation and climate change a "flavor of the month" approach, at the expense of the Iraq and Palestine issues.[14] In response, the former director of the Al-Ahram Center for Strategic and Political Studies, `Abdel Moneim Said, declared that it was up to Arab political elites—rulers, the civilian bureaucracy, the military establishment, and the culture and media agencies—to recognize how bad things were and to take responsibility for changing them, as other elites in other countries and regions have done in similar circumstances. "At some point," he stated, "our elites, who are brave and smart, have to put two and two together and get four."[15]

Still, notwithstanding the serious shortcomings enumerated in the Reports, most Arab regimes appeared to be firmly ensconced. Leaders and allied elites seemed to have accumulated sufficient resources to maintain the existing bureaucratic-authoritarian order, at least for the time being. The mix of factors that provided them with a necessary measure of legitimacy varied from country to country, but "being Arab" was certainly a part of the package. Regimes as diverse as Syria and Jordan had devoted much effort to deepening the Arab identity of its citizens, creating what Christopher Phillips called "everyday Arabism," which was an integral part of their territorial nationalism package, one which implicitly seemed to bridge longstanding sectarian, ethnic, or tribal fault lines. With pan-Arabism having faded away as a viable political ideology, ruling regimes could openly pursue *raison d'état*, and claim legitimacy for doing so on "national-territorial" grounds without it being in contradiction of "Arab" values.

However, the decline of pan-Arabism and the loss of hope that it represented left Arab regimes bereft of an important legitimizing tool. Arab nationalism as an expressive ideology was not enough by itself. The regimes had to perform, and as the Arab Human Development Reports consistently showed, they had not delivered. Many Arab states had essentially "stalled."[16] Public opinion polls conducted in a cross section of Arab states during the decade after the 2003 Iraq war consistently showed a higher level of identification with transnational identities (Arab and Muslim) than with the respondents' countries.[17]

At the same time, although pan-Arabism had proven not to be a workable political ideology, the domination of al-Jazeera television news broadcasts throughout the Arab Middle East and North Africa, the proliferation of all-Arab mass culture markers like the "Arab Idol" music competition, and the spread in recent years of the Internet and attendant social media had created new types of identification among Arab citizens of different countries. Without these links, new and old, and the accompanying widespread identification with a broad Arab space that was suffering from common shortcomings for which they held their repressive rulers responsible,[18] the tsunami of mass protests that cascaded back and forth across the Arab and Middle East North Africa, after having been sparked by the self-immolation of a young, despairing, unemployed Tunisian in a dusty provincial town in December 2010, would not have taken place. By way of comparison, Arab publics had watched keenly as the abortive "Green Revolution" in Iran unfolded eighteeen months earlier, but from the sidelines.

FIRST RESPONSES TO THE UPRISINGS

Tunisia's "Revolution of Dignity" that toppled the country's long-serving autocratic president Zine al-`Abidine Ben `Ali on January 14, 2011, after three weeks of steadily building protests, was dramatic, entirely unexpected, and even shocking. Even more shocking was the fact that it immediately became a model of emulation, inspiring large numbers of Egyptians to succeed in bringing down the regime of Husni Mubarak, the second-longest-serving ruler (twenty-nine years) in the entire region (Qaddafi was the first, having seized power in 1969). The vivid scenes of protest and confrontation with the security forces, and the energy and euphoria of the many hundreds of thousands of Tunisians and Egyptians gathered in the centers of Tunis and Cairo, was palpable, and similar challenges to ruling regimes quickly spread in all directions—to Bahrain,

Yemen, Libya, and Syria, with not insignificant protests in a number of other countries as well.

There is no little irony in the fact that Tunisia might even be considered a model to emulate. Throughout its fifty-five years of independence, Tunisia was mostly at the margins of Arab politics as the ruling elites sought to keep at bay potentially subversive influences, whether leftist pan-Arab or Islamist. As early as 1991, Samuel Huntington had identified Tunisia as one of the Arab world's prime candidates for future democratization.[19] Its assets included the country's compactness and ethnic and religious homogeneity, a well-defined collective identity, a relatively large middle class, a tradition of active civil society (e.g., unions, lawyers, teachers), and a tradition of cultural openness to the outside world. However, Ben `Ali had essentially struck a bargain with the country's middle class in the early 1990s—harsh repression of the Islamist opposition and the maintenance of stability and economic growth in return for continued authoritarian rule.[20] Thus, it would take another twenty years before Huntington's supposition would begin to be realized. And while Ben `Ali's overthrow inspired others, no Arab country would prove capable of emulating Tunisia's post-revolutionary success between 2011 and 2014 in transitioning toward a fragile, but nonetheless meaningfully institutionalized pluralist and democratizing order.

As the protest movements spread, the GCC emerged as the only relatively cohesive bloc of Arab states. Having banded together in 1981 in the shadow of the Iran-Iraq war, this club of pro-Western, oil-rich, tribally based, geopolitically vulnerable Sunni Arab monarchies was generally like-minded on major strategic issues. The exception in recent years was Qatar, which was determined to carve out its own niche in regional affairs. As the Arab Spring upheavals unfolded, Qatar's differences with the rest of the GCC countries, led by Saudi Arabia, would become ever more pronounced.

Already at the outset, the Saudis were upset with Qatar, owing to al-Jazeera's unabashed support for, and 24/7 coverage of the protests in Tunis and Cairo, which was crucial in building their momentum. For the Saudi leadership, the toppling of Ben 'Ali, to whom it quickly gave asylum, was bad enough. The deposal, just four weeks later, of Egypt's Mubarak, the Saudis' prime regional ally for more than twenty years, shook them profoundly, all the more so in light of what they viewed as the US Obama Administration's failure to stand firmly behind him.

Egypt's changing political fortunes over the next few years would be the source of much tension between Riyadh and Doha.

For the moment, however, the Saudis could console themselves with the fact that the Egyptian military command remained in charge. Of more immediate concern were three emerging hot spots—Bahrain, Libya, and Yemen. Bahrain, of course, was one of the GCC's own, a member of the club. Unlike the others, however, it had a marginalized and increasingly vocal Shi`i majority, which in mid-February 2011 took to the streets in emulation of the protest movements in Tunisia and Egypt. After three weeks of demonstrations, the loosely organized youthful protestors, backed by smaller, organized opposition factions, became more confrontational and radicalized, both in word and deed. Hearing the voices calling for the toppling of the monarchy and seeing the protestors march on the royal palace itself and move to lock down Manama's financial district, old-guard elements in the government, backed by the increasingly anxious and defensive Sunni minority, took charge. In what was essentially a palace coup, Prime Minister Khalifa bin Salman Al Khalifa reasserted his authority. Blatantly disregarding Western urgings to reach agreement with the protestors, Bahrain welcomed the dispatch of a thousand-man Saudi-led GCC force, which crossed the Bahrain-Saudi Arabian causeway on March 14, setting the stage for a government crackdown.[21]

All along, the Saudis had viewed the unrest in Bahrain not through the lens of civic assertion, as it was seen in the West, but rather as a religious-communal struggle with potential to inflame the Saudis' own Shi`i population in the kingdom's neighboring oil-rich Eastern Province. Moreover, the Bahrain crisis also carried profound geopolitical ramifications: periodic Iranian claims to Bahrain and Tehran's vocal support for the Bahraini protestors posed a clear and present danger in Saudi eyes—the possible extension of Iranian power and influence across the Persian Gulf and onto the peninsula itself. Hence, for the Saudis, and thus the other GCC members, the choice was clear.

Whereas the purpose of the GCC's intervention in Bahrain policy was to restore the status quo ante, stabilizing Yemen, Saudi Arabia's soft underbelly on its southeast border, required a different strategy. As in Bahrain, February 2011 witnessed the beginning of widespread popular protests against Yemen's long-ruling autocratic president, `Ali `Abdallah Saleh. These quickly became expressions of rivalries within factionalized, tribally based elite groups. Given the concurrent rebellions in the formerly independent southern region[22] and the northwest, the latter by the Houthis, a Zaydi Shi`i movement suspected by the Saudis of receiving support from Iran, plus the active presence in portions of the countryside of al-Qa`ida's Arabian peninsula branch, Yemen was quickly falling into the category of being a "failed state," and a prime source for potentially destabilizing influences in the region.[23]

Seeking to cope with the crisis, the GCC took the lead in seeking a dignified exit of Saleh from power. Within two months, it had formulated a document, with American, British, and EU input, that offered Saleh immunity from prosecution in return for transferring power to his deputy. It also provided a multi-step path for political reform. But Saleh's reluctance to sign the agreement extended the crisis for many months. He himself was seriously wounded in a bomb explosion and spent months in Saudi Arabia convalescing. It was only in late November 2011, under the threat of UN-sponsored international sanctions, that he signed the agreement, under Saudi auspices in Riyadh. Two months later, he departed Yemen for the US for further medical treatment. For the Saudis and the rest of the GCC, it was the optimal outcome.[24] However, Yemen would remain a shell of a state, Saleh would eventually return to the country, seeking to make a comeback, and Houthi rebels, who had been left out of the GCC-brokered deal that established a governing coalition, consolidated their control in the north and continued to push southward. A UN-sponsored National Dialogue Conference, in which the Houthis participated, produced a number of agreed-on principles to guide Yemen's transition toward genuine power sharing in a federal-type arrangement, but implementation was another matter. Tapping into "widespread frustration with the corruption, favoritism, and injustices of the old regime," the Houthis attracted new followers and expanded their areas of control. In fact, they turned out to be the big winner of the 2011 uprising against Saleh, as the power of the state contracted and the military split between supporters of Saleh and of Gen. `Ali Muhsin.[25] At the end of 2014, the Houthis stunned everyone by taking over San`a, the capital, and in 2015 marched southward, provoking a Saudi bombing campaign to try to roll back the Houthis, who were seen in Riyadh as Tehran's proxy. As it had in the 1960s, the land ironically once known as "Árabia Felix" was now the battleground for a geopolitical and ideological conflict between rival regional powers.

Libya was another story. As opposed to intervening to preserve the status quo as in Bahrain, or to brokering a leadership change in order to maintaining the overall status quo as in Yemen, the GCC's goal in Libya was to demolish Qaddafi's personal rule and achieve regime change. The Libyan ruler had never made any bones about his disdain for the Gulf Arab monarchies: his media had branded the late Saudi King Fahd the "pig of the peninsula" (*khanzirat al-jazira*),[26] and Qaddafi and Saudi King 'Abdullah had exchanged personal invectives on a number of occasions in recent years at Arab summits, in front of the television cameras.[27] Sensitive to charges that they were opposed to the demands for change bubbling up from below, Gulf Arab monarchs jumped at the chance to support the Libyan uprising. Unlike the protests in Bahrain and Yemen, however, the demands of Libyan protestors quickly precipitated a civil war. Benghazi, in the eastern part of the country, became the base for the opposition, while Qaddafi and his loyalists held fast to Tripoli, in the west.

The challenge of toppling Qaddafi was an entirely different order of business for the GCC states. At best, they could only play a supporting role, with the heavy lifting to be done by Western powers. To that end, Saudi Arabia and Qatar, now on the same side, activated the Arab League, a matter of no small irony, as Qaddafi had hosted the annual Arab summit conference in his hometown of Sirte just one year earlier. Accordingly, on February 22, 2011, Arab League foreign ministers condemned the Libyan government's violent crackdown of anti-regime protesters and suspended it from participation in League meetings. This marked the first occasion when a League member had been barred due to actions taken against its own citizens within its sovereign territory, and it portended further measures. On March 12, as Qaddafi threatened to reconquer the rebellious eastern region of the country and hunt down his opponents "like rats," Qatar and Riyadh spearheaded a League resolution calling on the UN Security Council to impose a no-fly zone to protect Libyan civilians from Qaddafi's promised retributions. The situation was reminiscent of the 1990 Arab summit's actions against Saddam Husayn. Then, as now, the League provided vital Arab legitimacy for Western governments' subsequent actions. Qatar and the UAE would even provide small contingents from their respective air forces to participate in the NATO-led attacks on Qaddafi's forces, and the two countries, along with Kuwait, recognized the rebels' Transitional Council as the legitimate Libyan government well before Qaddafi's ultimate capture and summary execution on October 20, 2011.

Four years later, however, the situation in Libya was far from what the anti-Qaddafi coalition had hoped for. Notwithstanding a series of elections and the writing of a new constitution, viable state institutions had not been fashioned, the country was awash in competing armed militias, and radical Islamist groups were finding Libya to be a gold mine for arms, recruits, and a base for operations, to the consternation of its immediate neighbors—Algeria, Tunisia, and Egypt. Ethnic Touareg mercenaries serving in Qaddafi's armed forces moved out of Libya with their weapons and eventually seized a large portion of northern Mali, under a radical Islamist banner, before being driven back by French forces in early 2013.[28] Near the end of 2014, Libya was in the midst of a new civil war: Egypt, the UAE, and Saudi Arabia all provided active military support for a Libyan general, Khalifa Haftar, in his conflict with the Islamist-dominated post-Qaddafi authorities established in Tripoli, who were supported by Qatar. Qaddafi's four decades of brutal dictatorship and state-building efforts, underpinned by oil-generated revenues, had failed to produce a cohesive national identity where there hadn't been one before, and like Yemen, the future of the country's territorial integrity and corporate identity was very much in doubt.

MOROCCO—CONTAINING THE PROTESTS, RECONFIGURING NATIONAL IDENTITY

Morocco has always been *sui generis* within the Arab collective, an entity with a distinct geographical core stretching back more than 1,200 years; a ruling dynasty more than 350 years old whose legitimacy is based on direct descent from the Prophet Muhammad; religious homogeneity (98 percent Sunni Islam); and a particular material and popular culture, modes of religious practice, and linguistic configuration, much of which stems from Morocco's large Berber population and heritage. As with Algeria and Tunisia, the experience of French colonialism had a lasting impact that further distinguished Morocco from the Arab East. At the same time, the modern national identity project of Morocco's ruling elites, like their Algerian counterparts, was Arab-oriented, linguistically, culturally, and religiously, and sought to gradually Arabize their Berber-speaking populations. Under the long reign of King Hassan II (1961–1999), Morocco became firmly ensconced in the club of conservative pro-Western Arab monarchies, and played an active role in Arab politics, hosting numerous Arab summit conferences. Under his son and successor, Muhammad VI (1999——), it lowered its regional profile.

Morocco also suffered from many of the same underlying ills that had driven the protests elsewhere—corruption, poverty, unemployment, the overwhelming concentration of wealth in the hands of a small stratum of elite families intertwined with the authorities, the absence of real democracy, and closed horizons for its large youthful population, which suffered from disproportionately high rates of unemployment and underemployment. Not surprisingly, then, the unfolding of events in Tunisia and Egypt at the beginning of 2011 were keenly watched in Morocco and generated a protest movement that brought tens of thousands of demonstrators into the streets across the country. While positively mild compared to the rest of the region, the protests raised the specter of Morocco going down the same road as so many other Arab states, thus unnerving the authorities. But the protests were contained, as the king seized the initiative by promoting constitutional reform that bought much needed time and took the wind out of the protests' sails.

A new constitution was officially ratified in July 2011 in a nationwide referendum. Regarding the issue of Moroccan collective identity, its most innovative aspect was that it explicitly recognized Tamazight, the language of the country's Berber-speaking populations (an estimated forty percent of the total), as an official language, and required the passage of an "organic law" to translate that status into reality, in education and other spheres of public life. In that same vein, it emphasized that the Amazigh (Berber) people and culture constituted an integral component of Moroccan identity, which had been forged over the course of history, alongside the Arab-Islamic and Saharan-Hassanian components, and enriched along the way by "African, Andalusian, Hebraic, and Mediterranean currents." To be sure, some Amazigh activists failed to be excited by the new constitution. For them, the constitutional upgrade was just the latest in a series of the state's pseudo-embraces of the Amazigh movement in order to co-opt and neutralize it. Nonetheless, from a broader perspective, the officialization of Tamazight by the state, along with the explicit recognition of Amazigh identity as central to the Moroccan historical and social fabric, was nothing less than historic. Morocco now joined Iraq in the club of Arab League members in which Arab identity was now officially attenuated.[29]

THE STRUGGLE FOR SYRIA REDUX

Following the uprising in Tunisia, and in the midst of the protests in Egypt and Bahrain, Bashar al-Asad gave a memorable interview to the *Wall Street Journal*, in which he confidently asserted that Syria was immune from unrest because, unlike elsewhere, his policies were in tune with the Syrian people's desire to promote "resistance."[30] Within a few short weeks, however, this self-assuredness proved to be profoundly misconceived. Initial naïve protests by youth in a Sunni peripheral town were harshly repressed by the authorities, sparking further protests and repression, and, within the year, Syria descended into a brutal civil war. As of spring 2015, the war had cost over 220,000 lives and turned close to fifty percent of its population into refugees: 7.6 million, who had been displaced but were still inside Syria, and nearly four million, who had fled the country, primarily to Jordan, Turkey, and Lebanon.[31] Taken together, they constituted the largest number of refugees from one Arab country in history. The centralized Syrian state that had painfully emerged over the previous decades and become a regional actor with considerable clout had vanished. As of spring 2015, the Asad regime maintained effective control over only 25 percent of its territory, with the rest held by a collection of rival rebel groups dominated by radical Islamists, headed by the "Islamic State" (IS) and *Jabhat al-Nusra*. In addition, Syria's long-neglected Kurdish population (c. two million) now established control over their areas in the northeast (West) Kurdistan; "Rojoava" in the parlance of Kurdish nationalists. As had been the case in the 1940s and 1950s, much of the region's future seemed to hinge on the struggle within, and over, Syria.

As the Asad regime pulled out all stops in its battle to survive, it became estranged to an unprecedented degree from nearly all Arab states, and Turkey as well. In particular, the conservative Arab monarchies, facing their own restless populations, found it useful to identify with the predominantly Sunni Muslim Syrian opposition. Even more importantly, they recognized the potential geostrategic implications of the fall of the house of Asad. Having failed for three decades to pry Syria loose from the Iranian embrace, the prospect of regime change in favor of a Sunni-dominated government more attuned to Saudi, Turkish, Egyptian, and Western sensibilities and interests (not that these were identical, by any means) was extremely enticing. Tehran recognized what was at stake as well and acted accordingly. Iranian arms supplies, ferried via a compliant Shi'i-led government in Iraq, Iranian advisers, Iraqi Shi`i volunteers, and thousands of Hizballah fighters from Lebanon proved to be crucial in preventing the Asad regime's collapse. So did Russia's military, economic, and diplomatic assistance. In addition to the numerous other bones of contention between Moscow and the NATO alliance, Vladmir Putin had been angered that the West had used the Security Council's resolution to protect Libyan civilians as a cover to engineer Qaddafi's overthrow, and was determined not to allow the West to have its way in Syria, Moscow's longtime ally.

The Evolving Crisis

To be sure, many months would pass before the bridges would be entirely burned between Asad and the anti-Iranian, Arab Sunni bloc. Indeed, one of the first acts by the new Arab League Secretary-General Nabil al-`Arabi upon officially assuming his post in July 2011, after Moussa stepped down to run for the Egyptian presidency, was to meet Asad in Damascus. There he denounced "foreign intervention" in Syria, and specifically, US president Barak Obama for declaring that Asad had lost all legitimacy. At that point in time, a reform process that Asad had pledged to implement appeared to `Arabi to be the best hope for avoiding a conflagration in Syria.[32]

But the belief in Asad's commitment to reform withered away in subsequent months, and `Arabi organized an Arab diplomatic effort to apply pressure on Asad to make concessions. The proffered "Arab solution" to the crisis put the onus on the Asad regime: It was required to end its violence and killing, release prisoners, withdraw the army from cities, allow free access to foreign journalists, open a dialogue with the opposition under Arab League auspices, and accept the entry of a multi-national League monitoring mission that would report on compliance with its plan.

Damascus's slowness in responding and efforts to limit the number and purview of the monitors resulted in Syria's suspension from League activities, as had been done with Libya. Eighteen states voted in favor of the suspension, with only Lebanon and Yemen opposing and Iraq abstaining. That same day, November 12, 2011, Jordan's King `Abdallah became the first Arab head of state to suggest that Asad should step down. On November 27, the League announced the imposition of sanctions on Syria, including the banning of senior Syrian officials from traveling to other Arab countries, freezing Syrian assets in Arab countries, and halting financial operations with major Syrian banks. Further sanctions were announced the following week.

While clearly unhappy with the turn of events, the Syrians kept the door open and eventually agree to receive an Arab monitoring mission. Its very establishment was a novelty. Syrian forces intervening in Lebanon in 1976 had received the Arab League's qualified stamp of approval. Now, Syria was on the receiving end of collective Arab policies, though this was hardly a case of collective Arab will being imposed on Syria. The 165-member mission was led by a retired Sudanese general who had been involved in the genocidal actions in Darfur and was sympathetic to the official Syrian version of events. The regime's efforts to manage the mission's itinerary apparently included sending prostitutes to the hotel housing the monitors, secretly photographing them in their own rooms and bathrooms, and posting the pictures online in order to blackmail them.[33] Moreover, a number of monitors were attacked and injured by pro-regime elements. The chaotic nature of the mission led to the very vocal resignation of an Algerian participant, who called it "a farce."[34] The fifty-strong GCC contingent was demonstratively withdrawn in opposition to extending the mission's activities into a second month, followed quickly by Jordan's withdrawal, and the operation was closed down. Most importantly, the mission had failed to staunch the bloodshed.

Bashar's response to Arab condemnations was predictably dismissive. Much more than them, he declared, it was Syria that represented Arab identity and had advanced Arab interests, politically and culturally. Suspending Syria from the Arab League simply meant that the League had suspended its Arabness. Syria, he insisted, was the victim of an international conspiracy hatched by regional and global powers who, as in the past, wanted to destabilize the country and advance their interests. What passed for the international community, he declared, was "a group of big colonial countries which view the whole world as an arena full of slaves who serve their interests."[35]

   In response to the mission's failure, Arab League foreign ministers called on Asad to step down in favor of his vice president and for the establishment of a national unity government.[36] The plan, officially tendered to the Security Council by Morocco, was endorsed by the United States, the European Union, and Turkey but vetoed by Russia and China. The veto emboldened the Asad regime to take the offensive to try to stamp out its opponents, as had been brutally done in the early 1980s to a Muslim Brotherhood-sponsored insurgency. Qatar's emir Hamad suggested that troops from Arab countries be dispatched to quell the violence; League officials called for a joint Arab-UN peacekeeping force, and Saudi leaders spoke out forcefully in favor of arming the Syrian opposition. Riyadh's frustration with the absence of action was evidenced by Foreign Minister Sa'ud al-Faysal's very public complaint and demonstrative early exit from the Friends of Syria international conclave, held in Tunisia on February 24, 2012, for the purpose of applying additional pressure on the regime and mobilizing support for the Syrian opposition. The gathering produced few results. Similarly, the efforts of former UN Secretary-General Kofi Annan, jointly sanctioned by the UN and the Arab League, and his successor, Lakhdar Brahimi, the veteran Algerian and UN diplomat, generated little.

   As the Syrian civil war intensified during the latter half of 2012, the GCC and Arab League were drawn ever further onto the side of the opposition. On November 11, 2012, the fractious Syrian opposition came together in Qatar to proclaim the establishment of a new umbrella organization, the National Coalition for Syrian Revolutionary and Opposition Forces. The GCC immediately recognized it as "the legitimate representative of the Syrian people." Arab League foreign ministers, meeting in Cairo two days later, welcomed the establishment of the new group and praised Qatar's efforts, but stopped short of recognizing it as Syria's sole representative, following the objections of Iraq and Algeria. The organization's head, Ahmad al-`Asi al-Jarba, was granted the Syrian seat at the March 2013 Arab summit conference in Doha, thanks in part to host Qatar's influence. However, at the following year's summit, in Kuwait, he was prevented from doing so, although he was allowed to address the conference.

   As of mid-2015, the tides of the war appeared to have shifted again in favor of the various rebel forces, benefitting from the increased flow of weapons via Saudi Arabia, Qatar, and Turkey, and from the serious attrition of the Syrian military. Speculation about a possible abandonment of Damascus and regrouping in the `Alawi heartland of northwest Syria increased. Regardless of the outcome, rebuilding the broken Syrian polity would be an onerous, and perhaps impossible, task in the years ahead.

EGYPT CONSUMED WITH ITSELF

Meanwhile, the four years following Husni Mubarak's overthrow witnessed wild swings of the political pendulum. From the first days following Mubarak's removal, it was clear that the Islamist current, although not having been primarily responsible for Mubarak's downfall, would become a major player in determining the country's future. Unlike in Tunisia, where the process of constitution-writing and establishing governing institutions was painstakingly deliberate and fairly civil in tone, in Egypt, the process was hasty, highly charged, and extremely polarizing.

Throughout the first eighteen months of the post-Mubarak era, the Muslim Brotherhood and the governing Supreme Council of the Armed Forces (SCAF) engaged in a delicate dance, as each sought to shape Egypt's political evolution according to its preferences while avoiding all-out confrontation with the other. A watershed was reached in in June 2012, as the Brotherhood's Mohammed Morsi was elected to the presidency, with 51.73 percent of the vote (26.4 million out of 50.95 million), barely beating Mubarak's last prime minister and former air force commander, Ahmed Shafiq. Egyptian Islamists, and by extension, Islamists throughout the region, had reason to believe that the wind was at their backs. But over the next year, the Egyptian political scene would become even more polarized as Morsi overreached in his effort to consolidate Islamist hegemony over the country and confine the military to the barracks. Incompetence in governing, particularly in the economic realm, undermined his standing as well. Hence, just one year later, massive street demonstrations provided the military, led by Field Marshal and Defense Minister `Abd al-Fatah al-Sisi with the necessary legitimacy to carry out a coup, depose and arrest Morsi, and crack down massively on his supporters. Apart from Qatar, GCC state elites were overjoyed. The Saudis, the UAE, and Kuwait together provided $20 billion to Sisi's regime in the months after the coup in order to help him stabilize his rule and stave off economic collapse, and would continue to do so in 2014–2015.[37]

Over the next year, Sisi shed his uniform, was elected president by ninety-seven percent of the approximately twenty-five million Egyptians who, according to official figures, went to the polls on May 25–27, 2014, and reasserted the primacy of the military, and allied economic and administrative elites—Egypt's "deep state." Sisi was also supported by the Copt minority (c. 10 percent of the population),which deeply feared the Islamists, and many ordinary middle- aged and older people who yearned for stability, security, and a sense of normalcy after three years of postrevolutionary upheaval. Riding a wave of nostalgia for `Abd al-Nasir,[38] Sisi was trumpeted as Nasir's heir, representing Egyptian pride, dignity, and self-assertion against both radical Islamists and meddling Western powers, particularly the United States. Thousands of Brotherhood members and sympathizers, and the entire leadership were incarcerated, with the state showing no interest in dialogue of any kind. History never exactly repeats itself, but as Mark Twain supposedly once said, "it does rhyme." The crackdown evoked the early years after the 1952 Egyptian revolution, when the ruling military junta, led by the popular young Nasir, imprisoned, tortured, and even eventually executed some of the Brotherhood's leading figures, including the theoretician still revered by radical Sunni Islamists everywhere, Sayyid Qutb. State repression also extended to liberal critics of the regime, including Egypt's articulate and politically conscious youth, who played crucial roles in undermining both Mubarak and Morsi, and who dared to challenge what they viewed as the betrayal of the ideals of the Tahrir Square Revolution.

The unfolding of events in Egypt in 2013–2014 was somewhat reminiscent of what happened in Algeria in the 1990s. In Egypt, some Islamists drew the same conclusions that Algerian Islamists had after the military's crackdown, taking up arms, although not on the same scale. Moreover, just as young Algerians returned from the anti-Soviet jihad in Afghanistan with military training and a will to fight their own "infidel" regime, so too did Egyptians return from the new jihadi battlefront, Syria, with the kind of prowess that promised more bloodshed in the future. The Sinai desert region had already become a comfortable operating zone for these jihadis, and the confrontation with the Egyptian state now entered into higher gear.

To be sure, Sisi appeared to possess a degree of popular legitimacy and unified support within the ruling elite that the Algerian junta never had. Salafi-jihadi terrorism in Egypt only reinforced his standing, enabling the state media to successfully tar the Brotherhood with the "terrorist" label. Following the murderous radical Islamist attacks in France in January 2015, pro-government journalists in *Al-Ahram* stressed that "the horror that unfolded in Paris was written in big letters on Cairo's walls all along. We read it, but the West refused to take notice."[39] Sisi also framed the issue as a problem within Islam: a "revolution" in Islamic thought was needed, he declared at al-Azhar University, just a week before the Paris attack, one that would not "rely on a discourse that has not changed for 800 years...and had become a source of anxiety, danger, killing, and destruction for the rest of the world."[40]

Parliamentary elections were planned in 2015 that were intended to complete Sisi's institutional consolidation of power. What would he do with it? No one expected economic miracles—Egypt's problems were too deep-seated to be amenable to quick fixes. But Sisi would undoubtedly need to be able to point to interim achievements in both the security and economic realms in order to avoid a renewal of social and political protests. He already invoked the Nasirist legacy of greater state involvement in the economy, as a counter to the crony capitalism that characterized the Mubarak era.[41] In the same vein, he expressed a desire to direct more of the state's massive food and fuel subsidies to those who really needed it. And just as Nasir had his big-ticket economic development project—the Aswan High Dam—Sisi trumpeted one of his own, the large-scale widening of the Suez Canal.

Egypt, Hamas, and the Israeli-Hamas Confrontation

For Hamas, the Palestinian offshoot of the Egyptian Muslim Brotherhood, the rise to power of the Brotherhood in Egypt in 2011–2012 seemed to herald a new dawn. But it was a false one. During his year in power, Morsi did not fully open the Gaza-Egyptian border while struggling to cope with an Islamist insurgency in Sinai, and Sisi's regime accused Hamas of providing vital support to Islamist militants, drawing the blood of Egyptian security forces there. Consquently, it moved forcefully to close down the network of tunnels between Sinai and Gaza vital to the Gazan economy. Not surprisingly, Israeli-Egyptian security cooperation reached an unprecedented level. Hence, during the fifty-one-day war in summer 2014 in Gaza, Sisi clearly hoped that Israel's military would deal a sharp, and even fatal blow to Hamas. Throughout the conflict, the Sisi-directed Egyptian media, pro-regime public figures, and generally more circumspect Saudi commentators kept up a steady stream of withering criticism of Hamas for repeatedly bringing disaster to the Palestinian public. Their critique resembled that leveled against the Lebanese Shi`ite, Iranian-backed Hizballah for provoking the Israel-Lebanon war in 2006. But this time, it was an all-Sunni affair. On the other side of the divide within the Sunni Arab world stood Turkey and Qatar, as unlike as two countries can be, both of which aspired to play major regional roles. The Tahrir Square uprising and the Muslim Brotherhood's subsequent rise to power had been warmly welcomed in Ankara, as they were in line with Erdoğan's promotion of political Islam through the ballot box. Understandably, the Brotherhood's removal, and then the Israel-Gaza war, raised the level of mutual of invective between Cairo and Ankara to new heights, while Cairo (and Israel) rejected efforts by Turkey and Qatar to replace Egypt as the primary mediator to an end of the war. Near the end of 2014, Qatar acceded to Saudi pressure to close down al-Jazeera's Egyptian channel, whose continuous anti-Sisi coverage outraged the Egyptian authorities, suggesting that the Egyptian-Saudi alliance was making its weight felt in the region. In March 2015, Cairo hosted the annual Arab League summit conference. Although Egypt remained consumed with internal affairs, and its regional influence paled in comparison to past decades, Sisi's assertiveness as summit host, which included a proposal for the establishment of a joint Arab force to combat terror, indicated that Egypt remained intent on playing a leadership role in the Arab world and the Middle East as a whole, and that this intent was an integral part of the country's political DNA. However, as had been true throughout modern Arab history, establishing a multi-nation military force required a degree of agreement and common purpose that seemed absent. Once again, Egyptian desires and intentions did not seem to match its capabilities.

THE "ISLAMIC STATE," THE KURDISH FACTOR, AND THE BLURRING OF BOUNDARIES IN THE FERTILE CRESCENT

During the early days of the Arab Spring protests, many analysts had proclaimed that they constituted a definitive rejection of al-Qa`ida's ideology of waging violent jihad against corrupt Arab regimes and their Western backers.[42] Indeed, Osama bin Laden's former popularity, as measured by public opinion polls, had already declined sharply by then.[43] Hence, at first glance, his liquidation by US forces in May 2011 seemed to herald the organization's demise. However, the organization demonstrated an ability to adapt and even reshape itself, while maintaining a core message that retains its appeal in some Muslim circles. Moreover, the subsequent breakdown of order across the Middle East and North Africa, and concomitant sharpening of the age-old Sunni-Shi`i fault line in the Muslim world, provided new arenas and opportunities for al-Qa`ida and like-minded Sunni Salafi-jihadi groups, from Iraq and Syria, to Yemen, Sinai, and across North and East Africa.

In 2013, the renewal of large-scale sectarian-based violence in Iraq became intertwined with the ongoing brutal civil war in Syria in new and unforeseen ways. In the process, the very nature of the post-World War I Arab and Middle East order was called into question, thanks to two diametrically opposed developments: the emergence of the jihadi "Islamic State" (*al-dawla al-Islamiyya;* IS) organization, which seized control over a large swath of territory in Iraq and Syria, and proclaimed the creation of a caliphate there; and the expansion of a pan-Kurdish space and collective consciousness.

IS was first established as the Islamic State of Iraq in 2006, emerging from the Iraqi franchise of al-Qa`ida that had been founded by Abu Mus`ab al-Zarqawi, a colleague and ultimately rival of Osama bin Laden. Zarqawi's brutal executions, including personal beheadings, of uncooperative Muslims, was too much for even Bin Laden and his deputy Ayman al-Zawahiri to bear. In 2007–2008, the Iraqi Sunni insurgency had lost steam, as Iraqi's Sunni tribes turned against them, with the promise of having their needs addressed by the Iraqi authorities. But over time, Nuri al-Maliki government's increasingly marginalized and persecuted the disenfranchised Sunni Arab minority, wiping away the gains of 2007–2008. For Iraqi Sunnis, the Shi`i-dominated state and army was now the enemy. Whereas Bashar Asad's regime in Damascus had turned a blind eye to the steady stream of Sunni young men from Syria into Iraq in support al-Qa`ida's Iraqi franchise's jihad against US forces and the Shi`ite-dominated government in Baghdad between 2005–2007, the tables were turned during 2013. Young Iraqi Sunnis, along with others from across the region, now made their way to Syria to join Islamist radicals that were taking a leading role in the war against the Asad regime and its Shi`i Hizballah and Iranian supporters. The umbrella organization of Iraqi jihadi Islamists was rebranded in 2013 as the Islamic State of Iraq and *al-Sham* (the Levant/greater Syria; ISIS or ISIL) and began taking an active role in Syria's northern regions, against not only government forces but also other Syrian opposition forces, including armed groups of the Syrian Kurdish Democratic Union Party (*Partiya Yekîtiya Demokrat*; PYD). Earlier generations of militant Arab nationalists had bemoaned the Western powers' perfidy in artificially carving up the former Ottoman Arab lands after World War I, and advocated their reunification in the name of pan-Arab ideals. Now, the Syrian-Iraqi boundary was being effaced, but by true believers of a different sort, radical Salafi Sunnis proclaiming the establishment of an Islamic caliphate, the long-held utopic ideal of political Islam.

Initially, ISIS was ostensibly part of *Jabhat al-Nusra*, al-Qa`ida's franchise in Syria. In fact, however, its head, a shadowy figure named Abu Bakr al-Baghdadi, made a power play to take over the organization and expand his reach into Syria. Eventually, this morphed into a full-fledged violent conflict between the two organizations, with ISIS gaining the upper hand in Syria. In June 2014, it changed its name again, to the Islamic State (IS). The new name emphasized the organization's vision of a universal caliphate, not limited to a particular territory. As if to bolster the point, jihadi groups in Libya and Egypt's Sinai desert proclaimed their loyalty to IS.

In June–July 2014, IS forces suddenly seized control of Mosul, Iraq's second-largest city, and up to one-third of the country's territory, while American-equipped Iraqi forces collapsed and fled, leaving behind vast quantities of advanced weapons. IS forces in Syria took control of Tabqa air force base in Raqqa province, confirming its dominance in northeastern Syria. The boundary between Syria and Iraq, entities established in the aftermath of World War I, was now effectively erased.

The list of IS's nightmarish acts was long: pursuit of genocide against the Yezidi minority in northern Iraq, brutal persecution of native Christian communities in Syria including crucifixions, beheadings, rape and enslavement of women and forced conversions, mass executions of Iraqi and Syrian soldiers, and extermination of a whole Syrian tribe that resisted its conquest. Horrific videoed beheadings of foreign journalists and of gay men being pushed to their deaths off the roof of a building were all manifestations of IS's apocalyptic vision of the future. In its regional capital in Syria, Raqqa, it practiced what the Arab-American analyst Husayn Ibish described as "thoroughgoing totalitarianism."[44]

In Iraq, ex-Ba`thi military commanders and bureaucrats came to play key roles in the building of IS's quasi-state, in terms of weapons procurement, training, and administration of areas under their control. In addition to the massive amounts of booty seized from the Iraqi and Syrian armies, it funded itself through the sale of oil from captured oil fields. An analysis by the Institute of the Study of War concluded that ISIS had a disciplined military command and unified, coherent leadership structure dedicated to pursuing a controlled military campaign in both Syria and Iraq in order to establish a transnational emirate in the widest possible area. IS was also supported by wealthy Gulf Arabs to the tune of hundreds of millions of dollars. Conversely, some members of Kuwait's Shi`i community are similarly raising funds for pro-regime elements.[45] Indeed, both Lebanese and Iraqi Shi`is have mirrored their Sunni counterparts in joining the struggle for Syria, further sharpening its sectarian aspect.

Between their terror tactics, alliances with local Sunni groups, and sometimes cooperation with other Syrian insurgent factions, their achievements were nothing short of spectacular. These in turn served as a vital recruiting tool for disconsolate and alienated Sunni youth throughout the region and beyond. So no doubt did American-led bombing raids against IS targets, which commenced in August 2014 in order to blunt ISIS's advances and bolster Iraqi government forces and, more immediately, the *peshmerga* of the KRG. Ironically, a year earlier, US war planes had been on the verge of bombing regime targets to punish it for employing chemical weapons against Syrian rebels. Now, the calibrated bombings in Syria were being carried out against Asad's opponents.

The International Centre for the Study of Radicalisation and Political Violence estimated in 2014 that the total number of foreign fighters in radical Islamist ranks (including returnees and fatalities) as 8,500 to 11,000 persons (c. ten percent of the total number of opposition fighters). They originated from seventy-four different countries, 70 percent from the Middle East and eighteen percent from Western Europe, presumably children of Muslim immigrants. The largest number (over two thousand) came from neighboring Jordan, followed by Saudi Arabia (over one thousand), Tunisia (970), Lebanon (890), and Libya (556). Based on the Afghanistan experience of the 1980s, the possible blowback effects once these battle-hardened, and ideologically motivated fighters return home are considerable.[46]

The porous Jordanian-Syrian border was one avenue of entry. Another was the Turkish-Syrian one. Turkish authorities made little or no effort to interdict the transit of foreign fighters whose destination was obviously the battlefront. The Saudis apparently turned a blind eye as well, enabling prospective jihadi fighters to depart from Riyadh airport for northern Syria (via Turkey). Exporting their own jihadis served as a safety valve of sorts for the regime, as well as a legitimizing tool at home. It also confirmed that, the battle for Syria was deemed crucial by the Saudis for checking Iran's hegemonic ambitions and for the regime's survival. In this sense, it was the struggle for Syria all over again. On the other hand, by 2015, the specter of a large IS entity to the north was a nightmare as well. It was for the Jordanian state as well. One of its air force pilots, participating in US-led coalition air strikes against IS (as were UAE warplanes) was taken prisoner. Efforts to broker his release failed, and he was ceremoniously burned alive in January 2015. Chillingly, IS made sure to disseminate the video of his immolation across the globe. For the moment, Jordanians were almost uniformly outraged, and King 'Abdallah ordered large-scale bombing raids against IS targets. The longer-term domestic and regional effects of Jordan's direct involvement in the war against IS remained to be seen.

The rise of IS was both a consequence and a cause of the deepening salience of the Sunni-Shi'i divide in Arab and regional affairs. It also played a key role in the sharpening of Kurdish ethno-national consciousness. To be sure, the swift breakdown of the Syrian state in 2011–2012 had already made Syrian Kurds, numbering perhaps 10 percent of the Syrian population, many of them deprived of Syrian citizenship and living in the remote northeast of the country, an integral part of the Kurdish ethno-national assertion across the region. The PYD had established autonomous governing mechanisms and defense units to fill the vacuum left by the contracting Syrian state. The war's spread to their region generated a flow of more than two hundred thousand Syrian Kurdish refugees to the relative safety of the Kurdish Regional Government in northern Iraq, which was increasingly a de facto independent entity, and spearheading the broader movement for Kurdish self-assertion across the region. In 2014 the Syrian Kurdish city of Kobane, located on the border with Turkey, became a symbol for Kurds everywhere, as it successfully withstood besieging IS forces, with the help of American airstrikes and *peshmerga* reinforcements sent by the KRG.

Overall, the state of the Arab world in mid-2015 was a far cry from the heady "Spring" days of four years earlier. Of all the countries touched by the upheavals, only Tunisia had translated them into something that appeared to be sustainable and approved of by the bulk of the populace. Egypt had experienced wild swings of the political pendulum, and at considerable human cost, before restoring the old order. Saudi Arabia served as the bulwark for Egypt and other conservative Arab regimes while trying unsuccessfully to bring about regime change in Syria. Yemen and Libya had become "failed" states. The reform movement in Bahrain had been crushed. Morocco's 2011 cosmetic constitutional reforms had been enough to defuse the heterogeneous protest movement there, while ruling authoritarian elites in Algeria had maintained themselves as well. Most dramatically, the Syrian civil war, which was spilling over into always fragile Lebanon as well, and the sectarian conflict in Iraq had resulted in the governments' loss of control over wide swaths of territory in both entities. The Arab League had still been shown to have some limited instrumental value, being employed in a number of instances by the Saudi-led grouping of states and providing important legitimacy for international action in Libya, but primarily remained a reflection of the overall balance of power within the Arab world, and of Arab collective weakness. The vacuum in the Fertile Crescent, the historic cradle of modern Arabism, was being filled, at least partially, by the apocalyptic IS and Kurdish ethno-nationalist forces.

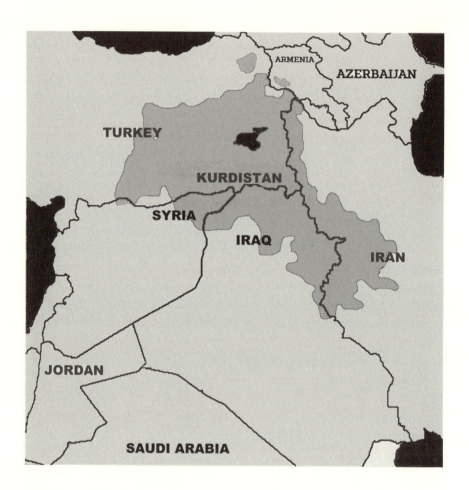

Figure 11.1.   Greater Kurdistan.

CONCLUDING OBSERVATIONS

Whither the Arab System? Whither the Arab State?

One hundred years after the outbreak of World War I and the collapse of the Ottoman Empire, the system of Arab states that had emerged in the subsequent decades, underpinned by an overarching Arab national identity and loosely organized under the rubric of the League of Arab States, appeared to have reached a Shakespearean moment, "to be or not to be." What had happened? Arab nationalism had achieved hegemonic status among the emerging Arab entities in the period between the two world wars, decisively shaping both domestic and regional politics. However, the new Arab states were led by narrow-based elites, their governing capacity was severely limited, and the level of national cohesion extremely low. All of this became amply clear in 1948. The colossal failure in the 1948 Arab-Israeli war, the first major challenge to the newly formed Arab collective, helped to catalyze the overthrow of a number of Arab regimes in the 1950s, inaugurating a new era of both hope and conflict. However, the vision of revolutionary pan-Arabism, which had had such an electrifying effect on the younger generation of increasingly politicized Arab youth in the 1950s and 1960s, had proven impossible to realize, owing to the durability of competing and more parochial interests, as well as the limited capacities of its champions. Of course, the overlapping of the Cold War and the Arab-Israeli conflict with Arab politics exacerbated the situation immeasurably. By the end of the 1960s, it was clear that territorial-based Arab national entities had survived the assault of radical pan-

Arabism. Over the subsequent decades, Arab states seemed to have reached a critical mass in terms of organizational capacity and political legitimacy, while continuing to compete with one another over both concrete and symbolic matters connected to their identity as Arab states. Political and economic integration remained a far-off dream; at the same time, state Arabization policies and developments in the media realm deepened the cultural connections and interactions within the broad realm of the "Arab space," from the Atlantic Ocean to the Persian Gulf.

Throughout the vicissitudes of inter-Arab relations, Egypt's role, both politically and culturally, was generally outsized, usually in alliance with Saudi Arabia. This was true during the first decade after the Arab League's founding in 1945, when the two countries kept Hashimite ambitions in check, and almost continuously after the 1967 debacle, excepting Egypt's suspension from the League between 1979 and 1989. The revolution in the oil market after 1967 shifted the center of economic gravity to the Gulf region, and conferred the Saudis and the other Gulf Arab principalities with considerable influence, while also engendering palpable resentment among poorer Arabs and in the older established centers of Arab culture At the same time, Gulf Arab states were well aware of their vulnerabilities to threats emanating from ambitious and covetous neighbors, and were in constant need of both global and regional allies to balance those threats. Matters came to a head in 1990–1999, when Iraq's second bid for regional hegemony within a decade crashed and burned. The Gulf War effectively removed Iraq from any meaningful regional role and seemed to clear the way for a pro-Western Arab order led by Cairo and Riyadh, which could now get to work at building more effective collective Arab institutions and addressing the pressing needs of Arab societies.

However, whereas the reality of multiple Arab states had finally won out over the proponents of pan-Arab unity, the accompanying state-building projects had proven to be severely deficient. Arab states were "fierce," and not genuinely strong. At the dawn of the new millennium, Arab states had failed to jump on the globalization train, instead maintaining the existing systems of economic oligarchy and political autocracy and hereditary dynasty. Islamist movements had reemerged and become the prime opposition political force in most Arab states. Consequently, the meaning of Arab identity was increasingly bound up with Islam. Arab nationalism, therefore, lost its role both as a platform for secular politics and as a cohesive force overriding more traditional forms of collective identity. Regional politics were marked by Arab fragmentation and collective weakness, the concurrent increasing regional influence of Turkey and Iran, the two other non-Arab states in the Middle East besides Israel, and an expanding ethno-national Kurdish space.

It was this combination of factors that set the stage for the Arab Spring upheavals. Arab societies now essentially "kicked back" against their "over-stated" states. But apart from Tunisia, no country possessed the capability of translating the initial achievements of the protests into a durable and potentially stable and consensual order. And the resulting disorder resulted in state disintegration in many cases, the sharpening of geopolitical and ideological conflicts along both religious (Sunni-Shi`a) and national (Saudi-Iranian) fault lines, and further Kurdish self-assertion, with the Kurdish Regional Government in northern Iraq becoming independent in all but name. As for the Palestinian issue, the traditional pole for expression of common Arab identity, this too had faded in salience.

Yezid Sayigh noted in 2014 that "the most powerful ideological discourse of the independence period, Arab nationalism, ha[d] now given way to variants of Islamism that are increasingly militant and sectarian." Many Arab states, he said, were at a "tipping point," and some had already passed it, having failed "to evolve in ways that were responsive to social change and democratic economic restructuring."[1] Similarly, Paul Salem pointed to the collapse of the Sykes-Picot divisions and functional disintegration of Syria and Iraq, their replacement by predominantly `Alawi and Shi`i rump states, a rising Kurdish entity, and an emerging Sunni Arab "Syriaq" one. In addition, Yemen and Libya were essentially failed states, being wracked by ongoing violence grounded in sectarian, tribal, and geographical divisions.[2] Taking issue with this gloomy outlook, the Egyptian political scientist `Ali El Deen Hilal Dessouki expressed cautious optimism that the challenges facing the Arab regional system would be successfully addressed and that the Arab order would be maintained, organizationally, and in the realm of Arab identity. To be sure, he emphasized that the efficacy of collective Arab institutions was dependent on genuine political reform within Arab countries, one that would be based on "the principles of wise government, the rule of law and institutions, and respect for human rights." The Arab League's "political and ethical message," he declared, needed to be one that followed the lead of the Organization of American States and the Association of Southeast Asian nations in their promotion of democratic systems among their members as a condition for realizing the aims of their organization. Arabism, Dessouki said, did not stand in contrast to respect for ethnic identities and diversity, but should serve as a cultural framework that includes that diversity.[3] At this point of time, his cautious optimism for the Arab region's future seemed badly out of tune with the course of events on the ground. Picking up the pieces and refashioning the numerous fractured and fragmented Arab states that littered the region would be at the very least a herculean task in the coming years.

NOTES

INTRODUCTION

1. This chapter draws, in part, on Bruce Maddy-Weitzman and Asher Susser, "State Cohesion in the Middle East: Historical and Contemporary Perspectives," in *Inglorious Revolutions: State Cohesion in the Middle East After the Arab Spring*, Brandon Friedman and Bruce Maddy-Weitzman (eds.) (Tel Aviv: The Moshe Dayan Center, 2014), pp. 13–36.

2. For the systematic cultivation of territorial nationalism by state authorities via the vehicle of national celebrations, see Elie Podeh, *The Politics of National Celebration in the Arab Middle East* (New York: Cambridge UP, 2011).

3. Hisham Sharabi, *Neo-patriarchy: A Theory of Distorted Change* (Oxford: Oxford UP, 1988).

4. Paul Noble, "The Arab System: Pressures, Constraints, and Opportunities," in *The Foreign Policies of Arab States: The Challenge of Change*, Bahgat Korany and Ali E. Hillal Dessouki (eds.) (Boulder, CO: Westview Press, 1991), p. 56.

5. Paul Noble, "From Arab System to Middle East System?: Regional Pressures and Constraints," in *The Foreign Policies of Arab States*, Bahgat Korany and Ali E. Hillal Dessouki (eds.), third edition (Cairo and New York: AUC Press, 2008), p. 84.

6. Elie Kedourie, *In the Anglo-Arab Labyrinth* (Cambridge: Cambridge University Press, 1976).

7. Israel Gershoni, "Rethinking the Formation of Arab Nationalism in the Middle East, 1920–1945: Old and New Narratives;" in James Jankowski and Israel Gershoni (eds.), *Rethinking Nationalism in the Arab Middle East* (New York: Columbia University Press, 1997), pp. 3–25; Phillip Khoury, "The Para-

doxical in Arab Nationalism: Interwar Syria Revisited," in Jankowski and Gershoni (eds.), *Rethinking Nationalism*, pp. 273–87.

8. Ilya Harik,"The Origins of the Arab State System," in *The Arab State*, Giacomo Luciani (ed.) (Berkeley: University of California Press, 1990), pp. 1–28.

9. J. P. Nettl, "The state as a conceptual variable," *World Politics* 20, 4 (1968), pp. 559–592; Gabriel Ben-Dor, *State and Conflict in the Middle East* (New York: Praeger, 1983); Joseph Kostiner, "Solidarity in the Arab State: An Historical Perspective," in *Challenges to the Cohesion of the Arab State*, Asher Susser (ed.) (Tel Aviv: The Moshe Dayan Center, 2008), pp. 21–39.

10. For instructive discussions on the value of Arabism in promoting territorial, state-centered nationalism, see Michael Barnett, *Dialogues in Arab Politics* (New York: Columbia University Press, 1998); Cyrus Schayegh, "1958 Reconsidered: State Formation and the Cold War in the Early Postcolonial Arab Middle East," *International Journal of Middle East Studies*, 45, 3 (August 2013), pp. 421–443; Christopher Phillips, *Everyday Arab Identity: The Daily Reproduction of the Arab World* (London: Routledge, 2013).

11. Malik Mufti, *Sovereign Creations: Pan-Arabism and Political Order in Syria and Iraq* (Ithaca and London: Cornell University Press, 1996).

12. Emanuel Sivan, "Arab Nationalism in the Age of Islamic Resurgence," in Jankowski and Gershoni (eds.), *Rethinking Nationalism*, pp. 207–228.

13. Raymond Hinnebusch, "Introduction: The Analytical Framework," in *The Foreign Policies of Middle East States*, Raymond Hinnebusch and Anoushiravan Ehteshami (eds.) (London: Lynne Rienner Publishers, 2002), p. 10.

14. E.g., Hamied Ansari, *Egypt, The Stalled Society* (Albany, New York: SUNY Press, 1986).

15. Marc Lynch, *The Arab Uprising: The Unfinished Revolutions of the New Middle East* (New York: Public Affairs, 2012), p. 8.

16. R. Stephen Humphreys, *Between Memory and Desire: The Middle East in a Troubled Age* (Berkeley: University of California Press, 1999).

17. Martin Kramer, "Arab Nationalism: Mistaken Identity," *Daedalus*, 122, 3 (Summer 1993), pp. 171–206.

1. ARAB NATIONALISM

1. Anthony Smith, *The Ethnic Origins of Nations* (Oxford: Blackwell, 1996).

2. Bernard Lewis, *The Arabs in History*, revised edition (New York: Harper & Row, 1967).

3. Kemal Karpat, "The Ottoman Ethnic and Confessional Legacy in the Middle East," in *Ethnicity, Pluralism, and the State in the Middle East*, Milton J. Esman and Itamar Rabinovich (eds.) (Ithaca, NY: Cornell University Press, 1988), pp. 35–53.

4. Bruce Masters, *The Arabs of the Ottoman Empire* (New York: Cambridge University Press, 2013), pp. 11–12.

5. George Antonius, *The Arab Awakening* (London: H. Hamilton, 1938).

6. Israel Gershoni, "Rethinking the Formation of Arab Nationalism in the Middle East, 1920-1945. Old and New Narratives," in James Jankowski and Israel Gershoni (eds.), *Rethinking Nationalism in the Arab Middle East* (New York: Columbia University Press, 1977), pp. 11–12

7. C. Ernest Dawn, *From Ottomanism to Arabism* (Urbana: University of Illinois Press, 1973), and *idem*, "The Origins of Arab Nationalism," in *The Origins of Arab Nationalism*, Rashid Khalidi, et al. (eds.) (New York: Columbia University Press, 1991), pp. 3–30.

8. Adeed Dawisha, *Arab Nationalism in the 20th Century: From Triumph to Despair* (Princeton, NJ: Princeton University Press, 2003), pp. 33–34; Eliezer Tauber, *The Arab Movements in World War I* (London: Frank Cass, 1993), pp. 1–9. While accepting this thesis, Rashid Khalidi argues that growing Arab opposition in Beirut to the CUP's centralization policies has been ignored by scholars focusing on developments in Damascus. Rashid Khalidi, "Ottomanism and Arabism in Syria Before 1914: A Reassassment," in Khalidi, et al., ibid, pp. 50–69.

9. Thomas Phillip, *Jurji Zaidan and the Foundations of Arab Nationalism*, (Syracuse, NY: Syracuse University Press, 2014); John W. Jandora and Butrus al-Bustani, "Arab Conscousness and Arabic Revival," *The Muslim World*, LXXIV, 2 (April 1984), pp. 71–84; Butrus Abu-Manneh, "The Christians between Ottomanism and Syrian Nationalism: The Ideas of Butrus Al-Bustani," *International Journal of Middle East Studies*, 11, 3 (May 1980), pp. 287–304.

10. Dawn, "The Origins of Arab Nationalism," pp. 3–11.

11. Albert Hourani, *A History of the Arab Peoples* (Cambridge, MA: Belknap Press, 1991), pp. 304–10.

12. Hasan Kayali, *Arabs and Young Turks: Ottomanism, Arabism and Islamism in the Ottoman Empire, 1908–1918* (Berkeley: University of California Press, 1997), p. 50.

13. The term *salifism* was originally synonymous with Islamic modernism. In recent decades, its meaning has been transformed and is now associated with extremely conservative, literal-minded Islam, both the nonviolent and the violent varieties.

14. He was actually of Persian, and not Afghan origin, as his name suggested.

15. Hourani, *History of the Arab Peoples*, pp. 307–8; Nikki Keddie, *Sayyid Jamal al-Din "al-Afghani": A Political Biography* (Berkeley: University of Cal-

ifornia Press, 1972); Mark Sedgwick, *Muhammad Abduh* (Oxford: Oneworld, 2009).

16. Kayali, *Arabs and Young Turks*, p. 46.

17. Masters, *The Arabs of the Ottoman Empire*, pp. 209–11.

18. In addition, he postulated, they were, of all Muslims, the ones most guided by the socialist way of life and the most ancient people to practice *shura* ("consultation"); in this he differs from Afghani. "The Excellences of the Arabs," in Sylvia Haim, *Arab Nationalism, An Anthology* (Berkeley: University of California Press, 1962), pp. 83–87.

19. Haim, *Arab Nationalism*, pp. 27–29; Elie Kedourie, "The Politics of Political Literature: Kawakibi, Azoury and Jung," in *idem*, *Arabic Political Memoirs and Other Studies* (London: Frank Cass, 1980), pp. 107–11.

20. Stephen Wild, "Negib Azoury and his Book *Le Reveil de la Nation Arabe*," in Marwan R. Buheiry (ed.), *Intellectual Life in the Arab East, 1890–1939* (Beirut: American University of Beirut, 1981), pp. 62–83.

21. William Cleveland, "Sources of Arab Nationalism: An Overview," *Middle East Review*, xi (1979), pp. 25–33. Reprinted in Michael Curtis (ed.), *Religion and Politics in the Middle East* (Boulder, CO: Westview Press, 1981), pp. 55–67.

22. Neville Mandel, *The Arabs and Zionism Before World War I* (Berkeley: University of California Press, 1976).

23. Kayali, *Arabs and Young Turks*, p. 72.

24. To be sure, the number of actual members was extremely small. Kayali, p. 178 and footnotes 35 and 36; Dawn, "Origins," p. 13.

25. Scholars differ over the importance of these newspapers as an indicator of the rising tide of Arab nationalism at that time. For the debate on the issue, see Dawn, "The Origins of Arab Nationalism of Arab Nationalism," and Khalidi, "Ottomanism and Arabism,"

26. Kayali, *Arabs and Young Turks*, p. 138; Masters, *The Arabs of the Ottoman Empire*, p. 216.

27. Kayali, *Arabs and Young Turks*, pp. 138–9.

28. Zeine Zeine, *The Emergence of Arab Nationalism,* 3rd ed. (New York: Caravan, 1978), quoted by Kayali, *Arabs and Young Turks*, p. 6.

29. Dawn, *From Ottomanism to Arabism,* pp. 169–74. Kayali says that CUP supporters among Arabs had resented Hamidian favoring of wealthy bureaucratic and 'ulama families (pp. 78–79).

30. Masters, *The Arabs of the Ottoman Empire*, p. 213.

31. Benedict Anderson, *Imagined Communities*, 2nd ed. (London: Verso, 1991).

32. Kayali, *Arabs and Young Turks*, p. 79.

33. Kayali, *Arabs and Young Turks*, p. 79.

34. "I knew I was an Arab Ottoman Muslim, though I only possessed the most ill-defined sense of myself as Arab. Hence, if I was in this position despite belonging to an illustrious family of noble origins, what must have been the experience of those around me?" Tawfiq al-Suwaydi, *My Memoirs: Half a Century of the History of Iraq and the Arab Cause* (Boulder, CO: Lynne Rienner, 2013), p. 60.

35. William Ochsenwald, *The Hijaz Railroad* (Charlottesville: University of Virginia, 1988).

2. WORLD WAR I AND ITS AFTERMATH

1. Antonious, *passim*; Abu Khaldun Sati` al-Husri, *The Day of Maysalun* (Washington, DC: Middle East Institute, 1966), p. 12.

2. For the text of the Mandate for Palestine, see http://unispal.un.org/UNISPAL.NSF/0/2FCA2C68106F11AB05256BCF007BF3CB.

3. Efraim Karsh, *Empires of the Sand: The Struggle for Mastery in the Middle East, 1789–1923*, with Inari Karsh (Cambridge, MA: Harvard University Press, 1994), pp. 185–243.

4. Kedourie, *In the Anglo-Arab Labyrinth*, p. 98.

5. The word also means "province" (*velayet*, in Turkish), creating no end of controversy in subsequent years.

6. Kedourie, *In the Anglo-Arab Labyrinth*, pp. 98–99.

7. The text of the correspondence can be found in J.C. Hurewitz, *The Middle East and North Africa in World Politics, A Documentary Record*, 2nd ed. (New Haven, CT: Yale University Press, 1979), pp. 46–56.

8. Kedourie, *In the Anglo-Arab Labyrinth*, pp. 230–31.

9. Khoury, *Syria Under the French Mandate*, p. 35.

10. Ibid., pp. 27–32.

11. Eliezer Tauber, *The Formation of Modern Syria and Iraq* (London: Frank Cass, 1995), p. 174–75.

12. Muhammad Muslih, "The Rise of Local Nationalism in the Arab East," in Khalidi, et al. (eds.), pp. 167–85.

13. James Gelvin, *Divided Loyalties: Nationalism and Mass Politics in Syria at the Close of Empire* (Berkeley: University of California Press, 1998), *passim*.

14. Ibid., p. 32–47.

15. Ibid., p. 46.

16. Ali A. Allawi, *Faysal of Iraq* (New Haven, CT: Yale University Press, 2014), p. 289; Gelvin, *Divided Loyalties*, pp. 1–3.

17. Gelvin, *Divided Loyalties*, pp. 296–97.

3. STATE-BUILDING AND NATION-BUILDING IN ADVERSE CIRCUMSTANCES

1. Michael Barnett, *Dialogues in Arab Politics: Negotiations in Regional Order* (New York: Columbia University Press, 1998), p. 56.

2. Gershoni, "Rethinking the Formation of Arab Nationalism," pp. 3–25; Khoury, "The Paradoxical in Arab Nationalism," pp. 273–87.

3. C. Ernest Dawn, "The formation of Pan-Arab Ideology in the Inter-War Years," *International Journal of Middle East Studies*, 20, 1 (1988), pp. 67–91.

4. Israel Gershoni, "The Evolution of National Culture in Modern Egypt: Intellectual Formation and Social Diffusion, 1892–1945," *Poetics Today*, 13, 2 (1992), p. 328.

5. Bassam Tibi, *Arab Nationalism: A Critical Enquiry*, 2nd ed. (New York: St. Martin's Press, 1991), pp. 118–98; Dawisha, Adeed, *Arab Nationalism in the 20th Century: From Triumph to Despair* (Princeton, NJ: Princeton University Press, 2003). pp. 49–74.

6. Walid Kazziha, "Another Reading into Husari's Concept of Arab Nationalism," in Buheiry (ed.), pp. 154–64.

7. Kedourie, "The Kingdom of Iraq, 1917–1958: A Retrospect," in *idem*, *The Chatham House Version and other Middle-Eastern Studies* (Hanover, NH: University Press of New England, 1984), p. 273.

8. Ibid., pp. 273–74.

9. Franck Salameh, *Language Memory and Identity in the Middle East* (Lanham, MD: Lexington Books, 2010), pp. 191–258.

10. Mohamed Chtatou, "The influence of the Berber language on Moroccan Arabic," *International Journal of the Sociology of Language,* 123, 1 (January 1997), pp. 101–18.

11. Harik, *passim.*

12. Allawi, Ali A., *Faisal I of Iraq* (New Haven, CT: Yale University Press, 2014), pp. 356–60.

13. Ofra Bengio, "Faysal's Vision of Iraq: A Retrospect," in *The Hashemites in the Modern Arab World: A Festschrift in Honor of the Late Professor Uriel Dann*, Asher Susser/Aryeh Shmuelevitz (eds.) (London: Frank Cass, 1995), pp. 139–52.

14. Kedourie, "The Kingdom of Iraq: A Retrospect."

15. Yehoshua Porath, *In Search of Arab Unity, 1930–1945* (London: Frank Cass, 1986), pp. 1–2, 39–57, 216–23; Dawisha, *Arab Nationalism in the 20th Century*, pp. 75–79.

16. Michael Provence, *The Great Syrian Revolt and the Rise of Arab Nationalism* (Austin: University of Texas Press, 2005), pp. 100–7.

17. Phillip Khoury, "The Paradoxical in Arab Nationalism: Inter-war Syria Revisited," in *Rethinking Nationalism*, Jankowski and Gershoni (eds.), pp. 280–82.

18. Itamar Rabinovich, "Inter-Arab Relations Foreshadowed: The Question of the Syrian Throne in the 1920s and '30s," in *idem, The View from Damascus: State, Political Community and Foreign Relations in Twentieth-Century Syria* (London: Valentine Mitchell, 2011), p. 54–67.

19. Aaron S. Kleiman, *Foundations of British Policy in the Arab World: The Cairo Conference of 1921* (Baltimore: Johns Hopkins University Press, 1970).

20. Joshua Teitelbaum, *The Rise and Fall of the Hashimite Kingdom of Arabia* (London: Hurst & Co. 2001), pp. 249–82; Allawi, *Faisal I of Iraq*, pp. 466–67.

21. Joseph Kostiner, *The Making of Saudi Arabia, 1916–1936: From Chieftaincy to Monarchical State* (New York: Oxford University Press, 1993), pp. 100–17, 163.

22. Not to be confused with the Egypt-based *al-Ikhwan al-Muslimin* ("Muslim Brotherhood").

23. Dawisha, *Arab Nationalism in the 20th Century*, p. 103.

24. Israel Gershoni and James Jankowski, *Egypt, Islam, and the Arabs: The Search for Egyptian Nationhood, 1900–1930* (New York: Oxford University Press, 1986), pp. 43, 91, 155, 157.

25. The term is Nadav Safran's. *Egypt in Search of Political Commmunity* (Cambridge, MA: Harvard University Press, 1961).

26. For varying perspectives see ibid., pp. 164–80; Charles D. Smith, "The 'Crisis of Orientation': The Shift of Egyptian Intellectuals to Islamic Subjects in the 1930s," *International Journal of Middle East Studies*, 4, 4 (October 1973), pp. 382–410; Israel Gershoni and James Jankowski, *Redefining the Egyptian Nation, 1930–1945* (Cambridge: Cambridge University Press, 1995), pp. 35–142.

27. Porath, *In Search of Arab Unity*, pp. 149–59.

28. Michael Brett and Elizabeth Fentress, *The Berbers* (Oxford: Blackwell, 1996).

29. William L. Cleveland, *Islam Against the West* (Austin: University of Texas Press, 1985), pp. 90–114; Mohamed El Mansour, "Salafis and Modernists in the Moroccan Nationalist Movement," in John Ruedy (ed.), *Islamism and Secularism in North Africa* (New York: St. Martin's Press, 1999), pp. 53–72; Jamil M. Abun-Nasr, 'The Salafiyya movement in Morocco: The Religious Bases of the Moroccan Nationalist Movement,' in Albert Hourani (ed.), "St. Antony's Papers No. 16," *Middle Eastern Affairs*, No. 3. (London: Chatto and Windus, 1963), pp. 91–105; on the salafi current in Algeria, see James McDougall, *Histo-*

ry and the Culture of Nationalism in Algeria (Cambridge: Cambridge University Press, 2006).

30. Hala Khamis Nassar and Marco Boggero, "Omar al-Mukhtar: The Formation of Cultural Memory and the Case of the Militant Group that Bears His Name," *The Journal of North African Studies*, 13, 2 (June 2008), pp. 201–17.

31. Charles Tripp, *A History of Iraq*, 3rd ed. (Cambridge: Cambridge University Press, 2007), pp. 86–96.

32. Phillip Khoury, *Syria and the French Mandate, The Politics of Arab Nationalism 1920–1945* (Princeton, NJ: Princeton University Press, 1987), pp. 485–93.

33. Barnett, *Dialogues in Arab Politics*, pp. 55–56.

34. Phillip Khoury, "Divided Loyalties? Syria and the Question of Palestine, 1919–1939," *Middle Eastern Studies*, 21, 3 (July 1985), pp. 324–48; Yehoshua Porath, *In Search of Arab Unity, 1930–1945* (London: Frank Cass, 1986), pp. 162–75.

35. Elie Kedourie, "Great Britain and Palestine: The Turning Point," in *idem, Islam in the Modern World and Other Studies* (London: Mansell, 1980), pp. 93–170.

36. George Kirk, *The Middle East in the War* (Oxford: Oxford University Press, 1953), p. 334.

37. Michael Barnett, *Dialogues in Arab Politics: Negotiations in Regional Order* (New York: Columbia University Press, 1998), p. 75.

38. Elie Kedourie, "Pan-Arabism and British Policy," in *idem, The Chatham House Version and other Middle-Eastern Studies* (Hanover, NH: University Press of New England, 1984), pp. 213–35.

39. Porath, *In Search of Arab Unity*, pp. 256–311; Ahmed Gomaa, *The Foundation of the League of Arab States* (London: Longman, 1977*), passim;* Israel Gershoni, "The Arab League as an Arab Enterprise," *The Jerusalem Quarterly,* 40 (1986), pp. 88–101.

40. For `Abdallah's efforts up until 1945, see Yehoshua Porath, "Abdallah's Greater Syria Program," *Middle Eastern Studies*, 20, 2 (1984), pp. 172–89.

41. Porath, "Nuri al-Sa`id's Arab Unity Programme," *Middle Eastern Studies* 20, 4 (1984), pp. 76–98.

42. Since 1899, Sudan had officially been ruled by an Anglo-Egyptian condominium.

43. For Nahhas's consultations, see Bruce Maddy-Weitzman, *The Crystallization of the Arab State System, 1945–1954* (Syracuse, NY: Syracuse University Press, 1993), pp. 15–18.

44. To this day, Egypt insists on maintaining the privilege of having an Egyptian hold the post.

45. Maddy-Weitzman, *Crystallization of the Arab State System,* pp. 19–20; for the text of the Charter, see http://avalon.law.yale.edu/20th_century/arableag.asp.

46. Wadsworth to Secretary of State, Baghdad tel. no. 800, June 13, 1947, NA, RG64/350, box 680.

47. Albert Hourani, "Ottoman Reform and the Politics of Notables," in *The Beginnings of Modernization in the Middle East,* William R. Polk and Richard L. Chambers (eds.) (Chicago: University of Chicago Press, 1968), pp. 41–68.

48. Barnett, *Dialogues in Arab Politics,* pp. 55–83.

49. Gabriel Ben-Dor, "Stateness and Ideology in Contemporary Middle East Politics," *Jerusalem Journal of International Relations,* 9, 3 (1987), p. 21.

50. Clifford Geertz, *The Interpretation of Cultures* (New York: Basic Books, 1973), pp. 269–70.

51. Charles Issawi, *An Economic History of the Middle East and North Africa* (New York: Columbia University Press, 1982), pp. 41–43.

52. Alfred G. Mursey, *An Arab Common Market: A Study in Inter-Arab Trade Relations, 1920–1967* (New York: Praeger, 1969), pp. 11–22, 30–39; Issawi, *An Economic History of the Middle East and North Africa,* p. 161.

4. THE DYNASTIC ERA

1. Over 400 people were killed in Damascus by French shelling (Khoury, *Syria and the French Mandate,* p. 617).

2. Cosmetic alterations were made to the treaty in 1948.

3. Avi Shlaim, *Collusion Across the Jordan* (Oxford: Clarendon Press, 1988), p. 33, citing Larry Collins and Dominique Lapierre, *O Jerusalem* (New York: Pocket Books, 1972), p. 87.

4. Hinton to State Department, Damascus dispatch no. 775, September 22, 1947 (NA, RG59/890D.001, enclosure no. 1).

5. For details of the debate, see Daniel Dishon and Bruce Maddy-Weitzman, "Inter-Arab Relations," in *Middle East Contemporary Survey, Vol. V, 1980–81,* Colin Legum, Haim Shaked, and Daniel Dishon (eds.) (New York: Holmes and Meier, 1982), pp. 236–38.

6. `Abd al-Ilah was the son of `Ali, the eldest son of Sharif Husayn, and briefly king of the Hijaz.

7. Barry Rubin, *The Arab States and the Palestine Conflict* (Syracuse, NY: Syracuse University Press, 1981), p. 15.

8. Although the country's official name has always been "The Hashemite Kingdom of the Jordan," the name "Jordan" only gradually replaced "Transjordan" in common usage. In this work, "Jordan" is used for everything that refers

to events subsequent to the signing of the Armistice Agreement with Israel on April 4, 1949.

9. For Safwat's reports and activities, see Hashemite Kingdom of Iraq, *Meahorey Haparagod: Va`ada Parlementarit `Iraqit `al Hamilhama Beyisrael*, Shmuel Segev, trans. (Tel Aviv: Ma`arakhot, 1954), pp. 66–103.

10. Joshua Landis, "Syria and the Palestine War: Fighting King `Abdullah's 'Greater Syria Plan'," in *The War for Palestine, Rewriting the History of 1948*, Eugene L. Rogan and Avi Shlaim (eds.) (Cambridge: Cambridge University Press, 2001), pp. 178–205.

11. Maddy-Weitzman, *The Crystallization of the Arab State System*, pp. 64–65.

12. John Norton Moore (ed.), *The Arab-Israeli Conflict*, Vol. 3 (Princeton, NJ: Princeton University Press, 1974), pp. 352–57.

13. For an explanation of Jordanian actions, see Benny Morris, *1948, A History of the First Arab-Israeli War* (New Haven, CT: Yale University Press, 2008), pp. 286–92.

14. Campbell to Foreign Office, Cairo tel. no. 1717, December 11, 1948, PRO, FO371, 68644/E15734.

15. Benny Morris, *The Birth of the Palestinian Refugee Problem Revisited* (Cambridge: Cambridge University Press, 2004), pp. 1, 7.

16. Qustantin Zurayq, *Ma`na al-Nakba* (Beirut: Dar al-`Ilm lil-Malayin, 1948). [English translation by R. Bayly Winder, *The Meaning of the Disaster* (Beirut: Khayat's College Book Cooperative, 1956)].

17. Patrick Seale, *The Struggle for Syria*, 2nd ed. (New Haven, CT: Yale University Press, 1986).

18. UN Security Council Resolution 242, adopted on November 22, 1967, gave this more formal expression.

19. Morris, *1948*, p. 388.

20. The proposed agreement was actually a salvage operation, following the failure of the two sides to conclude a more far-reaching agreement.

21. The texts of the resolutions can be found in Mohamed Khalil (ed.), *The Arab States and the Arab League*, Vol. II (Beirut: Al-Khayat, 1962), pp. 165–67.

22. Text of the resolution in ibid., vol. I, p. 54.

23. Za`im was motivated by a combination of factors. These included high-minded national goals, but also a need to defend the army's prerogatives and image, which had been damaged by its poor performance in the war, and perhaps even to forestall corruption charges against Za`im personally.

24. Patrick Seale, *The Struggle for Syria*, new edition (New Haven, CT: Yale University Press, 1987), p. 46.

25. Maddy-Weitzman, *The Crystallization of the Arab State System*, p. 111.

26. The party is also known as the SSNP (Syrian Social Nationalist Party), in accordance with its Arabic name. For the deep attraction of the party to a portion of politically conscious Arab youth, see Hisham Sharabi, *Embers and Ashes: Memoirs of an Arab Intellectual* (Northampton, MA: Olive Branch Press, 2007), pp. 49–66, 141–86.

27. Maddy-Weitzman, *The Crystallization of the Arab State System*, pp. 114–15.

28. For the differences between Nuri's approach and Crown Prince `Abd al-Ilah's, see Reeva S. Simon, "The Hashemite 'Conspiracy': Hashemite Unity Attempts, 1921–1956," *International Journal of Middle East Studies*, 5, 3 (1974), pp. 314–27.

29. Bruce Maddy-Weitzman, "Jordan and Iraq: Efforts at Intra-Hashimite Unity," *Middle Eastern Studies*, 26, 1 (January 1990), pp. 65–75.

30. For the text of the treaty, see http://avalon.law.yale.edu/20th_century/arabjoin.asp.

31. Yusuf A. Sayigh, *The Arab Economy* (New York: Oxford University Press, 1982).

5. THE RADICAL HEYDAY (1955–1967)

1. Hanna Battatu, *The Old Social Classes and the Revolutionary Movements of Iraq* (Princeton, NJ: Princeton University Press, 1982).

2. Nadav Safran, *From War to War* (New York: Praeger, 1969), pp. 83–88.

3. Fouad Ajami, "The End of Pan-Arabism," *Foreign Affairs,* 52, 1 (Winter 1978–1979), p. 355.

4. Barnett, *Dialogues in Arab Politics*, pp. 7–8, 10–11.

5. Clement Henry Moore, "On Theory and Practice Among the Arabs," *World Politics*, 24, 1 (1971), pp. 106–26.

6. The term is P. J. Vatikiotis's, *Nasir and His Generation* (London: Croon Helm, 1978).

7. Elie Podeh, *The Quest for Hegemony in the Arab World* (Leiden, The Netherlands: E.J. Brill, 1995), pp. 98–99.

8. Nuri would maintain that in his talks with Nasir in 1954, the latter had agreed that Iraq could proceed as long as the door was left open for Egypt and others to join. Waldemar J. Gallman, *Iraq Under General Nuri* (Baltimore: The Johns Hopkins University Press, 1964), p. 38.

9. Barnett, *Dialogues in Arab Politics*, p. 113, quoting Khalil, *The Arab States and the Arab League*, Vol. 2, pp. 236–37.

10. Ibid., p. 112.

11. Dawisha, *Arab Nationalism in the 20th Century*, pp. 140–41.

12. Benny Morris, *Israel's Border Wars* (Oxford: Clarendon Press, 1993), pp. 324–54.

13. Uriel Dann, *King Hussein and the Challenge of Arab Radicalism, 1955–67* (New York: Oxford University Press, 1989), pp. 3, 26.

14. Ibid., pp. 31–77; Phillip Robins, A *History of Jordan* (Cambridge: Cambridge University Press, 2004), p. 94–101.

15. The phrase is a twist on the title of Joel Gordon's authoritative book on the Free Officers' movement and the early years of Nasir's rule, *Nasir's Blessed Movement: Egypt's Free Officers and the July Revolution* (New York: Oxford University Press, 1991).

16. The term is Elizabeth Monroe's. *Britain's Moment in the Middle East, 1914–1956* (London: Johns Hopkins Press, 1963).

17. Robert E. Osgood, *Ideals and Self-Interest in American Foreign Relations* (Chicago: University of Chicago Press, 1953).

18. Miles Copeland, *The Game of Nations* (London: Weidenfeld and Nicholson, 1969), pp. 47–60. The CIA's Stephen Meade had been on intimate terms with Husni Za`im before his coup in Syria as well, but Miles Copeland recanted his earlier claim that the CIA had masterminded that coup. Copeland, *The Game Player: Confessions of the CIA's Original Political Operative* (London: Aurum, 1989), pp. 94–95. For details of Za`im's contacts with Meade before the coup, see Sami Moubayed, *Syria and the USA* (London: I.B Tauris, 2013), pp. 77–80.

19. The attitude of the United States toward Ba`thi Iraq and Syria would be similar. See Weldon C. Matthews, "The Kennedy Administration, Counterinsurgency, and Iraq's First Ba`thist Regime," *International Journal of Middle East Studies*, 43, 4 (November 2011), pp. 635–53; Malik Mufti, *Sovereign Creations: Pan-Arabism and Political Order in Syria and Iraq* (Ithaca, NY: Cornell University Press, 1995), pp. 143–45, 154, 156, 177.

20. Shimon Shamir, "The Collapse of Project Alpha," in Wm. Roger Louis and Roger Owen (eds.), *Suez 1956; The Crisis and its Consequences* (Oxford: Clarendon Press, 1989), pp. 73–100.

21. Donald Neff, *Warriors at Suez* (New York: The Linden Press/Simon & Schuster, 1981), pp. 134–36.

22. Benny Morris, *Righteous Victims* (New York: Alfred A. Knopf, 1999), pp. 266–67.

23. Suwaydi, *My Memoirs*, p. 448.

24. Avner Cohen, *Israel and the Bomb* (New York: Columbia University Press, 1998).

25. For the text of the doctrine, see http://coursesa.matrix.msu.edu/~hst306/documents/eisen.html.

26. David Lesch, *Syria and the United States: Eisenhower's Cold War in the Middle East* (Boulder, CO: Westview, 1992), pp. 104–209.

27. For a good sense of the belief that the UAR's establishment was a formative, and even transformational, moment in modern Arab history, see Fayez Sayegh, *Arab Unity: Hope and Fulfillment* (New York: Devin-Adair, 1958).

28. Dawisha, *Arab Nationalism in the 20th Century*, pp. 197–98.

29. Barnett, *Dialogues in Arab Politics*, pp. 130–31.

30. Quwatli was independent Syria's first president. Deposed by Husni Za'im in 1949, he had been restored to office in 1955. Ironically, he was now potentially the country's last president as well.

31. Dawisha, pp. 198–204; Elie Podeh, *The Decline of Arab Unity* (Brighton, UK: Sussex Academic Press, 1999), pp. 42–51.

32. Uriel Dann, *Iraq Under Qassem: A Political History, 1958-1963* (New York: Praeger, 1969), p. 12.

33. For the texts of the Federation's proclamation and constitution, see Khalil, *The Arab States and the Arab League*, Vol. I, pp. 79–91.

34. Gallman, *Iraq Under General Nuri*, p. 222.

35. Dann, *King Hussein and the Challenge of Arab Radicalism,* p. 52.

36. Malcolm Kerr, *The Arab Cold War*, 3rd ed. (Oxford: Oxford University Press, 1971).

37. *Majzarat Qasr al-Rihab*, an account written and published by the Beirut newspaper *al-Hayat* (Beirut, 1960), pp. 32–36.

38. Roger Owen, "Class and Class Politics in Iraq Before 1958: The Colonial and Post-Colonial State," in Robert A. Fernea and Wm. Roger Louis (eds.), *The Iraqi Revolution of 1958: The Old Social Classes Revisited* (London: I.B. Taurus, 1991), p. 169. See also Toby Dodge, *Inventing Iraq: The Failure of Nation-Building and a History Denied* (London: Hurst, 2012).

39. Drawing from a memoir written by 'Abd al-Ilah's royal guard who was present at the time, Elie Kedourie points to the Regent's lack of resistance as stemming from his belief that the regime was alien and illegitimate, and a fatalism that he would somehow survive by not resisting, as his father 'Ali had when he abandoned his short-lived Kingdom of the Hijaz to Ibn Sa'ud in 1925. Kedourie, "Arabic Political Memoirs," in *idem, Arabic Political Memoirs and Other Studies* (London: Frank Cass, 1980), p. 80.

40. Dann, *King Hussein*, pp. 168–69.

41. Samuel P. Huntington, *Political Order in Changing Societies* (New Haven, CT: Yale University Press, 1968), pp. 177–91.

42. Yitzhak Oron (ed.), *Middle East Record* (MER), Vol. 1, 1960 (London: Weidenfeld and Nicholson, 1965), pp. 144–48.

43. Ibid., pp. 132–38.

44. The image is from Kerr, *The Arab Cold War*, p. 126.

45. Jason Hillman, *A Storm in a Tea-Cup, The Iraq-Kuwait Crisis of 1961: From Gulf Crisis to Inter-Arab Dispute* (Tel Aviv: The Moshe Dayan Center for

Middle Eastern and African Studies, 2014), pp. 61–71; Helene von Bismarck, "The Kuwait Crisis of 1961 and Its Consequences for Great Britain's Persian Gulf Policy," *Britain and the World: Historical Journal of The British Scholar* 2, 1 (2009), pp. 75–96; Elie Podeh, "Suez in Reverse: The Arab Response to the Iraqi Bid for Kuwait, 1961-1963," *Diplomacy & Statecraft*, 14, 1 (2003), pp. 103–30.

46. Hillman, *A Storm in a Tea-Cup*, pp. 46–50.

47. *Records of Iraq: 1914-1966*, Henniker-Major to Foreign Office, tel. 573, July 18, 1961.

48. Yassine-Hamdan and Pearson, *Arab Approaches to Conflict Resolution*, pp. 117–26.

49. Kerr, *The Arab Cold War*, pp. 28–29.

50. Uzi Rabi, *Yemen: Revolution, Civil War, and Unification* (London: I.B. Tauris, 2015), p. 39; Leigh Douglas, *The Free Yemeni Movement, 1935–1962* (Beirut: American University of Beirut Press, 1987), pp. 9–15, 30–33; Manfred W. Werner, *Modern Yemen, 1918–1966* (Baltimore: The Johns Hopkins University Press, 1967), pp. 176–89.

51. Lt. Cdr. Youssef Aboul-Enein, "The Egyptian-Yemen War (1962–67): Egyptian Perspectives on Guerrilla Warfare," http://onceagreenberet.com/Word-Press/publications/Egyptian%20Perspectives.pdf.

52. Rabi, *Yemen*, p. 42.

53. For a discussion of casualty estimates and the economic costs of the war, see Jesse Ferris, *Nasir's Gamble: How Intervention in Yemen Caused the Six-Day War and Decline of Egyptian Power* (Princeton, NJ: Princeton University Press, 2012), pp. 194–99.

54. Aboul-Enein, "The Egyptian-Yemen War (1962-67)."

55. Kerr, *The Arab Cold War*, pp. 44–76. Elie Podeh, "To Unite or Not to Unite: That is Not the Question: The 1963 Tripartite Talks Reassessed," *Middle Eastern Studies*, 39, 1 (2003), pp. 150-85.

56. Ferris, *Nasir's Gamble*, pp. 87, 109, 111, 188, 260.

57. Barnett, *Dialogues in Arab Politics*, pp. 146–59.

58. The reverse acronym of *Harakat al-Tahrir [al-Watani] al-Filastini* ("Movement for Palestinian [National] Liberation"). The word "*fatah*" means "opening" or "conquest," which references the initial spread of Islam.

59. Michael Oren, *Six Days of War: June 1967 and the Making of the Modern Middle East* (Oxford: Oxford University Press, 2002), p. 19; Kerr, *The Arab Cold War*, p. 126.

60. Traditionally one of Syria's most marginal sectarian groups, military service had provided a means of upward mobility for its young males, ultimately leading to the center of power. Eyal Zisser, "The 'Alawis, Lords of Syria: From Ethnic Minority to Ruling Sect," in Ofra Bengio and Gabriel Ben-Dor (eds.),

Minorities and the State in the Arab World (Boulder, CO: Lynne Rienner, 1999), pp. 129–45.

61. Kerr, *The Arab Cold War*, pp. 117–22.

62. Michael Oren, *Six Days of War; June 1967 and the Making of the Modern Middle East* (Oxford: Oxford University Press, 2002).

63. Safran, *From War to War*, p. 292; Nasser's speech at UAR Advanced Headquarters, May 25, 1967, contained in Walter Laqueur and Barry Rubin (eds.), *The Israeli-Arab Reader: A Documentary History of the Middle East Conflict*, 5th ed., (New York: Penguin Books, 1995), pp. 144–49.

64. Laqueur and Rubin (eds.), ibid., pp. 158–60.

6. AFTER THE JUNE 1967 DEBACLE

1. For the text of the speech, see Laqueur and Rubin (eds.), *The Israeli-Arab Reader*, pp. 158–65.

2. For the full text of the Khartoum resolutions, see www.mideastweb.org/khartoum.htm.

3. Dawisha, *Arab Nationalism in the 20th Century*, p. 256.

4. Barnett, *Dialogues in Arab Politics*, p. 163.

5. Samir A. Mutawi, *Jordan in the 1967 War* (Cambridge, MA: Cambridge University Press, 2002), pp. 128–29.

6. Adopted on November 22, 1967, it has served as the basis for all subsequent diplomatic efforts to resolve the Arab-Israeli conflict. For the text of the resolution, see http://unispal.un.org/unispal.nsf/0/7D35E1F729DF491C85256EE700686136.

7. Avraham Sela, "'Abd al-Nasser's Regional Politics: A Reassessment," in Elie Podeh and Onn Winckler (eds.), *Rethinking Nasserism: Revolution and Historical Memory in Modern Egypt* (Gainesville: University Press of Florida, 2004), p. 198.

8. Patrick Seale, *Asad: The Struggle for the Middle East* (Berkeley: University of California Press, 1989), pp. 157–65.

9. Fouad Ajami, *The Arab Predicament* (Cambridge: Cambridge University Press, 1981), pp. 25–40, 50–63.

10. Sadiq al-Azm, *Self-Criticism After the Defeat, 1967* (London: Saqi Books, 2011, *en passim*; first published in Arabic in 1968).

11. Tareq Ismael, *The Arab Left* (Syracuse, NY: Syracuse University Press, 1976).

12. John Calvert, *Sayyid Qutb and the Origins of Radical Islamism* (New York: Columbia University Press, 2010).

7. DIMINISHED LEADERSHIP

1. Ajami, *The Arab Predicament,* pp. 95–97. For a broader critique from liberal intellectuals after 1967, and their struggle against the ascending Islamist current, see Shimon Shamir, "From Liberalism to Postrevolution," in *idem* (ed.), *From Monarchy to Revolution* (Boulder, CO: Westview Press, 1995), pp. 200–11.

2. Historians will continue to debate whether opportunities for a diplomatic breakthrough that would have prevented the outbreak of war were missed. One thing is clear: neither Israel nor the US believed that Sadat was in possession of a military option.

3. Here, too, historians will continue to debate the nature of Husayn's message to Israeli leaders and how it was understood. In any case, the accumulating indications that Egypt and Syria were heightening their military preparations did not translate into Israeli or American conclusions that they were bent on war, until it was too late.

4. Patrick Seale, *Asad: The Struggle for the Middle East* (Berkeley: University of California Press, 1989); Avraham Sela, *The Decline of the Arab-Israeli Conflict* (Albany, NY: SUNY Press, 1998), pp. 140–41.

5. Seale, ibid., pp. 202–25.

6. Sela, *The Decline of the Arab-Israeli Conflict*, pp. 165–70.

7. For details of the agreement and its significance, see Kenneth W. Stein, *Heroic Diplomacy* (London: Routledge, 1999).

8. www.sadat.umd.edu/archives/speeches.htm.

9. Seale, *Asad*, pp. 304–6.

10. For a full account, see William Quandt, *Camp David: Peacemaking and Politics* (Washington, DC: Brookings Institution, 1986).

11. EIU, *Country Report, Jordan*, no. 2, 1989. The total amount of combined debt was more than $80 billion, a sum that did not include up to $60 billion in wartime loans extended to Iraq by Saudi Arabia and Kuwait. Joseph Kostiner, *Conflict and Cooperation in the Gulf Region* (Wiesbaden, Germany: Verlag, 2009), p. 78.

12. Bruce Maddy-Weitzman, "Inter-Arab Relations," in *Middle East Contemporary Survey*, Vol. XVI, 1990, Ami Ayalon (ed.), (Boulder, CO: Westview Press, 1992), pp. 134–35. Fahd had ascended to the throne in 1985, following the death of King Khalid in June 1982.

13. Yezid Sayigh, "The Gulf Crisis: Why the Arab Regional Order Failed," *International Affairs*, 67, 3 (1991), pp. 487–507.

14. According to one source, Kuwait's ruler suspected that the Egyptians and Saudis would apply pressure on Sa`d at the Jeddah meeting, which he was instructed to rebuff. Majid Khadduri and Edmond Ghareeb, *War in the Gulf*

(1997), quoted by Nahla Yassine-Hamdan and Frederic S. Pearson, *Arab Approaches to Conflict Resolution* (London: Routledge, 2014), p. 115.

15. Saudi Press Agency (SPA), January 6, 1991 (FBIS-DR, January 7, 1991).

16. Michael R. Gordon and General Bernard E. Trainor, *The General's War* (Boston: Little Brown and Co., 1995).

17. For the text of the declaration, see *Middle East Contemporary Survey*, Vol. XV, 1991, Ami Ayalon (ed.) (Boulder, CO: Westview Press, 1993), pp. 163–65.

18. Joel S. Migdal, *Strong Societies and Weak States: State-Society Relations and State Capabilities in the Third World* (Princeton, NJ: Princeton University Press, 1988).

19. Nazih N. Ayubi, *Over-stating the Arab State* (London, New York: I.B. Tauris, 1995).

20. Samuel Huntington, *The Third Wave: Democratization in the Late Twentieth Century* (Norman: Oklahoma University Press, 1991).

21. Not surprisingly, King Husayn took offense, and quickly responded that the problem was not haste, but that the Arab world had waited too long in making peace. Bruce Maddy-Weitzman, "Inter-Arab Relations," and Asher Susser, "Jordan" in *MECS* , Vol. XIX, 1995 (Boulder, CO: Westview, 1997), pp. 70–71, 419.

22. Edward Said, "The Morning After," *London Review of Books*, October 21, 1993.

23. Fouad Ajami, *Dream Palace of the Arabs* (New York: Pantheon Books, 1998), pp. 253–312.

24. Telhami, Shibly, "2008 Annual Arab Public Opinion Poll"www. brookings.edu/~/media/events/2008/4/14%20middle%20east/0414_middle_ east_telhami.pdf.

8. FAILED ASPIRATIONS, FAILED STATE

1. Ayubi, pp. 449–50.

2. Kanaan Makiya, *The Republic of Fear*, updated edition (Berkeley: University of California Press, 1998).

3. Ofra Bengio, *The Kurds of Iraq: Building a State Within a State* (Boulder, CO: Lynne Reinner, 2012).

4. Daniel Dishon, "Inter-Arab Relations," in *Middle East Contemporary Survey*, Vol. III, 1978–1979, Colin Legum, et al. (eds.) (New York: Holmes and Meier, 1981), p. 215.

5. Ibid., p. 237; for the text of the Charter, see pp. 268–70. For an account of the two decades of hostility that preceded the agreement, see Eberhard Kienle,

Ba'th Versus Ba'th: The Conflict Between Syria and Iraq, 1968–1989 (London: I.B. Tauris, 1991).

6. Dishon, ibid., pp. 238–40; Seale, *Asad*, pp. 354–55.

7. Esther Webman, "The Gulf States", in *Middle East Contemporary Survey*, Vol. V, 1980–1981, Colin Legum, et al. (eds.) (New York: Holmes and Meier, 1982), pp. 458–64.

8. Daniel Dishon and Bruce Maddy-Weitzman, "Inter-Arab Relations," and Ofra Bengio and Yitzhak Gal, "Iraq," *Middle East Contemporary Survey*, Vol. VI, 1981–1982, Colin Legum, et al. (eds.) (New York: Holmes and Meier, 1984), pp. 233, 612.

9. For the text of his announcement, see www.cfr.org/iran/letter-ayatollah-khomeini-regarding-weapons-during-iran-iraq-war/p11745.

10. Amin al-Huwaydi, *Zilzal `Asifa al-Sahra'a Watawabi`hu* (Cairo: Dar al-Shuruq, 1998).

11. Iraqi News Agency (INA), July 18, 1990 (FBIS-DR).

12. Bruce Maddy-Weitzman and Joseph Kostiner, "From Jidda To Cairo: The Failure of Arab Mediation in the Gulf Crisis," *Diplomacy & Statecraft*, 7, 2 (Summer 1996), pp. 466–90.

13. Laurie A. Brand, *Jordan's Inter-Arab Relations, the Political Economy of Alliance Making* (New York: Columbia University Press, 1994), pp. 210–24.

14. Ofra Bengio (ed.), *Saddam Speaks on the Gulf Crisis* (Tel Aviv: The Moshe Dayan Center, 1992), pp. 100–18, 127–43; Saddam's widespread popularity was measured in reliable public opinion polls covering six different countries, Shibly Telhami, *The World Through Arab Eyes* (New York: Basic Books, 2013), pp. 5–6.

15. Curtis R. Ryan, *Inter-Arab Alliances: Regime Security and Jordanian Foreign Policy* (Gainesville: University Press of Florida, 2009), pp. 127–44.

16. Senem Aslan, *Nation-Building in Turkey and Morocco* (New York: Cambridge University Press, 2014), pp. 36–79, 114–55.

17. Kanan Makiya, *Cruelty and Silence* (New York: W.W. Norton & Co., 1993), *passim.*

18. http://edition.cnn.com/2003/WORLD/meast/03/01/sprj.irq.arab.ministers/
.

19. Yitzhak Nakash, *The Shi`is of Iraq* (Princeton, NJ: Princeton University Press, 1994).

20. For the text of the constitution, see www.wipo.int/wipolex/en/text.jsp?file_id=230000.

9. SYRIA UNDER THE ASAD DYNASTY

1. Podeh, *The Politics of National Celebrations*, p. 162.

2. Christopher, Phillips, *Everyday Arab Identity* (London: Routledge, 2013), p. 40.

3. Eyal Zisser, *Asad's Legacy: Syria in Transition* (London: Hurst & Co, 2001).

4. Lisa Wedeen, *Ambiguities of Domination* (Chicago: Chicago University Press, 1999).

5. Michael C. Hudson, *The Precarious Republic: Political Modernization in Lebanon* (New York: Random House, 1968).

6. Itamar Rabinovich, *The War for Lebanon, 1970–1983* (Ithaca, NY: Cornell University Press, 1984), pp. 34–88.

7. For the text of the speech, see ibid., pp. 183–218.

8. The meeting was attended by Asad, Sadat, `Arafat, Lebanon's president Elias Sarkis, and Kuwait's Amir Sabah al-Salim al-Sabah.

9. *Tishrin,* November 17, 1980, quoted by R. Damascus, November 1980 (FBIS-DR, 18/11/80).

10. R. Monte Carlo, November 14, 1980.

11. Dishon and Maddy-Weitzman, *Middle East Contemporary Survey*, Vol. V, p. 236; Maddy-Weitzman, "The Fragmentation of Arab Politics: Inter-Arab Affairs Since the Afghanistan Invasion," *Orbis*, 25, 2, (Summer 1981), pp. 389–407.

12. For the text of the plan, see *Middle East Contemporary Survey*, Vol. V, pp. 163–64.

13. Dishon and Maddy-Weitzman, *Middle East Contemporary Survey,* Vol. VI, 1981–1982, pp. 224–27.

14. Ibid., pp. 253–58.

15. The Pact stipulated that "any [act of] armed aggression made against any one or more of [the signatory countries] or their armed forces, [would be considered as] directed against them all," requiring immediate collective and individual steps to repel it. For the text of the treaty, see http://avalon.law.yale.edu/20th_century/arabjoin.asp.

16. William H. Harris, "Lebanon", in *Middle East Contemporary Survey*, Vol. XIII, 1989, Ami Ayalon (ed.) (Boulder, CO: Westview Press, 1991), pp. 519–22.

17. William H. Harris, "Lebanon," in *Middle East Contemporary Survey*, Vol. XIV, 1990, Ami Ayalon (ed.) (Boulder, Co: Westview Press, 1992), pp. 536–44.

18. Itamar Rabinovich, *The Brink of Peace* (Princeton, NJ: Princeton University Press, 1998), pp. 54–119; Bouthaina Shaaban, *Damascus Diary: An Inside Account of Hafez al-Assad's Peace Diplomacy*, 1990–2000 (Boulder, CO: Lynne Rienner Publishers, 2013).

19. Ofra Bengio, *The Turkish-Israeli Relationship: Changing Ties of Middle Eastern Outsiders* (New York: Palgrave MacMillan, 2004), pp. 144–56.

20. The term is Moshe Maoz's. *The Sphinx of Damascus* (London: Weidenfeld and Nicolson, 1988).

10. SYMBOL VERSUS SUBSTANCE

1. For a cogent analysis of these events by a Palestinian-Jordanian member of Jordan's governing elite, see Adnan Abu-Odeh, *Jordanians, Palestinians & the Hashemite Kingdom in the Middle East Peace Process* (Washington DC: United States Institute of Peace, 1999), pp. 169–208.

2. Published by *al-Nahar*, December 4, 1973, www.jewishvirtuallibrary.org/jsource/History/arabsum73.html.

3. On the history of the PLO, see Yezid Sayigh, *Armed Struggle and the Search for State, The Palestinian National Movement, 1949–1993* (Oxford: Oxford University Press, 1997); Moshe Shemesh, *The Palestinian Entity 1959–1974: Arab Politics and the PLO* (Portland, OR: Frank Cass, 1996); Barry Rubin, *Revolution Until Victory? The Politics and History of the PLO* (Cambridge, MA: Harvard University Press, 1994).

4. Asher Susser, *Israel, Jordan and Palestine; The Two-State Imperative* (Lebanon, NH: University Press of New England, 2001), pp. 30–35. UNSC Resolution 338 was passed in the last days of the October 1973 war. It reaffirmed the principles of Resolution 242, and stipulated the opening of negotiations to implement them. http://unispal.un.org/unispal.nsf/0/7FB7C26FCBE80A31852560C50065F878.

5. Jordan TV, October 25, 1994 (FBIS-DR, October 26, 2014),

6. The literature on the Oslo process and the Camp David negotiations of 2000 is vast. For a retrospective collection that includes contributions by some of the participants, as well as scholars, see Shimon Shamir and Bruce Maddy-Weitzman, *The Camp David Summit: What Went Wrong? Americans, Israelis and Palestinians Analyze the Failure of the Boldest Attempt Ever to Resolve the Palestinian-Israeli Conflict* (Brighton, UK: Sussex Academic Press, 2005). For an authoritative Palestinian perspective, see Akram Hanieh, "The Camp David Papers," *Journal of Palestine Studies*, 30, 2 (Winter 2001), pp. 75–97.

7. *Al-Quds al-`Arabi*, October 6, 2000 (*Mideast Mirror*).

8. In an interview with Thomas Friedman, *New York Times*, February 17, 2002.

9. Marwan Muasher, *The Arab Center The Promise of Moderation* (New Haven, CT: Yale University Press, 2009), pp. 120–21.

10. *"Diyarihim"* is the precise Arabic translation of the term used in UNGA Resolution 194, which speaks of enabling refugees "to return to their homes."

11. For a fuller discussion of the summit's dynamics, see Maddy-Weitzman, "Arabs vs. the Abdullah Plan," *Middle East Quarterly*, 17, 3 (Summer 2010), pp. 3–12.

12. UNSCR Resolution 1397, adopted just two weeks before the Beirut summit, called for an immediate cessation of the Israeli-Palestinian violence and affirmed the vision of two states, Israel and Palestine. Syria, which was a member of the Council at that time, abstained in the vote. www.un.org/press/en/2002/sc7326.doc.htm.

11. THE ARAB SPRING

1. Ahmad S. Moussali, "Regional Realities in the Arab World," in Helmut K. Anheier, Yudhishthir Raj Isa (eds.), *Cultures and Globalization: Conflicts and Tensions* (London: Sage Publications, 2007), pp. 133–42, and especially foootnote 1.

2. Paul Rivlin, *Arab Economies in the 21st Century* (New York: Cambridge University Press, 2009), p. 295.

3. *Al-Ahram,* January 14, 2000 (*Mideast Mirror*).

4. Rami G. Khouri, "Wisdom or Insolvency of the Contemporary Arab State?" *Jordan Times*, February 23, 1999.

5. Jordan TV, December 27, 1998 (FBIS-DR).

6. *Al-Quds al-`Arabi*, June 25, 1998 (*Mideast Mirror*).

7. *Al-`Alam*, August 8, 1998.

8. Ajami, *Dream Palace*, pp. 279–80, 304. Qabbani had taken up residence in Beirut in 1966 after two decades in the Syrian diplomatic service, leaving in 1982 after the Israeli invasion.

9. Paul Salem, *Bitter Legacy: Ideology and Politics in the Arab World* (Syracuse, NY: Syracuse University Press, 1994), pp. 89–146.

10. Martin Evans and John Phillips, *Algeria: Anger of the Dispossessed* (New Haven, CT: Yale University Press, 2008).

11. Huntington, *The Third Wave.*

12. In 2009, after a decade of bloody civil war in Sudan pitting the Arab-Muslim central government against the predominantly African Christian and animist south, the southern region seceded and established a new state: South Sudan.

13. www.arab-hdr.org.

14. Gihan Shahine, "Old wine in new bottles," *Al Ahram Weekly Online*, 30 July-August 5 2009, http://weekly.ahram.org.eg/2009/958/eg5.htm.

15. Abdel-Moneim Said, "Why are we so far behind?" *Al Ahram Weekly Online,* August 6-12, 2009, http://weekly.ahram.org.eg/2009/959/op1.htm.

16. Hamied Ansari, *Egypt, The Stalled Society* (Albany, NNY: SUNY Press, 1986).

17. Lebanon was the one exception, although there too the identification with the country grew weaker. Telhami, *The World Through Arab Eyes,* p. 77.

18. Ibid., p. 17.

19. Huntington, *The Third Wave*, pp. 25, 287, 313.

20. Michele Penner Angrist, "Whither the Ben Ali Regime in Tunisia?" in *The Maghrib in the New Century*, Bruce Maddy-Weitzman and Daniel Zisenwine (eds.) (Gainesville: University Press of Florida, 2007), pp. 179–82.

21. International Crisis Group, "Popular Protest in North Africa and the Middle East (VIII): Bahrain's Rocky Road to Reform," *Middle East/North Africa Report* N°111 – 28 July 2011 www.crisisgroup.org/en/regions/middle-east-north-africa/iraq-iran-gulf/bahrain.aspx.

22. The former PDRY (South Yemen) was incorporated into the Yemeni Arab Republic in 1990. For the difficulties in maintaining the union, climaxing in an unsuccessful attempt at southern secession, see Joseph Kostiner, *Yemen, The Tortuous Quest for Unity, 1990–94* (London: Royal Institute of International Affairs, 1996).

23. Rabi, *Yemen,* pp. 193–203.

24. International Crisis Group, "Yemen: Enduring Conflicts, Threatened Transition," Middle East Report N°125 – 3 July 2012, www.crisisgroup.org/en/regions/middle-east-north-africa/iraq-iran-gulf/yemen/125-yemen-enduring-conflicts-threatened-transition.aspx.

25. International Crisis Group, "The Huthis: From Saada to Sanaa," Middle East Report N°154 | 10 June 2014, www.crisisgroup.org/en/regions/middle-east-north-africa/iraq-iran-gulf/yemen/154-the-huthis-from-saada-to-sanaa.aspx.

26. Dishon and Maddy-Weitzman, "Inter-Arab Relations," in *Middle East Contemporary Survey*, Vol. VI, 1981–1982, pp. 258–59.

27. www.youtube.com/watch?v=eYY_ws6axKo, www.huffingtonpost.com/2009/03/30/gaddafi-storms-out-of-ara_n_180661.html.

28. Yehudit Ronen, "Libya, the Tuareg and Mali on the Eve of the 'Arab Spring' and in its Aftermath: An Anatomy of Changed Relations." *The Journal of North African Studies* 18, 4 (2013), pp. 544–59.

29. Maddy-Weitzman, "Is Morocco Immune to Upheaval?" *Middle East Quarterly*, 19, 1 (Winter 2012), pp. 87–93.

30. *The Wall Street Journal*, January 31, 2011.

31. www.ibtimes.com/syrian-civil-war-number-refugees-nears-4-million-un-estimates-1955475.

32. http://english.ahram.org.eg/NewsContent/2/8/16347/World/Region/Arab-League-chief-hits-back-at-Clinton-after-meeti.aspx.

33. Abdul Rahman al-Rashed, "How can we save Syria?" *al-Arabiya News* (Dubai), January 31, 2012, http://english.alarabiya.net/views/2012/01/31/191596.html

34. *The Guardian*, January 11, 2012.

35. Bashar al-Assad speech, Damascus University, January 10, 2012, www.globalresearch.ca/president-bashar-al-assad-s-2012-damascus-university-speech/31250.

36. *Washington Post*, January 22, 2012.

37. For a look at the dimensions of the problem, see Paul Rivlin, "Egypt's Economy: Sisi's Herculean Task*," Iqtisadi*, 4, 11 (November 29, 2014), www.dayan.org/iqtisadi-4-no-11-november-29-2014.

38. Joyce van de Bildt, "Nasser Nostalgia in post-Mubarak Egypt," in *Inglorious Revolutions: State Cohesion in the Middle East After the Arab Spring*, Brandon Friedman and Bruce Maddy-Weitzman (eds.) (Tel Aviv: The Moshe Dayan Center, 2014), pp. 203–16.

39. "Who Isn't Charlie," *Al-Ahram Weekly Online,* January 12, 2015, http://weekly.ahram.org.eg/Print/10126.aspx.

40. Jacques Neriah, "Egyptian President Sisi Calls for Reform of Islam," *Institute for Contemporary Affairs*, vol. 155, no. 5, February 15, 2015, http://jcpa.org/article/sisi-calls-for-reform-of-islam/.

41. Robert Springborg, *Mubarak's Egypt* (Boulder, CO: Westview, 1989).

42. Fawaz A. Gerges, *The Rise and Fall of al-Qaeda* (New York: Oxford University Press, 2011).

43. www.pewglobal.org/2011/05/02/osama-bin-laden-largely-discredited-among-muslim-publics-in-recent-years/.

44. Hussein Ibish, "Does the Islamic State pass the test of statehood?" *The National*, August 16, 2014 www.thenational.ae/opinion/comment/does-the-islamic-state-pass-the-test-of-statehood; and *idem* "Child Abuse, IS-style," *NOW,* September 2, 2014, https://now.mmedia.me/lb/en/commentary/562352-child-abuse-is-style.

45. A Brooking Institute study documents the assets that have flowed into Syria to support the rebellion. Each rebel group posted a representative in Kuwait to solicit funds, with Syrian expatriates providing facilitation services. At least one of the Kuwaiti groups providing the funds is currently under US Treasury sanctions for supporting terrorism. Elizabeth Dickinson, "Playing with Fire: Why Private Gulf Financing for Syria's Extremist Rebels Risks Igniting Sectarian Conflict at Home," December 6, 2013, www.brookings.edu/research/papers/2013/12/06-private-gulf-financing-syria-extremist-rebels-sectarian-conflict-dickinson.

46. Peter R. Neumann, "Foreign fighter total in Syria/Iraq now exceeds 20,000; surpasses Afghanistan conflict in the 1980s," January 26, 2015, http://icsr.info/2015/01/foreign-fighter-total-syriairaq-now-exceeds-*20000*-surpasses-afghanistan-conflict-1980s/.

CONCLUDING OBSERVATIONS

1. Yezid Sayigh, "The Arab Region at Tipping Point," http://carnegie-mec.org/2014/08/21/arab-region-at-tipping-point, originally published in in Arabic in *Al-Hayat*, August 21, 2014.

2. Paul Salem, "A Century After 1914," *al-Hayat,* October 31, 2014. www.mei.edu/content/article/century-after.

3. Ali El Deen Hilal Dessouki, "The Arab Regional System: A question of Survival," *Contemporary Arab Affairs*, 8:1, 96–108, DOI: 10.1080/17550912.2014.990797, published online: December 17, 2014 (an earlier version was published in Arabic in *Al Siyassa Al Dawliya*, no. 198, October 2014, pp. 42–48, www.siyassa.org.eg.

SOURCES

ARCHIVES AND PUBLISHED DOCUMENTS

Bengio, Ofra, *Saddam Speaks on the Gulf Crisis* (Tel Aviv: The Moshe Dayan Center, 1992).

Hashemite Kingdom of Iraq, *Meahorey Haparagod: Va`ada Parlementarit `Iraqit `al Hamilhama Beyisrael*, Shmuel Segev, trans. (Tel Aviv: Ma`arakhot, 1954).

Hurewitz, J.C. (ed.), *The Middle East and North Africa in World Politics, A Documentary Record*, 2nd ed. (New Haven, CT: Yale University Press, 1979).

Khalil, Mohamed (ed.), *The Arab States and the Arab League*, Vols. I and II (Beirut: Al-Khayat, 1962).

Laqueur ,Walter, and Barry Rubin (eds.), *The Israel-Arab Reader: A Documentary History of the Middle East Conflict*, 5th ed. (New York: Penguin Books, 1995).

Moore, John Norton (ed.), *The Arab-Israeli Conflict*, Vol. 3 (Princeton, NJ: Princeton University Press, 1974).

NA–US National Archives, Washington D.C.

PRO–Public Record Office, London

Records of Iraq, 1914–1966, A. de L. Rush and Jane Priestland (eds.) (Cambridge, UK: Archive Editions, 2001).

BOOKS AND ARTICLES

Aboul-Enein, Youssef, "The Egyptian-Yemen War (1962–1967): Egyptian Perspectives on Guerrilla Warfare," http://onceagreenberet.com/WordPress/publications/Egyptian%20Perspectives.pdf.

Abun-Nasr, Jamil M., "The Salafiyya movement in Morocco: the Religious Bases of the Moroccan Nationalist Movement," in Albert Hourani (ed.), St. Antony's Papers No. 16, *Middle Eastern Affairs*, no. 3. (London: Chatto & Windus, 1963), pp. 91–105.

Abu-Manneh, Butrus, "The Christians between Ottomanism and Syrian Nationalism: The Ideas of Butrus Al-Bustani," *International Journal of Middle East Studies*, 11, 3 (May, 1980), pp. 287–304.

Abu-Odeh, Adnan, *Jordanians, Palestinians & the Hashemite Kingdom in the Middle East Peace Process* (Washington, DC: United States Institute of Peace, 1999).

Ajami, Fouad, *The Arab Predicament* (Cambridge: Cambridge University Press, 1981).

_____, *Dream Palace of the Arabs* (New York: Pantheon Books, 1998).

_____, "The End of Pan-Arabism," *Foreign Affairs*, 52, 1 (Winter 1978–1979), pp. 355–73.

Allawi, Ali A., *Faisal I of Iraq* (New Haven, CT: Yale University Press, 2014).

Anderson, Benedict, *Imagined Communities*, 2nd ed. (New York: Verso, 1991).

Ansari, Hamied, *Egypt, The Stalled Society* (Albany, NY: SUNY Press, 1986).

Antonius, George, *The Arab Awakening* (London: H. Hamilton, 1938).

Ayubi, Nazih N., *Over-stating the Arab State* (New York: I. B. Tauris, 1995).

Al-Azm, Sadiq, *Self-Criticism After the Defeat, 1967* (London: Saqi Books, 2011).

Battatu, Hanna, *The Old Social Classes and the Revolutionary Movements of Iraq* (Princeton, NJ: Princeton University Press, 1982).

Barnett, Michael, *Dialogues in Arab Politics: Negotiations in Regional Order* (New York: Columbia University Press, 1998).

Ben-Dor, Gabriel, *State and Conflict in the Middle East* (New York: Praeger, 1983).

_____, "Stateness and Ideology in Contemporary Middle East Politics," *Jerusalem Journal of International Relations*, 9, 3 (1987), pp. 20–37.

Bengio, Ofra, "Faysal's Vision of Iraq: A Retrospect," in *The Hashemites in the Modern Arab World: A Festschrift in Honor of the Late Professor Uriel Dann*, Asher Susser/ Aryeh Shmuelevitz (eds.) (London: Frank Cass, 1995), pp. 139–52.

_____, *The Kurds of Iraq: Building a State Within a State* (Boulder, CO: Lynne Reinner, 2012).

_____, "Iraq," in *Middle East Contemporary Survey*, Vol. XX, 1996, Bruce Maddy-Weitzman (ed.) (Tel Aviv: The Moshe Dayan Center, 1996).

_____ and Yitzhak Gal, "Iraq," in *Middle East Contemporary Survey*, Vol. VI, 1981–1982, Colin Legum, Haim Shaked, Daniel Dishon (eds.) (New York: Holmes and Meier, 1984), pp. 582–630.

Berger, Anne-Emmanuelle Berger (ed.), *Algeria in Others' Languages* (Ithaca, NY: Cornell University Press, 2002).

Bismarck, Helene von, "The Kuwait Crisis of 1961 and Its Consequences for Great Britain's Persian Gulf Policy," *Britain and the World: Historical Journal of the British Scholar Society*, 2, 1 (2009), pp. 75–96.

Brand, Laurie A., *Jordan's Inter-Arab Relations, The Political Economy of Alliance Making* (New York: Columbia University Press, 1994).

Brett, Michael, and Elizabeth Fentress, *The Berbers* (Oxford: Blackwell, 1996).

Calvert, John, *Sayyid Qutb and the Origins of Radical Islamism* (New York: Columbia University Press, 2010).

Chtatou, Mohamed, "The influence of the Berber language on Moroccan Arabic," *International Journal of the Sociology of Language*, 123, 1 (January 1997), pp. 101–18.

Cleveland, William L., "Sources of Arab Nationalism: An Overview," *Middle East Review*, xi (1979), pp. 25–33. Reprinted in Michael Curtis (ed.), *Religion and Politics in the Middle East* (Boulder, CO: Westview Press, 1981), pp. 55–67.

_____, *Islam Against the West* (Austin: University of Texas Press, 1985).

Cohen, Avner, *Israel and the Bomb* (New York: Columbia University Press, 1998).

Copeland, Miles, *The Game of Nations* (London: Weidenfeld and Nicholson, 1969).

_____, *The Game Player: Confessions of the CIA's Original Political Operative* (London: Aurum, 1989).

Dann, Uriel, *Iraq Under Qassem: A Political History, 1958-1963* (New York: Praeger, 1969).

_____, *King Hussein and the Challenge of Arab Radicalism, 1955–67* (New York: Oxford University Press, 1989).

Dawisha, Adeed, *Arab Nationalism in the 20th Century: From Triumph to Despair* (Princeton, NJ: Princeton University Press, 2003).

Dawn, C. Ernest, *From Ottomanism to Arabism* (Urbana: University of Illinois Press, 1973).

_____, "The Origins of Arab Nationalism," in *The Origins of Arab Nationalism*, Rashid Khalidi, et al. (eds.) (New York: Columbia University Press, 1991), pp. 3–30.

_____, "The formation of Pan-Arab Ideology in the Inter-War Years," *International Journal of Middle East Studies*, 20, 1 (1988), pp. 67–91.

Dessouki, Ali El Deen Hilal, "The Arab Regional System: A Question of Survival," *Contemporary Arab Affairs*, 8:1, 96–108, DOI: 10.1080/17550912.2014.990797, published online: December 17, 2014 (an earlier version was published in Arabic in Al Siyassa Al Dawaliya, no. 198, October 2014, pp. 42–48, www.siyassa.og.eg.

Dickinson, Elizabeth, "Playing with Fire: Why Private Gulf Financing for Syria's Extremist Rebels Risks Igniting Sectarian Conflict at Home," December 6, 2013, www.brookings.edu/research/papers/2013/12/06-private-gulf-financing-syria-extremist-rebels-sectarian-conflict-dickinson.

Dishon, Daniel, "Inter-Arab Relations," *Middle East Contemporary Survey, Vol. 3, 1978–79*, Colin Legum, Haim Shaked, Daniel Dishon (eds.) (New York: Holmes and Meier, 1980), pp. 213–70.

_____, and Bruce Maddy-Weitzman, "Inter-Arab Relations," in *Middle East Contemporary Survey, Vol. V, 1980–81*, Colin Legum, Haim Shaked, and Daniel Dishon, eds. (New York: Holmes and Meier, 1982), pp. 227–90.

_____, "Inter-Arab Relations," in *Middle East Contemporary Survey*, Volume VI, 1981–82, Colin Legum, Haim Shaked, and Daniel Dishon, et al. (eds.) (New York: Holmes and Meier, 1984), pp. 221–82.

Dodge, Toby, *Inventing Iraq: The Failure of Nation-Building and a History Denied* (London: Hurst, 2012).

Doran, Michael, *Pan-Arabism before Nasir: Egyptian Power Politics and the Palestine Question* (New York: Oxford University Press, 1999).

Douglas, Leigh, *The Free Yemeni Movement, 1935–1962* (Beirut: American University of Beirut Press, 1987).

Evans, Martin, and John Phillips, *Algeria: Anger of the Dispossessed* (New Haven, CT: Yale University Press, 2008).

Ferris, Jesse, *Nasir's Gamble: How Intervention in Yemen Caused the Six-Day War and the Decline of Egyptian Power* (Princeton, NJ: Princeton University Press, 2012).

Gallman, Waldemar J., *Iraq Under General Nuri* (Baltimore: The Johns Hopkins University Press, 1964).

Geertz, Clifford, *The Interpretation of Cultures* (New York: Basic Books, 1973).

Gelvin, James, *Divided Loyalties: Nationalism and Mass Politics in Syria at the Close of Empire* (Berkeley: University of California Press, 1998).

Gerges, Fawaz A., *The Rise and Fall of al-Qaeda* (New York: Oxford University Press, 2011).

Gershoni, Israel, "Rethinking the Formation of Arab Nationalism in the Middle East, 1920–1945: Old and New Narratives," in *Rethinking Nationalism in the Arab Middle East,* James Jankowski and Israel Gershoni (eds.) (New York: Columbia University Press 1997), pp. 3–25.

_____, "The Arab League as an Arab Enterprise," *The Jerusalem Quarterly*, 40 (1986), pp. 88–101.

_____, "The Evolution of National Culture in Modern Egypt: Intellectual Formation and Social Diffusion, 1892–1945," *Poetics Today*, 13, 2 (1992), pp. 325–50.

_____ and James Jankowski, *Egypt, Islam, and the Arabs: The Search for Egyptian Nationhood, 1900–1930* (New York: Oxford University Press, 1986).

_____, *Redefining the Egyptian Nation, 1930–1945* (Cambridge: Cambridge University Press, 1995).

Gomaa, Ahmed, *The Foundation of the League of Arab States* (London: Longman, 1977).

Gordon, Joel, *Nasir's Blessed Movement: Egypt's Free Officers and the July Revolution* (New York: Oxford University Press, 1991).

Gordon, Michael R., and General Bernard E. Trainor, *The General's War* (Boston: Little Brown and Co., 1995).

Haim, Sylvia, *Arab Nationalism, An Anthology* (Berkeley: University of California Press, 1962).

Hanieh, Akram, "The Camp David Papers," *Journal of Palestine Studies*, 30, 2 (Winter 2001), pp. 75–97.

Harik, Ilya, "The Origins of the Arab State System," in *The Arab State,* Giacomo Luciani (ed.) (Berkeley: University of California Press, 1990), pp. 1–28.

Harris, William H., "Lebanon," in *Middle East Contemporary Survey,* Vol. XIII, 1989, Ami Ayalon (ed.) (Boulder, CO: Westview Press, 1991), pp. 499–533.

_____, "Lebanon," in *Middle East Contemporary Survey*, Vol. XIV, 1990, Ami Ayalon (ed.), (Boulder, CO: Westview Press, 1992), pp. 520–56.

Hillman, Jason, *A Storm in a Tea-Cup, The Iraq-Kuwait Crisis of 1961: From Gulf Crisis to Inter-Arab Dispute* (Tel Aviv: The Moshe Dayan Center, 2014).

Hinnebusch, Raymond, "Introduction: The Analytical Framework," in *The Foreign Policies of Middle East States,* Raymond Hinnebusch and Anoushiravan Ehteshami (eds.) (Boulder, CO: Westview Press, 2002), pp. 1–27.

Hourani, Albert, *A History of the Arab Peoples* (Cambridge, MA: Harvard University Press, 1991).

_____, "Ottoman Reform and the Politics of Notables," in *The Beginnings of Modernization in the Middle East*, William R. Polk and Richard L. Chambers (eds.) (Chicago: University of Chicago Press, 1968), pp. 41–68.

Hudson, Michael C., *The Precarious Republic: Political Modernization in Lebanon* (New York: Random House, 1968).

Humphreys, R. Stephen, *Between Memory and Desire: The Middle East in a Troubled Age* (Berkeley: University of California Press, 1999).

Huntington, Samuel, *Political Order in Changing Societies* (New Haven, CT: Yale University Press, 1968).

_____, *The Third Wave: Democratization in the Late Twentieth Century* (Norman: Oklahoma University Press, 1991).

al-Husri, Abu Khaldun Sati`, *The Day of Maysalun* (Washington, DC: Middle East Institute, 1966).

al-Huwaydi, Amin, *Zilzal `Asifa al-Sahra'a Watawabi`hu* (Cairo: Dar al-Shuruq, 1998).

Ibish, Hussein, "Child Abuse, IS-style," September 2, 2014, https://now.mmedia.me/lb/en/commentary/562352-child-abuse-is-style.

_____, "Does the Islamic State pass the test of statehood?" *The National*, August 16, 2014, www.thenational.ae/opinion/comment/does-the-islamic-state-pass-the-test-of-statehood.

International Crisis Group, "Popular Protest in North Africa and the Middle East (VIII): Bahrain's Rocky Road to Reform," Middle East/North Africa Report N°111 – 28 July 2011, www.crisisgroup.org/en/regions/middle-east-north-africa/iraq-iran-gulf/bahrain.aspx.

_____, "Yemen: Enduring Conflicts, Threatened Transition," *Middle East Report N°125–3 July 2012,* www.crisisgroup.org/en/regions/middle-east-north-africa/iraq-iran-gulf/yemen/125-yemen-enduring-conflicts-threatened-transition.aspx.

_____, "The Huthis: From Saada to Sanaa," *Middle East Report* N°154 | 10 June 2014, www.crisisgroup.org/en/regions/middle-east-north-africa/iraq-iran-gulf/yemen/154-the-huthis-from-saada-to-sa-naa.aspx.

Ismael, Tareq, *The Arab Left* (Syracuse, NY: Syracuse University Press, 1976).

Issawi, Charles, *An Economic History of the Middle East and North Africa* (New York: Columbia University Press, 1982).

Jandora, John W., Butrus al-Bustani, "Arab Conscousness and Arabic Revival," *The Muslim World*, LXXIV, 2 (April 1984), pp. 71–84.

Jankowski, James, and Israel Gershoni (eds.), *Rethinking Nationalism in the Arab Middle East* (New York: Columbia University Press, 1992).

Karpat, Kemal, "The Ottoman Ethnic and Confessional Legacy in the Middle East" in *Ethnicity, Pluralism, and the State in the Middle East*, Milton J. Esman and Itamar Rabinovich (eds.) (Ithaca, NY: Cornell University Press, 1988), pp. 35–53.

Karsh, Efraim, *Empires of the Sand: The Struggle for Mastery in the Middle East, 1789–1923* (with Inari Karsh) (Cambridge, MA: Harvard University Press, 1994).

Kayali, Hasan, *Arabs and Young Turks: Ottomanism, Arabism and Islamism in the Ottoman Empire, 1908–1918* (Berkeley: University of California Press, 1997).

Kazziha, Walid, "Another Reading Into Husari's Concept of Arab Nationalism," in Marwan R. Buheiry (ed.), *Intellectual Life in the Arab East, 1890–1939* (Beirut: American University of Beirut, 1981), pp. 154–64.

Keddie, Nikkie, *Sayyid Jamal al-Din "al-Afghani": A Political Biography* (Berkeley: University of California Press, 1972).

Kedourie, Elie, "Pan-Arabism and British Policy," in *idem, The Chatham House Version and other Middle-Eastern Studies* (Hanover, NH: University Press of New England, 1984), pp. 213–35.

_____, *In the Anglo-Arab Labyrinth*, (Cambridge: Cambridge University Press, 1976).

_____, "The Politics of Political Literature: Kawakibi, Azoury and Jung," in *idem, Arabic Political Memoirs and Other Studies* (London: Frank Cass, 1980), pp. 107–23.

_____, "Arabic Political Memoirs," in *idem, Arabic Political Memoirs and Other Studies* (London: Frank Cass, 1980), pp. 177–205.

_____, "The Kingdom of Iraq, 1917–1958: A Retrospect," in *idem, The Chatham House Version and other Middle-Eastern Studies* (Hanover, NH: University Press of New England, 1984), pp. 236–85.

_____, "Great Britain and Palestine: The Turning Point," in *idem, Islam in the Modern World and Other Studies* (London: Mansell, 1980), pp. 93–170.

Kerr, Malcolm, *The Arab Cold War*, 3rd edition (Oxford: Oxford University Press, 1971).

Khalidi, Rashid, Lisa Anderson, Muhammad Muslih, Reeva S. Simon (eds.), *The Origins of Arab Nationalism* (New York: Columbia University Press, 1991).

_____, "Ottomanism and Arabism in Syria Before 1914: A Reassessment," in Khalidi, et al. (eds.), *The Origins of Arab Nationalism* (New York: Columbia University Press, 1991), pp. 50–69.

Khouri, Rami G., "Wisdom or Insolvency of the Contemporary Arab State?" *Jordan Times*, February 23, 1999.

Khoury, Phillip, *Urban Notables and Arab Nationalism: The Politics of Damascus, 1860–1920* (Cambridge: Cambridge University Press, 2003).

_____, "The Paradoxical in Arab Nationalism: Interwar Syria Revisited," in Jankowski, James and Israel Gershoni, (eds.), *Rethinking Nation-*

alism in the Arab Middle East (New York: Columbia University Press, 1997), pp. 273–87.

_____, *Syria and the French Mandate, The Politics of Arab Nationalism 1920–1945* (Princeton, NJ: Princeton University Press, 1987).

_____, "Divided Loyalties? Syria and the Question of Palestine, 1919–1939," *Middle Eastern Studies*, 21, 3 (July 1985), pp. 324–48.

Kienle, Eberhard, *Ba'th Versus Ba'th: The Conflict Between Syria and Iraq, 1968–1989* (London: I. B. Tauris, 1991).

Kirk, George, *The Middle East in the War* (Oxford: Oxford University Press, 1953).

Kleiman, Aaron S., *Foundations of British Policy in the Arab World: The Cairo Conference of 1921* (Baltimore: Johns Hopkins University Press, 1970).

Kostiner, Joseph, "Solidarity in the Arab State: An Historical Perspective," in *Challenges to the Cohesion of the Arab State*, Asher Susser (ed.) (Tel Aviv: The Moshe Dayan Center, 2008), pp. 21–39.

_____, *The Making of Saudi Arabia, 1916–1936: From Chieftaincy to Monarchical State* (New York: Oxford University Press, 1993).

_____, *Yemen, The Tortuous Quest for Unity, 1990–94* (London: Royal Institute of International Affairs, 1996).

Kramer, Martin, "Arab Nationalism: Mistaken Identity," *Daedalus*, 122, 3 (Summer 1993), pp. 171–206.

Landis, Joshua, "Syria and the Palestine War: Fighting King `Abdullah's 'Greater Syria Plan'," in *The War for Palestine, Rewriting the History of 1948*, Eugene L. Rogan and Avi Shlaim (eds.) (Cambridge: Cambridge University Press, 2001), pp. 178–205.

Lesch, David, *Syria and the United States: Eisenhower's Cold War in the Middle East* (Boulder, CO: Westview, 1992).

Lewis, Bernard, *The Arabs in History*, revised edition (New York: Harper & Row, 1967).

Lynch, Mark, *Voices of the New Arab Public: Iraq, Al-Jazeera and Middle East Politics Today* (New York: Columbia University Press, 2006).

Maddy-Weitzman, Bruce, *The Crystallization of the Arab State System, 1945–1954* (Syracuse, NY: Syracuse University Press, 1993).

_____, *The Berber Identity Movement and the Challenge to North African States* (Austin: University of Texas Press, 2011).

_____, "Jordan and Iraq: Efforts at Intra-Hashimite Unity," *Middle Eastern Studies*, 26, 1 (January 1990), pp. 65–75.

_____, "Why Did Arab Monarchies Fall? An Analysis of Old and New Explanations," in *Middle East Monarchies: The Challenge of Modernity*, Joseph Kostiner (ed.) (Boulder: Lynne Rienner, 2000), pp. 37–52.

_____, "Islam and Arabism: The Iran-Iraq War," *The Washington Quarterly*, 5, 4 (Autumn 1982), pp. 181–88.

_____, "The Fragmentation of Arab Politics: Inter-Arab Affairs Since the Afghanistan Invasion," *ORBIS*, 25, 2 (Summer 1981), pp. 389–407.

_____, "Arabs vs. the Abdullah Plan," *Middle East Quarterly*, 17, 3 (Summer 2010), pp. 3–12.

_____, "Inter-Arab Relations," *Middle East Contemporary Survey*, Volume XIX, 1995, Bruce Maddy-Weitzman, (ed.) (Boulder, CO: Westview, 1997), pp. 60–96.

_____, "Inter-Arab Relations," *Middle East Contemporary Survey*, Vol. XVI, 1990, Ami Ayalon (ed.) (Boulder, CO: Westview Press, 1992), pp. 131–75.

_____, "Is Morocco Immune to Upheaval," *Middle East Quarterly*, 19, 1 (Winter 2012), pp. 87–93.

_____, and Asher Susser, "State Cohesion in the Middle East: Historical and Contemporary Perspectives," in *Inglorious Revolutions: State Cohesion in the Middle East After the Arab Spring,* Brandon Friedman and Bruce Maddy-Weitzman (eds.) (Tel Aviv: The Moshe Dayan Center, 2014), pp. 13–36.

_____, and Joseph Kostiner, "From Jidda To Cairo: The Failure of Arab Mediation in the Gulf Crisis," *Diplomacy & Statecraft*, 7, 2 (Summer 1996), pp. 466–90.

Makiya, Kanan, *The Republic of Fear*, 2nd ed. (Berkeley: University of California Press, 1998).

_____, *Cruelty and Silence* (New York: W. W. Norton & Co., 1993).

Mandel, Neville, *The Arabs and Zionism Before World War I* (Berkeley: University of California Press, 1976).

Mansour, Mohamed El, "Salafis and Modernists in the Moroccan Nationalist Movement," in John Ruedy (ed.) *Islamism and Secularism in North Africa* (New York: St. Martin's Press, 1999), pp. 53–72.

Maoz, Moshe, *The Sphinx of Damascus* (London: Weidenfeld and Nicolson, 1988).

Masters, Bruce, *The Arabs of the Ottoman Empire* (New York: Cambridge University Press, 2013).

Matthews, Weldon C., "The Kennedy Administration, Counterinsurgency, and Iraq's First Ba`thist Regime," *International Journal of Middle East Studies*, 43, 4 (November 2011), pp 635–53.

McDougall, James, *History and the Culture of Nationalism in Algeria* (Cambridge: Cambridge University Press, 2006).

Migdal, Joel S., *Strong Societies and Weak States: State-Society Relations and State Capabilities in the Third World* (Princeton, NJ: Princeton University Press, 1988).

Miller, Susan Gilson, *A History of Modern Morocco* (Cambridge: Cambridge University Press, 2013).

Monroe, Elizabeth, *Britain's Moment in the Middle East, 1914–1956* (London: Johns Hopkins Press, 1963).

Moore, Clement Henry, "On Theory and Practice Among the Arabs," *World Politics*, 24, 1 (1971), pp. 106–26.

Morris, Benny, *The Birth of the Palestinian Refugee Problem Revisited* (Cambridge: Cambridge University Press, 2004).

_____, *Israel's Border Wars, 1949–1956* (Oxford: Clarendon Press, 1993).

_____, *1948, A History of the First Arab-Israeli War* (New Haven, CT: Yale University Press, 2008).

Moubayed, Sami, *Syria and the USA* (London: I.B Tauris, 2013).

Moussali, Ahmad S., "Regional Realities in the Arab World," in Helmut K Anheier, Yudhishthir Raj Isa (eds.), *Cultures and Globalization: Conflicts and Tensions* (London: Sage Publications, 2007), pp. 133–42.

Muasher, Marwan, *The Arab Center: The Promise of Moderation* (New Haven, CT: Yale University Press, 2009).

Mufti, Malik, *Sovereign Creations: Pan-Arabism and Political Order in Syria and Iraq* (Ithaca, NY: Cornell University Press, 1995).

Mursey, Alfred G., *An Arab Common Market: A Study in Inter-Arab Trade Relations, 1920–1967* (New York: Praeger, 1969).

Muslih, Muhammad, "The Rise of Local Nationalism in the Arab East," in Rashid Khalidi, Lisa Anderson, Muhammad Muslih, Reeva S. Simon (eds.), *The Origins of Arab Nationalism* (New York: Columbia University Press, 1991), pp. 167–85.

Nakash, Yitzhak, *The Shi`is of Iraq* (Princeton, NJ: Princeton University Press, 1994).

Nassar, Hala Khamis and Marco Boggero, "Omar al-Mukhtar: The Formation of Cultural Memory and the Case of the Militant Group that Bears His Name," *The Journal of North African Studies*, 13, 2 (June 2008), pp. 201–17.

Neff, Donald, *Warriors at Suez* (New York: Simon & Schuster, 1981).

Neriah, Jacques, "Egyptian President Sisi Calls for Reform of Islam," *Institute for Contemporary Affairs*, vol. 155, no. 5, February 15, 2015.

Nettl, J. P. "The state as a conceptual variable," *World Politics* 20, 4 (July 1968), pp. 559–92.

Neumann, Peter R., "Foreign fighter total in Syria/Iraq now exceeds 20,000; surpasses Afghanistan conflict in the 1980s," *International Centre for the Study of Radicalisation and Political Violence,"* January 26, 2015,   http://icsr.info/2015/01/foreign-fighter-total-syriairaq-now-exceeds-20000-surpasses-afghanistan-conflict-1980s/.

Noble, Paul, "The Arab System: Pressures, Constraints and Opportunities," in *The Foreign Policies of Arab States: The Challenge of Change*, Bahgat Korany and Ali E. Hillal Dessouki (eds.) (Boulder, CO: Westview Press, 1991), pp. 167–65.

_____, "From Arab System to Middle East System?: Regional Pressures and Constraints," in *The Foreign Policies of Arab States*, Bahgat Korany and Ali E. Hillal Dessouki (eds.), 3rd ed. (New York: AUC Press, 2008), pp. 167–65.

Ochsenwald, William, *The Hijaz Railroad* (Charlottesville: University of Virginia, 1988).

Oren, Michael, *Six Days of War: June 1967 and the Making of the Modern Middle East* (Oxford: Oxford University Press, 2002).

Oron, Yitzhak (ed.), *Middle East Record*, Vol. 1, 1960 (London: Weidenfeld and Nicholson, 1965).

Osgood, Robert E., *Ideals and Self-Interest in American Foreign Relations* (Chicago: University of Chicago Press, 1953).

Owen, Roger, "Class and Class Politics in Iraq Before 1958: The Colonial and Post-Colonial State," in Robert A. Fernea and Wm. Roger Louis (eds.), *The Iraqi Revolution of 1958: The Old Social Classes Revisited* (London: I. B. Taurus, 1991), pp. 154–71.

Penner Angrist, Michele, "Whither the Ben Ali Regime in Tunisia?" in *The Maghrib in the New Century: Identity, Religion and Politics*, Bruce Maddy-Weitzman and Daniel Zisenwine (eds.) (Gainseville: University Press of Florida, 2007), pp. 175–93.

Phillip, Thomas, *Jurji Zaidan and the Foundations of Arab Nationalism* (Syracuse, NY: Syracuse University Press, 2014).

Phillips, Christopher, *Everyday Arab Identity* (London: Routledge, 2013).

Podeh, Elie, "To Unite or Not to Unite: That is Not the Question. The 1963 Tripartite Talks Reassesed," *Middle Eastern Studies*, 39, 1 (2003), pp. 150–85.

_____, "Suez in Reverse: The Arab Response to the Iraqi Bid for Kuwait, 1961-1963," *Diplomacy and Statecraft*, 14, 1 (2003), pp. 103–30.

_____, *The Quest for Hegemony in the Arab World* (Leiden: E.J. Brill, 1995).

_____, *The Decline of Arab Unity* (Brighton, UK: Sussex Academic Press, 1999).

_____, *The Politics of National Celebration in the Arab Middle East* (New York: Cambridge University Press, 2011).

Porath, Yehoshua, *In Search of Arab Unity, 1930–1945* (London: Frank Cass, 1986).

_____, "Abdallah's Greater Syria Program," *Middle Eastern Studies*, 20, 2 (1984), pp. 172–89.

_____, "Nuri al-Sa'id's Arab Unity Programme," *Middle Eastern Studies* 20, 4 (1984), pp. 76–98.

Provence, Michael, *The Great Syrian Revolt and the Rise of Arab Nationalism* (Austin: University of Texas Press, 2005), pp. 100–7.

Quandt, William, *Camp David: Peacemaking and Politics* (Washington DC: Brookings Institution, 1986).

Rabi, Uzi, *Yemen: Revolution, Civil War and Unification* (London: I.B. Tauris, 2015).

Rabinovich, Itamar, "Inter-Arab Relations Foreshadowed: The Question of the Syrian Throne in the 1920s and '30s," in *idem, The View from Damascus: State, Political Community and Foreign Relations in Twentieth-Century Syria* (London: Valentine Mitchell, 2011), pp. 54–67.

_____, *The War for Lebanon* (Ithaca, NY: Cornell University Press, 1984).

_____, *The Brink of Peace* (Princeton, NJ: Princeton University Press, 1998).

_____ and Hanna Zamir, "Lebanon," in *Middle East Contemporary Survey, Vol. I, 1976–7*, Colin Legum (ed.) (New York: Holmes and Meier, 1978), pp. 492–525.

Rivlin, Paul, *Arab Economies in the 21st Century* (New York: Cambridge University Press, 2009).

_____, "Egypt's Economy: Sisi's Herculean Task," *Iqtisadi* 4, no. 11 (November 29, 2014), www.dayan.org/iqtisadi-4-no-11-november-29-2014.

Robins, Phillip, *A History of Jordan* (Cambridge: Cambridge University Press, 2004).

Ronen, Yehudit, "Libya, the Tuareg and Mali on the Eve of the 'Arab Spring' and in its Aftermath: An Anatomy of Changed Relations," *The Journal of North African Studies* 18, 4 (2013), pp. 544–59.

Rubin, Barry, *The Arab States and the Palestine Conflict* (Syracuse, NY: Syracuse University Press, 1981).

_____, *Revolution Until Victory? The Politics and History of the PLO* (Cambridge, MA: Harvard University Press, 1994).

Ruedy, John, *Modern Algeria, The Origins and Development of a Nation* (Bloomington: Indiana University Press, 1992).

Ryan, Curtis R., *Inter-Arab Alliances: Regime Security and Jordanian Foreign Policy* (Gainesville: University Press of Florida, 2009).

Safran, Nadav, *From War to War* (New York: Praeger, 1969).

_____, *Egypt in Search of Political Community* (Cambridge, MA: Harvard University Press, 1961).

Said, Abdel-Moneim, "Why are we so far behind?" *Al Ahram Weekly Online*, August 6–12, 2009, http://weekly.ahram.org.eg/2009/959/op1.htm.

Said, Edward, "The Morning After," *London Review of Books*, October 21, 1993.

Salame, Ghassan, "The Return to Geography," in William B. Quandt (ed.), *The Middle East: Ten Years After Camp David* (Washington, DC: The Brookings Institute, 1988), pp. 319–53.

Salameh, Franck, *Language Memory and Identity in the Middle East* (Lanham, MD: Lexington Books, 2010).

Salem Paul, *Bitter Legacy: Ideology and Politics in the Arab World* (Syracuse, NY: Syracuse University Press, 1994).

_____, "A Century After 1914," *al-Hayat*, October 31, 2014, www.mei.edu/content/article/century-after.

Sayegh, Fayez, *Arab Unity: Hope and Fulfillment* (New York: Devin-Adair, 1958).

Sayigh, Yezid, *Armed Struggle and the Search for State, the Palestinian National Movement, 1949–1993* (Oxford: Oxford University Press, 1997).

_____, "The Arab Region at Tipping Point," http://carnegie-mec.org/2014/08/21/arab-region-at-tipping-point, originally published in Arabic in *Al-Hayat*, August 21, 2014.

_____, "The Gulf Crisis: Why the Arab Regional Order Failed," *International Affairs*, 67, 3 (1991), pp. 487–507.

Sayigh, Yusuf A., *The Arab Economy* (New York: Oxford University Press, 1982).

Schayegh, Cyrus, "1958 Reconsidered: State Formation and the Cold War in the Early Postcolonial Arab Middle East," *International Journal of Middle East Studies,* 45, 3 (August 2013), pp. 421–43.

Seale, Patrick, *The Struggle For Syria*, new edition (New Haven and London: Yale UP, 1987).

_____, *Asad: The Struggle for the Middle East* (Berkeley: University of California Press, 1989).

_____, *The Struggle for Arab Independence: Riad El-Solh and the Makers of the Modern Middle East* (Cambridge: Cambridge University Press, 2010).

Sedgwick, Mark, *Muhammad Abduh* (Oxford: Oneworld, 2009).

Sela, Avraham, *The Decline of the Arab-Israeli Conflict* (Albany, NY: SUNY Press, 1998).

_____, "Israel, Transjordan and the 1948 War: Myth, Historiography and Reality," *Middle Eastern Studies,* 28, 4 (1992), pp. 623–88.

_____, "'Abd al-Nasir's Regional Politics: A Reassessment," in Elie Podeh and Onn Winckler (eds.), *Rethinking Nasirism: Revolution and Historical Memory in Modern Egypt* (Gainesville: University Press of Florida, 2004), pp. 179–204.

Shahine, Gihan, "Old wine in new bottles," *Al Ahram Weekly Online*, July 30–August 5, 2009, http://weekly.ahram.org.eg/2009/958/eg5.htm.

Shamir, Shimon, "The Collapse of Project Alpha," in Wm. Roger Louis and Roger Owen (eds.), *Suez 1956: The Crisis and its Consequences* (Oxford: Clarendon Press, 1989), pp. 73–100.

_____, "From Liberalism to Postrevolution," in *idem* (ed.), *From Monarchy to Revolution* (Boulder, Co: Westview Press, 1995), pp. 195–212.

_____ and Bruce Maddy-Weitzman (eds.), *The Camp David Summit: What Went Wrong?* (Brighton, UK: Sussex Academic Press, 2005).

Shaaban, Bouthaina, *Damascus Diary: An Inside Account of Hafez al-Assad's Peace Diplomacy, 1990–2000* (Boulder, CO: Lynne Rienner Publishers, 2013).

Sharabi, Hisham, *Neo-patriarchy: A Theory of Distorted Change* (Oxford: Oxford University Press, 1988).

_____, *Embers and Ashes: Memoirs of an Arab Intellectual* (Northampton, MA: Interlink Publishing, 2007).

Shemesh, Moshe, *The Palestinian Entity 1959–1974: Arab Politics and the PLO* (Portland, OR: Frank Cass, 1996).

Shlaim, Avi, *Collusion Across the Jordan* (Oxford: Clarendon Press, 1988).

_____, *Lion of Jordan: The Life of King Hussein in War and Peace* (New York: Alfred Knopf, 2008).

Simon, Reeva S., "The Hashemite 'Conspiracy': Hashemite Unity Attempts, 1921–1956," *International Journal of Middle East Studies*, 5, 3 (1974), pp. 314–27.

Sivan, Emmanuel, *Radical Islam* (New Haven, CT: Yale University Press, 1990).

_____, "Arab Nationalism in the Age of Islamic Resurgence," in *Rethinking Nationalism in the Arab Middle East*, James Jankowski and Israel Gershoni (eds.) (New York: Columbia University Press), pp. 207–28.

Smith, Anthony D., *The Ethnic Origins of Nations* (Oxford: Blackwell, 1996).

Smith, Charles D., "The 'Crisis of Orientation': The Shift of Egyptian Intellectuals to Islamic Subjects in the 1930s," *International Journal of Middle East Studies*, 4, 4, (October 1973), pp. 382–410.

Springborg, Robert, *Mubarak's Egypt* (Boulder, CO: Westview, 1989).

Stein, Kenneth W., *Heroic Diplomacy* (London: Routledge, 1999).

Susser, Asher, *Israel, Jordan and Palestine; The Two-State Imperative* (Hanover, NH: University Press of New England, 2001).

_____, "Jordan" in *Middle East Contemporary Survey*, Vol. XIX, 1995, Bruce Maddy-Weitzman (ed.), (Boulder, CO: Westview, 1997), pp. 384–431.

Al-Suwaydi, Tawfiq, *My Memoirs: Half a Century of the History of Iraq and the Arab Cause* (Boulder, CO: Lynne Rienner, 2013).

Tauber, Eliezer, *The Arab Movements in World War I* (London: Frank Cass, 1993).

_____, *The Formation of Modern Syria and Iraq* (London: Frank Cass, 1995).

Teitelbaum, Joshua, *The Rise and Fall of the Hashimite Kingdom of Arabia* (London: Hurst & Co., 2001).

Telhami, Shibly, *The World Through Arab Eyes* (New York: Basic Books, 2013).

_____, "2008 Annual Arab Public Opinion Poll," www.brookings.edu/~/media/events/2008/4/14%20middle%20east/0414_middle_east_telhami.pdf.

Tibi, Bassam, *Arab Nationalism, A Critical Enquiry* (New York: St. Martin's Press, 1991).

Tripp, Charles, *A History of Iraq,* 3rd ed. (Cambridge: Cambridge University Press, 2007).

Van de Bildt, Joyce, "Nasser Nostalgia in post-Mubarak Egypt," in *Inglorious Revolutions: State Cohesion in the Middle East After the Arab Spring*, Brandon Friedman and Bruce Maddy-Weitzman (eds.) (Tel Aviv: The Moshe Dayan Center, 2014), pp. 203–16.

Vatikiotis, P.J., *Nasir and His Generation* (London: Croon Helm, 1978).

Webman, Esther, "The Gulf States," in *Middle East Contemporary Survey*, Vol. V, 1980–1981 (Colin Legum, Haim Shaked, Daniel Dishon (eds.) (New York: Holmes and Meier, 1982), pp. 458–66.

Werner, Manfred W., *Modern Yemen, 1918–1966* (Baltimore: The Johns Hopkins University Press, 1967).

Wedeen, Lisa, *Ambiguities of Domination* (Chicago: Chicago University Press, 1999).

Wild, Stephen, "Negib Azoury and his book Le Reveil de la Nation Arabe," in Marwan R. Buheiry (ed.), *Intellectual Life in the Arab East, 1890–1939* (Beirut: American University of Beirut, 1981), pp. 62–83.

Yassine-Hamdan, Nahla, and Frederic S. Pearson, *Arab Approaches to Conflict Resolution* (London: Routledge, 2014).

Zisser, Eyal, "The 'Alawis, Lords of Syria: From Ethnic Minority to Ruling Sect," in Ofra Bengio and Gabriel Ben-Dor (eds.), *Minorities and the State in the Arab World* (Boulder, CO: Lynne Rienner, 1999), pp. 129–45.

_____, *Asad's Legacy: Syria in Transition* (London: Hurst & Co, 2001).

Zurayq, Qustantin, *Ma`na al-Nakba* (Beirut: Dar al-`Ilm lil-Malayin, 1948). [English translation by R. Bayly Winder, *The Meaning of the Disaster* (Beirut: Khayat's College Book Cooperative, 1956)].

WEBSITES

www.arab-hdr.org
http://avalon.law.yale.edu/20th_century/
www.carnegie-mec.org
www.cfr.org
http://coursesa.matrix.msu.edu
www.crisisgroup.org
http://edition.cnn.com
http://english.ahram.org.eg
www.globalresearch.ca
www.huffingtonpost.com
www.ibtimes.com
www.jewishvirtuallibrary.org
http://jcpa.org
www.markdanner.com
www.mei.edu
www.mideastweb.org
https://now.mmedia.me
www.pewglobal.org
www.sadat.umd.edu/archives/speeches.htm
www.securitycouncilreport.org/
www.thenational.ae
www.un.org
http://weekly.ahram.org.eg
http://unispal.un.org
www.wipo.int/

www.youtube.com

PERIODICALS, PRINT AND BROADCAST MEDIA, NEWS AGENCIES, AND MEDIA ORGANIZATIONS

Agence France Presse
Al-Ahram
Al-Arabiya News
Al-Hayat
Al-`Alam
Al-Quds al-`Arabi
BBC Summary of World Broadcasts (SWB), The Middle East
Economic Intelligence Unit (EIU), *Country Reports*
Foreign Broadcast and Information Service (FBIS-Daily Report), The
Middle/Near East and Africa/South Asia
Egyptian Space Channel TV
The Guardian
Iraqi News Agency (INA)
Jordan Times
Jordan TV
Mideast Mirror
Middle East Contemporary Survey (MECS)
Middle East Record (MER)
Middle East Media and Research Institute (MEMRI)
New York Times
Radio Damascus
Radio Monte Carlo
Saudi Press Agency (SPA)
Tishrin
Wall Street Journal

INDEX

`Abdallah I, King of Jordan: All-Palestine Government threat to, 55–56; during Arab-Israeli war (1948), 51–54, 54–55; assassination of, 61, 65; as Jordan king, 33, 65, 74, 233n21; as proposed king of Iraq, 17; son of Husayn bin `Ali, 16; for Syria reunification, 40

`Abdallah II, King of Jordan, 128, 200, 210

`Abduh, Mohammed: as luminary of *salafism*, 7–8, 8, 219n13; *al-Manar*, 8; *al-`Urwa al-Wuthqa*, 8

Abdulhamid II, 5, 5–6, 8

`Abd al-Ilah, Prince, 40, 65, 82, 227n28, 229n39

al-Afghani, Jamal al-Din: as luminary *of salafism*, 7–8, 219n13; *al-`Urwa al-Wuthqa*, 8

al-`Ahd, Arab secret society, 10, 16

Algeria: in Arab-Israeli war (1973), 112–113; independence of, 73, 85; nation- and state-building in, 36; as pro-Palestinian, 113–114; in Steadfastness Front, 116, 137, 159, 160

al-watan al-`arabi. See Arab homeland

Amman. *See* Jordan

The Anglo-Arab Labyrinth (Kedourie), xiii

Antonius, George, 6, 16

Arab awakening: Arab Revolt (1916-1918), xi–xii; Arab Spring, xvi–xvii; *nahda* of Arab identity, 6; *The Arab Awakening* (Antonius), 6, 16

Arab Cold War, 82–91

Arab Congress (1913), 10–11

Arab Federation, countering UAR, 81

Arab homeland (*al-watan al-`arabi*), xii, 29–30

Arab Human Development Reports, 189–191

Arabian Peninsula: oil-rich conservative states of, xv; *al-Qa`ida* in, 195

Arabic language: Arab Congress for, 10–11; *nahda* as modernization of, 6; standardization of, 29; Turkish *vs.*, 11

Arab identity: cultural borrowing corrupting, 27; Lebanon's "Arab face", 155; as mostly Sunni, 4; new form of, 123–126, 136–138; Ottoman Turks contrasted with, 4, 9

Arabism (*`uruba*): Arab nationalism contrasted with, 6, 25, 218n10; Arab nationalism superseded by, 25; of Ba`th Party, xiv, 67; beating heart of (*qalb al-nabid lil-`uruba*), xvii; key focus of, 38, 49; of Nasir, xiv, 69, 69–70, 101–107; origin of, 5–13; Young Turks providing impetus for, 10–11, 221n34

Arab-Israeli diplomacy: by Egypt, 57–59; by Iraq, 58; by Jordan, 57–59; Madrid framework for, 154, 166, 176, 182; Peace efforts, failure of, 72–73; "Three No's" of Khartoum Summit, 102, 161, 163; US as peacemaker in, 75, 77, 78

ABOUT THE AUTHOR

Bruce Maddy-Weitzman is a professor in the Department of Middle Eastern & African History, and senior research fellow at the Moshe Dayan Center for Middle Eastern and African Studies, Tel Aviv University, and a senior fellow at the Foreign Policy Research Institute. He is the author of *The Berber Identity Movement and the Challenge to North African States* (2011), *The Crystallization of the Arab State System, 1945–1954* (1993), and articles on regional Arab politics and Maghrib affairs. He has edited or co-edited fifteen volumes, including the annual *Middle East Contemporary Survey* (1994–2000), *Religious Radicalism in the Greater Middle East* (1997), *The Camp David Summit—What Went Wrong?* (2005), *Turkish-Israeli Relations in a Trans-Atlantic Conference: Wider Europe and the Greater Middle East* (2005), *The Maghrib in the New Century: Identity, Religion and Politics* (2007), *Contemporary Morocco: State, Politics and Society under Mohammed VI* (2012), *Nationalism, Identity and Politics: Israel and the Middle East* (2014), and *Inglorious Revolutions: State Cohesion in the Middle East After the Arab Spring* (2014).

His email is bmaddy@post.tau.ac.il